"Americans have been turning to organizations, education, famous personalities, and ultimately government in an effort to address the ongoing racial strife in our nation. In 2008 many hoped the election of an African-American president would finally bridge the racial divide. Today, we are left wondering why racial tensions have not abated. John Piper argues from specific biblical texts that the only solution powerful enough to overcome racial strife and bring about reconciliation and harmony is the gospel of Jesus Christ. It is this gospel that announces that, through his blood, Jesus has demolished the dividing wall that separates humanity along racial lines and has brought all ethnicities together as brothers and sisters into one body—the church. Yet Piper does not end there. He carefully shepherds us through the various implications of the gospel in relation to race and ethnicity. In this sense, the book you hold in your hands is so much more than a book about race and ethnicity. *Bloodlines* is a prime example of how we are to do the hard work of renewing our minds by replacing old ways of thinking with gospel ways of thinking. Read this book and let it serve as a model of how to prepare your mind for action and to think soberly about God, your sin, Christ, the gospel, and one another for the sake of your soul, Christ's church, and God's glory."

Juan R. Sanchez Jr., Preaching Pastor, High Pointe Baptist Church, Austin, Texas

"John Piper has given us an exquisite work on the matter of race. He addresses the issue with biblical and theological soundness coupled with personal sensitivity and practical advice. This is a must read for those who wish to pursue unity God's way."

Tony Evans, President, The Urban Alternative; Senior Pastor, Oak Cliff Bible Fellowship

"For years, I have yearned for a biblically sound, theologically anchored resource on race. God has answered that prayer. Leaping off the pages of *Bloodlines* is the power of the gospel to overcome and defeat racism and a call to cross-centered, holy justice in our attitudes and actions toward those who are not like us. This is an important, foundational work, and I am sure it will be used of God to remind all of us of the power and precious, priceless dignity of the gospel."

Crawford W. Loritts Jr., author; speaker; radio host; Senior Pastor, Fellowship Bible, Roswell, Georgia

"Piper bequeaths an outstanding—and at times, *risky*—work on race and ethnicity, thoroughly soaked in the biblical Christian Hedonism worldview. I found that Piper's personal testimony from the 1960s until now and his exploration of African-American writers past and present demonstrate the complexity of dealing honestly with the topic for those who seek to honor the Savior. He is right: on race, 'we have fallen together.' The only question that remains is whether or not individual members of the church will take deeply to heart this sincere analysis of the cross of Christ and race and then become a steadfast holy force for undoing the problems of racism in the world."

Eric C. Redmond, author, *Where Are All the Brothers?*
Straight Answers to Men's Questions about the Church;
council member, The Gospel Coalition

BLOODLINES

Other Crossway Books by John Piper

What's the Difference?
A Hunger for God
God's Passion for His Glory
The Innkeeper
Seeing and Savoring Jesus Christ
The Legacy of Sovereign Joy
The Hidden Smile of God
Counted Righteous in Christ
The Misery of Job and the Mercy of God
The Roots of Endurance
Don't Waste Your Life
Fifty Reasons Jesus Came to Die
The Prodigal's Sister
When I Don't Desire God
God Is the Gospel
What Jesus Demands from the World
When the Darkness Will Not Lift
Contending for Our All
The Future of Justification
Spectacular Sins
This Momentary Marriage
Filling Up the Afflictions of Christ
John Calvin and His Passion for the Majesty of God
Velvet Steel
Ruth
Sweet and Bitter Providence
Think

BLOODLINES

RACE, CROSS, AND THE CHRISTIAN

JOHN PIPER

FOREWORD BY TIM KELLER

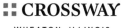

CROSSWAY

WHEATON, ILLINOIS

Cover design: Josh Dennis

First printing 2011

Printed in the United States of America

Hardcover ISBN: 978-1-4335-2852-1
PDF ISBN: 978-1-4335-2853-8
Mobipocket ISBN: 978-1-4335-2854-5
ePub ISBN: 978-1-4335-2855-2

Library of Congress Cataloging-in-Publication Data
Piper, John, 1946–
   Bloodlines : race, cross, and the Christian / John Piper ; foreword
by Tim Keller.
     p. cm.
   Includes bibliographical references and index.
   ISBN 978-1-4335-2852-1 (hc)
     1. Reconciliation—Religious aspects—Christianity. 2. Race
discrimination—Religious aspects—Christianity. 3. Church and
minorities. I. Title.
BT738.27.P57   2011
270.089—dc22   2011010732

Crossway is a publishing ministry of Good News Publishers.

LB		20	19	18	17	16	15	14	13	12	11
14	13	12	11	10	9	8	7	6	5	4	3	2	1

To
Talitha Ruth
Daughter by love and law,
sister in the Great Bloodline

CONTENTS

FOREWORD

I was excited when I learned that John Piper was writing a book on race and the gospel of the cross. When John gave me the privilege of reading the manuscript, I devoured it and found that despite my high expectations I was not disappointed. It was helpful to me personally, helpful to me theologically (in understanding the relevance of the gospel to racial conflict), and it was especially encouraging to me to think that many in the evangelical world would read it.

John and I are both old enough to remember the complicity of evangelical churches and institutions with the systemic racism in the US before the civil rights movement. I took my first church in a small town in the South in the early 1970s. The courts had recently ruled that the whites-only public swimming pool, operated by the town with taxpayers' money, had to be integrated. So what did the town do? It shut the pool down completely, and the white people of the town opened a new private swimming pool and club, which of course, did not have to admit racial minorities. Because I was a young pastor, our family was often invited to swim there, and swim we did, not really cognizant of what the pool represented.

One of the reasons I think this book is so important is that conservative evangelicals (particularly white ones) seem to have become more indifferent to the sin of racism during my lifetime. Why? One reason, of course, is the stubbornness of the sinful heart. We never want to hear about what is wrong with us. Another factor may be cultural. Many have made racism and prejudice virtually the only thing they will still call a "sin," and they often lay the guilt for the sin of racism at the doorstep of those who are social conservatives. Because of that, many who identify themselves as conservatives simply don't want to hear about racism anymore. They give lip service to it being a sin, but they associate any sustained denunciation of racism with the liberal or secular systems of thought. John's book, which you have in your hands, is a strong antidote to this misconception. His motivation is simply as a preacher of the Word to bring to light what God says in it regarding race and racism.

There are many ways in which this book will help the church in its struggle with the sin of racism. First, John takes us to all the biblical texts that speak most directly to the subject of race. But—and this was most helpful to me—John does not stop there. He then goes to most of the central doctrines and themes of our faith and shows the implications of each one for our understanding of race. He demonstrates how Jesus's proclamation of the kingdom, his substitutionary atonement, the doctrine of conversion, of union with Christ, of justification by faith—all transform our attitude toward our own race and culture as well as to those belonging to other races and cultures.

I won't ever forget how one of the elders in my first church, who had been growing in his understanding of the gospel and of the cross of Jesus, said to me, "You know, I realize I've been a racist all my life." I hadn't spoken to him of racism at all, but as he was going deeper into the theology of grace, he connected the dots for himself. I must say that most of us are not that insightful, and that's why we need this volume. Let John Piper connect the dots for you.

Tim Keller
February 2011

PREFACE

As I prepare to send *Bloodlines* into a world of ethnic and racial discord, I thank God that he has spoken. We are not left to ourselves. We humans have never had the resources in ourselves to love each other well across ethnic lines. There is too much selfishness in all of us.

But God has told us what we must do. And he has sent his Son, Jesus Christ, to do what we can't and to give us new power to do what we must. His death for us, and his Spirit in us, can make a world of difference.

God has told us not to murder (Ex. 20:13). He has told us to love our neighbor as ourselves (Lev. 19:18; Gal. 5:14)—including the neighbor who is an enemy (Matt. 5:44). He has told us to do good to everyone (Gal. 6:10)—including those who hate us (Luke 6:27). He has told us to be peacemakers (Matt. 5:9) and to treat others the way we would like to be treated (Matt. 7:12).

He has revealed to us that every human is created in the image of God (James 3:9). He has shown us that we all have the same human father and are therefore kinsmen by blood (Acts 17:26). And he has made clear that, when his Son died on the cross for our sins, he "ransomed people for God from every tribe and language and people and nation" (Rev. 5:9). Racial harmony is a blood issue, not just a social issue.

God has spoken. And he has acted. He has entered our world in the person of his Son. His word, his action, and his incarnation are the end of ethnic arrogance for those who embrace him as the Treasure of their lives.

* * *

The bloodline of Jesus Christ is deeper than the bloodlines of race. The death and resurrection of the Son of God for sinners is the only sufficient power to bring the bloodlines of race into the single bloodline of the cross.

* * *

Therefore, this book has a center. It has a heart. If I had to boil it down, I would send you to chapters 6, 9, 15, and the conclusion. But hearts don't exist without bodies. And so the rest of the book matters.

I tell my sad and thankful story in chapters 1 and 2 and set the stage globally in chapter 3. In chapter 4 I explain why black-white relations get prominence, when the contemporary picture of diversity is far more complex. Chapter 5 takes me in over my head to the complexities of personal and structural causes for race-related disadvantages. But better to aim at understanding and fall short than to surrender at the outset.

Chapter 6 is the center, where the gospel shines as the God-given remedy for ten deadly realities that lie at the root of racial strife. Chapters 7–14 give the biblical exposition that lies at the foundation of everything else. Chapter 15 tackles the issue of interracial marriage, which I think is still just beneath the surface of many racial tensions. And chapter 16 wrestles with the inevitability and necessity of forming pre-judgments and how they relate to negative prejudices.

* * *

Now there are stories to tell, and problems to solve, and complexities to ponder, but in the end the good news of what Jesus has done, in dying and rising again to bear our sins and bring us to God, will make all the difference. Only Jesus can bring the bloodlines of race into the single bloodline of the cross and give us peace. Everything was made through him and for him (Col. 1:16). Therefore he will get the glory for this too. "All the families of the nations shall worship before [him]" (Ps. 22:27).

* * *

I am thankful to my wife, Noël, and daughter, Talitha, for the support they have been to me during the writing of this book. Again the elders of our church have made this book possible by giving me a writing leave each year, and even a few extra days this time, because of the unusual challenges of this book. David Mathis, my fellow elder and executive pastoral assistant, along with Nathan Miller, has managed my life for me, and provided innumerable helps that freed me to do this kind of thinking and writing. Finally, the people of Bethlehem—the flock I love to feed—have been a joy to serve. Without their peace and partnership, I could not flourish in the ministry. God has been good to me.

John Piper
Minneapolis, Minnesota
Maundy Thursday 2011

A NOTE TO THE READER ON *RACE* AND *RACISM*

I'm a stickler for clear definitions. I like to know what I am talking about. If you would rather just pick up my meaning as you go along, feel free to skip this section and go straight to the introduction. Stories are always more interesting.

Believe it or not, the existence of the reality of *race* itself is disputed. I mean seriously by very wise people whom I admire. I deal with this in appendix 1. And, of course, the term *racism* is ambiguous as well.

It seems to me that it is a healthy sign to wish that the term *race* did not exist. It has not served well to enhance human relations. As we use it, it is not a biblical category. We may not be able to communicate in our day without the term, but we can at least try to show why it's a fuzzy term that has often been hijacked by ideology for racist purposes.

RACE IS MORE COMPLEX THAN COLOR—BUT NOT LESS

Nevertheless, in this book I have not tried to abandon the terms *race* and *racial*. As loaded as the terms are, they are too embedded in our language and in the thousands of books and articles and sermons and lectures and conversations that make up the world we must relate to. There is no escaping this historically, and, in the present day, the problems we face are conceived along racial lines understood mainly as color lines.

For example, in 1899 W. E. B. Du Bois delivered a speech to the First Pan-African Conference at Westminster Hall, London, and began like this:

> The problem of the twentieth century is the problem of the color line, the question as to how far differences of race—which show them-selves chiefly in the color of the skin and the texture of the hair—will

hereafter be made the basis of denying to over half the world the right of sharing to their utmost ability the opportunities and privileges of modern civilization.[1]

I will not begrudge Du Bois the use of the term *race* in this sense. This is history. And it is still the way the race issue is powerfully formulated today. Unless I explicitly differentiate *race* and *racial* from *ethnicity* and *ethnic*, I would like you, the reader, to think of both when I mention either—that is, *ethnicity* with a physical component and *race* with a cultural component. Very often I use the terms together to draw out this combination of ideas.

RACISM VALUES ONE RACE OVER ANOTHER

With regard to the term *racism*, it is possible to get oneself tied in so many knots that it feels hopeless to define. Several years ago, we spent months as a pastoral staff at our church trying to come up with a working definition. I never thought defining a single word could be so difficult. But I am simply going to cut the knot with a decision to work with someone else's definition.

In the summer of 2004, the Presbyterian Church in America settled on the following definition, which I find helpful: "Racism is an explicit or implicit belief or practice that qualitatively distinguishes or values one race over other races."[2] In spite of saying above that I usually use the term *race* with cultural connotations (*ethnicity*), in this definition I am thinking of race primarily in terms of physical features. I am making a distinction between *race* and *ethnicity*.

The reason is that, since *ethnicity* includes beliefs and attitudes and behaviors, we are biblically and morally bound to value some aspects of some ethnicities over others. Where such valuing is truly rooted in biblical teaching about good and evil, this should not be called *racism*. There are aspects of every culture, including our own (whoever "our" is), which are sinful and in need of transformation. So the definition of *racism* here leaves room for assessing cultures on the basis of a biblical standard.

The focus of this definition of racism is on the *heart* and *behavior* of the racist. The *heart* that believes one race is more valuable than another is a sinful heart. And that sin is called *racism*. The *behavior* that distinguishes one race as more valuable than another is a sinful behavior. And that sin is called *racism*. This personal focus on the term *racism* does not exclude the expression of this sin in structural ways—for example, laws and policies that demean or exclude on the basis of race. (See chapter 5 where I focus on the issue of structural racism.)

PART ONE

OUR WORLD: THE NEED FOR THE GOSPEL

MARTIN LUTHER KING JR.
What Was It Like for Those Who Weren't There?

A book on race written by a baby boomer,[1] who came of age in the 1960s, has to begin with the civil rights movement. It still grips us, defines us, in so many ways. After slavery itself and the Civil War, no event or movement in the last four hundred years has affected the racial climate in America today more than this movement. Things were done and said in those days that need to be known by those who weren't there. The most eloquent spokesman of the movement was Martin Luther King Jr. His vision and his description of the situation that gave rise to the movement help explain why this book exists—especially part 1, "Our World: The Need for the Gospel."

THE LEADER

Martin Luther King Jr. was born January 15, 1929. On April 4, 1968, at 6:00 p.m., just outside Room 306 of the Lorraine Motel in Memphis, Tennessee, the thirty-nine-year-old King stood by the railing looking out over some rundown buildings just beyond Mulberry Street. James Earl Ray took aim with a .30 caliber rifle and blew away the right side of King's face and neck. He was pronounced dead at St. Joseph's Hospital an hour and five minutes later. The nonviolent voice against the rage of racism was gone.

Why would a thirty-nine-year-old man be killed? We need to teach our children this history. Some of us lived it and will never forget it. Segregation was the world we grew up in—legally mandated separation of races at all kinds of levels. Separate schools, separate motels, separate restrooms, separate swimming pools, separate drinking fountains. How could you more clearly communicate the lie that being black was like a disease. It had an unbelievably oppressive and demeaning effect on the African-American community. And it had a deadening and defiling effect on the conscience of the white community.

King did not spark the movement. He was swept into it, almost against his will. The civil rights movement had many catalysts. One of the most important happened on May 17, 1954. That was the day that the Supreme Court decided the case called *Brown v. Board of Education.* It declared that state-imposed segregation in the public schools was a violation of the Fourteenth Amendment. Many scholars say that *"Brown* remains the most important Supreme Court decision in [the twentieth] century."[2] Some of us would say that the 1973 *Roe v. Wade* was equally important, only for opposite reasons. *Brown* tried to restore rights to an oppressed group. *Roe v. Wade* took rights away from an oppressed group.

Another catalyst happened about a year and a half later. On December 1, 1955, a forty-two-year-old black woman named Rosa Parks (who died October 24, 2005) refused to surrender her seat to a white man on an officially segregated bus in Montgomery, Alabama. The black community of Montgomery rallied behind her when she was put in jail. They boycotted the buses for 381 days. The leader of the movement—by no choice of his own—was the twenty-six-year-old pastor of Dexter Avenue Baptist Church, the Reverend Martin Luther King Jr. And with that leadership, he became the unrivaled leader of the movement until his death thirteen years later. No one spoke in that cause with more influence.

"THE MOST ELOQUENT AND LEARNED EXPRESSION"

Martin Luther King called for freedoms and rights and justice that were long overdue. And he did it with an appeal to historic Christian vision, with amazing rhetorical skill, without condoning violence, and with unprecedented and lasting success. That's why there is a holiday in his honor. One of his writings in particular provides a window on the mid-twentieth-century world of black Americans—"Letter from Birmingham Jail."

The place is Birmingham, Alabama. The time is April 11, 1963. I was seventeen years old in Greenville, South Carolina. At the Gaston

Motel, Room 30, Martin Luther King, Ralph Abernathy, Wyatt Walker, and Fred Shuttlesworth decided to lead a peaceful, nonviolent demonstration the next day, Good Friday, against the racial injustices of the city.

As in most Southern cities in those days (including the one I was growing up in 350 miles away) bus seating was segregated; schools, parks, lunch counters, restrooms, drinking fountains—they were almost all segregated. Some called Birmingham the most segregated city in the country. Its bombings and torchings of black churches and homes had given it the name "Bombingham"—and "the Johannesburg of the South."

There was one catch. The sheriff, Bull Connor, had served Martin Luther King with a state-court injunction that prohibited him and other movement leaders from conducting demonstrations. With a wife and four children back home in Atlanta, King decided to violate the injunction, pursue a peaceful, nonviolent demonstration, and willingly go to jail. On Good Friday, King led his fifty volunteers downtown, up to the police line, came face-to-face with Connor, and knelt down with Ralph Abernathy in prayer. He and all the demonstrators were thrown into paddy wagons and put in jail.

On Tuesday, April 16, King was shown a copy of the *Birmingham News*, which contained a letter from eight Christian and Jewish clergymen of Alabama (all white), criticizing King for his demonstration. In response, King wrote what has come to be called "Letter from Birmingham Jail" and which one biographer described as "the most eloquent and learned expression of the goals and philosophy of the nonviolent movement ever written."[3]

WHAT IT WAS LIKE—FOR THOSE WHO WEREN'T THERE

We need to hear the power and insight with which King spoke to my generation in the sixties—enraging thousands and inspiring thousands. The white clergy had all said he should be more patient, wait, and not demonstrate. He wrote:

Perhaps it is easy for those who have never felt the stinging darts of segregation to say, "Wait." But when you have seen vicious mobs lynch your mothers and fathers at will and drown your sisters and brothers at whim; when you have seen hate-filled policemen curse, kick, and even kill your black brothers and sisters; when you see the vast majority of your 20 million Negro brothers smothering in an airtight cage of poverty in the midst of an affluent society;

. . . when you suddenly find your tongue twisted and your speech stammering as you seek to explain to your six-year-old daughter why she cannot go to the public amusement park that has just been advertised on television, and see tears welling up in her eyes when she's told that Funtown is closed to colored children, and see ominous clouds of inferiority beginning to form in her little mental sky, and see her beginning to distort her personality by developing an unconscious bitterness toward white people;

. . . when you have to concoct an answer for a five-year-old son who is asking, "Daddy, why do white people treat colored people so mean?"; when you take a cross-country drive and find it necessary to sleep night after night in the uncomfortable corners of your automobile because no motel will accept you; when you are humiliated day in and day out by nagging signs reading "white" and "colored"; when your first name becomes "Nigger," your middle name becomes "Boy" (however old you are) and your last name becomes "John," and your wife and mother are never given the respected title "Mrs.";

. . . when you are harried by day and haunted by night by the fact that you are a Negro, living constantly at tiptoe stance, never quite knowing what to expect next, and are plagued with inner fears and outer resentments; when you are forever fighting a degenerating sense of "nobodiness"—then you will understand why we find it difficult to wait. There comes a time when the cup of endurance runs over, and men are no longer willing to be plunged into the abyss of despair. I hope, sirs, you can understand our legitimate and unavoidable impatience.[4]

To the charge that he was an extremist, he responded like this:

Was not Jesus an extremist for love: "Love your enemies, bless them that curse you, do good to them that hate you, and pray for them which despitefully use you, and persecute you"? Was not Amos an extremist for justice: "Let justice roll down like waters and righteousness like an ever-flowing stream"? Was not Paul an extremist for the Christian gospel: "I bear in my body the marks of the Lord Jesus"?

Was not Martin Luther an extremist: "Here I stand; I cannot do otherwise, so help me God"? And John Bunyan: "I will stay in jail to the end of my days before I make a butchery of my conscience." And Abraham Lincoln: "Thus this nation cannot survive half slave and half free." And Thomas Jefferson: "We hold these truths to be self-evident, that all men are created equal . . . " So the question is not whether we will be extremist, but what kind of extremist we will be. Will we be extremists for hate or for love?[5]

And finally he delivered a powerful call to the church, which rings as true today as it did in 1963:

There was a time when the church was very powerful—in the time when the early Christians rejoiced at being deemed worthy to suffer for what they believed. In those days the church was not merely a thermometer that recorded the ideas and principles of popular opinion; it was a thermostat that transformed the mores of society. . . . But the judgment of God is upon the church [today] as never before. If today's church does not recapture the sacrificial spirit of the early church, it will lose its authenticity, forfeit the loyalty of millions, and be dismissed as an irrelevant social club with no meaning for the 20th century.[6]

That is Martin Luther King's prophetic voice ringing out of the Birmingham jail in 1963.

HOW MUCH HAS CHANGED IN THE HEART?

Many things have changed since 1963. And some deep things have not changed. Let me illustrate. There are probably more vicious white supremacists in America today than there were in 1968. The victims are as likely to be Latinos or Somali immigrants as African Americans whose ancestors have been here for centuries. The Ku Klux Klan has no corner on hate any more.

On June 7, 1998—that's '98, not '68—outside Jasper, Texas, James Byrd, a forty-nine-year-old African American, was beaten and chained by his ankles to the back of a pickup truck and dragged two miles until his head ripped off. The perpetrators had racist tattoos, one of them depicting a black hanging from a tree. Many things have changed in the last forty years, but in some people some deep things haven't changed. There is still plenty of hate.

MORE THAN BLACK AND WHITE—BUT NOT LESS

I am aware that the issue of race relations is bigger and more complex than black and white relations in this country. I've devoted a chapter to the wider global reality we are facing (chapter 3), and another to why this book is especially (though not exclusively) focused on black-white relations (chapter 4). But we will do well not to speak in too many broad generalizations when dealing with race. Better to anchor our thoughts to the real world. And in the real world, people are one thing and not another. They may be complex, but they are not generalities. They are specific human beings. Focusing on my own history, and the black-white reality in particular, has helped me keep my feet on the ground and my heart connected to real people.

Part 1 of this book focuses on our world, as part 2 focuses on God's Word. Or we might say, part 1 deals with the issues raised by natural bloodlines, and part 2 deals with the new line stemming not from natural blood but from the shed blood of Jesus. What we will see in part 1 is that the world we live in is a world where only the gospel of Jesus Christ can bring the kind of racial and ethnic harmony that we were made to enjoy.

SECTION ONE

MY STORY, MY DEBT, MY WORLD:
WHY I WROTE THE BOOK

Remember not the sins of my youth
    or my transgressions;
according to your steadfast love remember me,
    for the sake of your goodness, O Lord!

PSALM 25:7

CHAPTER ONE

MY STORY: FROM GREENVILLE TO BETHLEHEM

Barack Obama, in a new preface to his older book *Dreams from My Father: A Story of Race and Inheritance,* quotes William Faulkner to show that history is never dead. He describes the difference between the time when the book was written and the time he was writing the new preface.

The book was first published in 1995 "against a backdrop of Silicon Valley and a booming stock market; the collapse of the Berlin Wall; Mandela—in slow, sturdy steps—emerging from prison to lead a country; the signing of peace accords in Oslo."[1] He observed that there was a rising global optimism as writers announced the end of our fractured history, "the ascendance of free markets, and liberal democracy, the replacement of old hatreds and wars between nations with virtual communities and battle for market share."[2]

"And then," he says, "on September 11, 2001, the world fractured."

"History returned that day with a vengeance; . . . in fact, as Faulkner reminds us, the past is never dead and buried—it isn't even past. This collective history, this past, directly touches my own."[3]

GROWING UP IN GREENVILLE

This is true about the story of race in America. It is certainly true in relation to me. "This collective history, this past, directly touches my own." I was born in 1946 in Chattanooga, Tennessee, and from the time I was six months old, I grew up in Greenville, South Carolina. I left for college eighteen years later and spent four years in Wheaton, Illinois; three years in Pasadena, California; three years in Munich, Germany; and the rest of my life in the Twin Cities of Minnesota. But those early years in South Carolina are the roots of my racial burden.

The population of South Carolina in 1860 was about 700,000. Sixty percent were African Americans (420,000), and all but 9,000 of these were slaves. That's a mere 150 years ago—only fifty-nine years before my father was born. On December 20, 1860, South Carolina was the first state to secede from the Union, largely in protest over Abraham Lincoln's election as an anti-slavery president and the implications that had for states' rights. Three weeks later, the Civil War began in Charleston, South Carolina.

Over four years later, on April 9, 1865, the war ended with the surrender of Southern general Robert E. Lee at Appomattox Court House. Ninety years later, when I was nine years old in Greenville, the enforced segregation was almost absolute: drinking fountains, public restrooms, public schools, public swimming pools, bus seating, housing, restaurants, hospital waiting rooms, dentist waiting rooms, bus station waiting rooms, and—with their own kind of enforcement—churches, including mine. I can tell you from the inside that, for all the rationalized glosses, it was not "separate but equal." It was not respectful, it was not just, it was not loving, and therefore it was not Christian. It was ugly and demeaning. And, as we will see, because of my complicity I have much to be sorry about.

Which is one reason this book focuses so heavily on the gospel of Jesus Christ. I owe my life and hope to the gospel. Without it I would still be strutting with racist pride, or I would be suffering the moral paralysis of "white guilt."[4] But the gospel has an answer to both pride and guilt. I hope this book makes that plain.

GROWING UP BLACK IN GREENVILLE

Three and a half miles across town from where I grew up, in the same city, five years older than I, another little boy was growing up on the other side of the racial divide. His name was Jesse Jackson.

Jackson was born October 8, 1941, at his home on 20 Haynie Street. When Jackson was thirteen the family moved to a newly constructed housing project, Fieldcrest Village (now Jesse Jackson Townhomes)—three miles to the east. His biographer describes the boyhood neighborhood:

> A dingy warren of flimsy little houses, with plank porch railings ranked with rusted coffee cans that, in the summer, held rufflings of geraniums and caladiums. Each house was perched on a tiny, grassless, rutted yard, some scattered with wood chips and upturned washtubs and old tires and bluish puddles of pitched-out dishwater, others whisked clean with straw brooms and enclosed by spindly fences assembled out of scraps of boards and wire, with walkways bordered by bits of brick and cement block and broken bottles set in neat parallel lines in the dirt.[5]

Our worlds were so close and yet so far apart. His mother, Helen, loved the same Christian radio station my mother did—WMUU, the voice of Bob Jones University. But there was a big difference. The very school that broadcast all that Bible truth would not admit blacks. And the large, white Baptist church four miles from Jesse Jackson's home wouldn't either. Nor would mine.

This was my hometown. And there is no mystery in it as to why a young black man growing up there—or a Martin Luther King growing up in Atlanta a generation earlier—would get his theological education at a liberal institution (such as Chicago Theological Seminary or Crozer Theological Seminary). Our fundamental and evangelical schools—and almost every other institution—especially in the South, were committed to segregation.

I WAS A RACIST

I was, in those years, manifestly racist. As a child and a teenager my attitudes and actions assumed the superiority of my race in almost every way without knowing or wanting to know anybody who was black, except Lucy. Lucy came to our house on Saturdays to help my mother clean. I liked Lucy, but the whole structure of the relationship was demeaning. Those who defend the noble spirit of Southern slaveholders by pointing to how nice they were to their slaves, and how deep the affections were, and how they even attended each other's personal celebrations, seem to be naïve about what makes a relationship degrading.

No, she was not a slave. But the point still stands. Of course, we were nice. Of course, we loved Lucy. Of course, she was invited to my sister's wedding. As long as she and her family "knew their place." Being nice to, and having strong affections for, and including in our lives is what we do for our dogs too. It doesn't say much about honor and respect and equality before God. My affections for Lucy did not provide the slightest restraint on my racist mouth when I was with my friends.

MY MOTHER: GUTSY YANKEE FUNDAMENTALIST

My demeaning attitude was not mainly my parents' fault. In fact, in some ways, it was in spite of my parents that I was a racist. My mother, who grew up in Pennsylvania, literally washed my mouth out with soap once for saying, "Shut up!" to my sister. She would have washed my mouth out with gasoline if she knew how foul my mouth was racially when she wasn't around.

In 1962 my home church voted not to allow blacks into the services.[6] The rationale, as I remember, was that in the heated context of the civil rights era, the only reason blacks would want to be there would be political, which is not what church is for. As I recall, my mother was the lone voice on that Wednesday night to vote no on this motion. I could be wrong about that. But she did vote no.

In December of that year, my sister was married in the church, and my mother invited Lucy's whole family to come. And they came. I remember an incredibly tense and awkward moment as they came in the door of the foyer (which must have taken incredible courage). The ushers did not know what to do. One was about to usher them to the balcony (which had barely been used since the church was built). My mother—all five feet, two inches of her—intervened and by herself took them by the arm and seated them on the main floor of the sanctuary.

She was, under God, the seed of my salvation in more ways than one. As I watched that drama, I knew deep down that my attitudes were an offense to my mother and to her God. Oh, how thankful I am for the conviction and courage of my gutsy, Yankee, fundamentalist mother.[7]

URBANA '67

My college years were fairly insulated. This was not the fault of Wheaton College. There was plenty of activism and political engagement among students and faculty at the time. It was owing to my own retiring and timid bent (another story that I tell elsewhere[8]). I would describe myself as simply disengaged from the wider social and political world for most of my college days. Large things were happening intellectually and spiritually, but they were happening in the furnace of my soul, not in the fires burning in urban America.[9]

One of the most memorable moments of my awakening from the sinful oblivion of racism was during my senior year in college. Noël, whom I married a year later, came with me to the great Urbana Missions Conference in December 1967. During a question-and-answer time before thousands of students, we heard Warren Webster, general director of the Conservative Baptist Foreign Mission Society, and former missionary to Pakistan, answer a student's question: *What if your daughter falls in love with a Pakistani while you're on the mission field and wants to marry him?*

The question was clearly asked from a standpoint of concern that this would be a racial or ethnic dilemma for Webster. (This was four months before Martin Luther King Jr. was killed.) With great forcefulness, Webster said something like: "Better a Christian Pakistani than a godless white American!" I think the answer was even more colorful than that (perhaps including a reference to a rich American *banker*. But I'm not sure.) Whatever the wording, the impact on Noël and me was profound. From that moment, I knew I had a lot of homework to do. The perceived wrongness of interracial marriage had been for me one of the unshakeable reasons why segregation was right.

THE FULLER SEMINARY YEARS

In the year that I finished Wheaton and started seminary in California, Martin Luther King Jr. was assassinated. It was April 4, 1968. These were explosive days, and I was fortunate to have seminary professors who cared about the issues and were committed to finding the biblical perspective on racial relations. One of those professors, Paul Jewett, compiled a 208-page syllabus of readings for us called "Readings in Racial Prejudice."

These readings were absolutely shocking. I had never seen or heard anything like this in my life. I still have this syllabus on the shelf across the room in front of me right now in my study. I could not read about the crimes of vicious hatred toward blacks and come away without trembling. Jewett's introduction to that syllabus ends like this:

> And now let us listen to the groans of Frederick Douglass, feel the lash with Amy, endure the satire of Du Bois, and measure the wrath of Malcolm X; let us contemplate the pathos of black childhood and the tragedy of black womanhood. And let us not forget that [as Martin Luther King Jr. said] "he who passively accepts evil is as much involved in it as he who helps to perpetrate it. He who accepts evil without protesting against it is really cooperating with it." And let us also remember that if God has given us a revelation of the true nature of man, surely we will render account if we do not live in the light of that revelation, and especially so if we are called to the holy office of the Christian ministry.[10]

Finally, in a class on ethics with the imposing figure of Professor Lewis Smedes in the spring of 1971, I faced head-on the biblical question of interracial marriage. I did a research project and wrote a paper called "The Ethics of Interracial Marriage." I have it here in front of me on the desk as I write. It was typed on the kind of sticky white paper that let you erase typing ink without using wite-out. He wrote six comments in the margin and gave me an A–.

Smedes was a realist, as the title of one of his best books shows (*Love within Limits: A Realist's View of 1 Corinthians 13*).[11] He approved of my exegesis and what I wrote in conclusion:

> Since . . . opposition to interracial marriage tends to perpetuate discrimination, the neighbors to whom one must be loving in this situation are not only the spouses and children of the interracial marriage. The welfare of society as a whole and the rights of the race discriminated against come into view.

However, his realism moved him to write in the margin:

> This is a tough question, I think, especially at the present [1971]. It is extremely hard to *see* the positive effect of specific interracial mar-

riages. Perhaps Black *identity* stress at present makes the positive effect of interracial marriage even less clear. I suspect we are left, for the present, with the burden of destroying discrimination while accepting the *minimal* of interracial marriage whose goodness has to be evaluated in terms of expediencies rather than absolute moral principles.

I doubt that Smedes would talk this way today (he died December 19, 2002). I don't know. His hesitancy to give a wholehearted affirmation to the goodness of interracial marriage was rooted in his desire not to minimize the struggle for the intrinsic worth of authentic black identity. My own take, then and now, given what I knew from my own background, is that affirming the beauty of interracial marriage, especially in real, concrete cases, carries a far greater dignity-affirming wallop than the more subtle threat to minority identity in marrying a person from the majority culture. But one can understand the concern.

That biblical study of interracial marriage that I did in seminary was for me a settling of the matter. I have not gone back from what I saw there. The Bible does not oppose or forbid interracial marriages but, as I will argue in chapter 15, sees them as a positive good for the glory of Christ.

IN THE SHADOW OF DACHAU

I spent the next three years (June 1971 to June 1974) in Germany, taking one trip home for Christmas in 1972. It is difficult to measure the effect of being removed from one's own country for three years—and feeling oneself becoming part of a much larger reality than America and the American church. Add to that the fact that Germany's history of horrific racist Nazism was only twenty-six years old. Hitler killed himself the year before I was born.

The Dachau concentration camp, preserved with its "Nie Wieder" (Never Again) memorial, lay ten miles northwest of where we lived in Munich. It was not the place you went for a Sunday outing. But we did go. Barbed wire, barrack rows, triple-decker trough beds, cremation furnaces and hanging rooms, the ostensible shower rooms—they are all there. This was the witness to the belief in the evolutionary superiority of an Aryan "master race." Living in the literal and figurative shadow of such horrific effects of racism solidified the merciful reorientation of my mind.

FROM SUBURBAN CLASSROOM TO URBAN PARISH

I took my degree from the University of Munich in the summer of 1974 and for the next six years taught Biblical Studies at Bethel College in a suburb of the Twin Cities of Minnesota. They were good years, but God's call to the pastorate became irresistible in late 1979. One of the impulses was the sense that my classrooms were too distant from the front lines of seeing the gospel change different kinds of people. The students represented a very small slice of humanity.

This is not a criticism. College education is necessarily self-selecting in many ways. Mostly the students will be between eighteen and twenty-two and well educated. I thank God for teachers who are called to give their lives to the task. I am deeply thankful for my own college days at a school much like Bethel.

But in the fall of 1979, the passion to preach and to apply God's Word to a wider range of people led me to a vocational crisis, and I gave my notice at Bethel and sought a church. In the summer of 1980, I accepted the call to Bethlehem Baptist Church, a 109-year-old center-city church on the edge of downtown Minneapolis. To my mind the location was perfect for the kind of impulses I felt. To the west was the upscale business district. To the north, the Metrodome (just being built) and light industrial district. To the east, the University of Minnesota. And to the south, the poorest and most diverse part of the city—Elliot Park and Phillips neighborhood.

We moved into the city and have lived within walking distance of the church in Elliot Park and Phillips ever since (now almost thirty years). The 2005 ethnic breakdown of our neighborhood was 24.6 percent Caucasian, 29 percent African American, 22 percent Hispanic, 11 percent Native American, 5.9 percent Asian, 7.4 percent other.[12] Immigration patterns have changed over the years with various groups swelling and shrinking from time to time. But that is pretty much what I see out of my study window on 11th Avenue South.

ADOPTION AT FIFTY

This is where I wanted to be. And this is where I would like to die. God could move me. But it will take a crystal-clear divine call to make me leave this kind of diversity. Noël and I raised four sons in this neighborhood. We used to joke that the reason we don't have a television is that the boys can watch the nightly news on the streets outside their house.

Not long after I turned fifty in 1996, Noël got a phone call from a friend and pro-life social worker in Georgia. "I have a little girl here who needs a family," she said, "I think she's for you." Was this the answer to Noël's prayer for a daughter that so far God had answered with four sons? It was not an easy decision. I was fifty, and this little girl was African American. Starting the parenting role again at age fifty was not in the plan. There were those who thought I was crazy to consider it.

Noël and I took long walks together in those days as we sought the Lord together. Finally, I knew the answer. Love your wife, love this little girl as your own, and commit yourself to the day of your death to the issue of racial harmony. Nothing binds a pastor's heart to diversity more than having it in his home. That was over fifteen years ago. In those years, we have tried to pursue as a church a deeper and wider racial and ethnic diversity and harmony. (You can see a few of the things we have done in Appendix 2.)

I AM NOT A MODEL MULTIETHNIC URBAN PASTOR

If any of this sounds valiant, don't be too impressed. I am not a good example of an urban pastor. Because of the way I believe God calls me to use my time, I don't have significant relationships with most of my neighbors. Nor does our church reflect the diversity of this neighborhood. There is diversity, but nothing like the statistics above.

Probably I could have been far more effective in immediate urban impact in this neighborhood if I had not written books or carried on a wider speaking ministry. Some thank me for this ministry, and others think I have made a mistake. Again, you may see why I cherish and cling to the gospel of Jesus.

The Lord will be my judge someday. I will give an account to him of how I served him. I expect that as he goes down the list of the choices I have made, none will have a perfectly pure motivation, and many will appear as unwise in the bright light of his holiness. I hope I have been a good steward of my gifts and time. But my confidence in the judgment is not in that. It's in the perfection of Jesus that God has credited to me through faith and in the punishment Jesus endured for me. And I believe there will be in my overall ministry sufficient, imperfect fruits of love that witness that my union with Jesus by faith was real.

I am not writing this book as a successful multiethnic leader. I am not successful. I am not an expert in diversity. If you came looking for the pragmatic silver bullet for the multiethnic congregation, I may as well bid you farewell. I don't have it. I write because of truth I see in the Scriptures, convictions I have in my mind, and longings I feel in my heart.

I believe that the gospel—the good news of Christ crucified in our place to remove the wrath of God and provide forgiveness of sins and power for sanctification—is our only hope for the kind of racial diversity and harmony that ultimately matters. If we abandon the fullness of the gospel to make racial and ethnic diversity quicker or easier, we create a mere shadow of the kingdom, an imitation. And we lose the one thing that can bring about Christ-exalting diversity and harmony. Any other kind is an alluring snare. For what does it profit a man if he gains complete diversity and loses his own soul?

I am debtor both to the Greeks, and to the Barbarians; both to the wise, and to the unwise.

ROMANS 1:14 (KJV)

Pay careful attention to yourselves and to all the flock, in which the Holy Spirit has made you overseers, to care for the church of God, which he obtained with his own blood.

ACTS 20:28

CHAPTER TWO

THE GOSPEL I LOVE, THE DEBT I OWE, AND THE CHURCH I SERVE

If, as I said in chapter 1, I am not a model multiethnic urban pastor, why am I writing this book? I said, "I write because of truth I see in the Scriptures, and convictions I have in my mind, and longings I feel in my heart." It may be helpful to spell out some of those truths, convictions, and longings.

I LOVE THE GLORY OF GOD IN THE CROSS OF CHRIST

First, I have come to see that love for the glory of God and reverence for the cross of Christ imply longing for racial and ethnic diversity and harmony in the body of Christ. This is what chapters 7–16 of this book aim to show. I do reverence the cross of Christ and love the glory of God. The cross is the solid *foundation* of my hope, and the glory of God is the ultimate *content* of my hope. "We have been justified by faith . . . and we rejoice in hope of the glory of God" (Rom. 5:1–2). Therefore, I long to see the followers of Christ, especially myself, living the kind of lives that advance the cause of Christ-exalting racial diversity and Spirit-enabled racial harmony. I pray this book serves that end.

I HAVE A DEBT TO PAY

Second, I have a debt to pay. I have already confessed in chapter 1 the racism of my youth. As much as I tore down, I would like to build up. This is not penance—as though I did not believe the blood of Christ were sufficient to cover all my sins. This book does not atone for anything. Christ is our only atonement. And he is enough. That is not the kind of debt I have to pay. If I slander a colleague and later I repent, I owe him the effort to restore his good name. If I break out your window in a drunken stupor, I owe you a new window and will work on it when I am sober. If I demean a racial group, I owe them the effort to affirm their dignity when I awake from my stupor.

But there is more to it than that. The debt I feel is not mainly to any particular group. This is a debt to all sinners. It is the kind of happy debt awakened by the experience of God's grace in Christ. Paul said in Romans 1:14, "I am debtor both to the Greeks, and to the Barbarians;[1] both to the wise, and to the unwise" (KJV). What did he mean by that? He meant that, owing to nothing in himself, Jesus had called him and forgiven him and accepted him and promised him everlasting joy in the presence of God.

As he looked around at the "Barbarians" and "Greeks," he saw people who were just as undeserving of grace as he was. Neither he nor they had any right to the grace of God. But here he was—the "foremost" of sinners (1 Tim. 1:15)—overwhelmed with Jesus's redeeming love. The effect this had on Paul was to give him a joyful sense of indebtedness to all other sinners like himself.

The debt was not to complete Jesus's payment for sin; it was the overflow of the fullness of that payment. "I owe you the gospel" did not mean "You deserve it." It meant, "I did not deserve it either, and by its very nature it cannot be hoarded. I *must* tell you the gospel or I will deny the grace reigning in me."

That is the way I feel about God's rescuing me from the sins of my youth, especially the sins rooted in racism. I am called and forgiven and accepted by God owing to nothing in me. When I met a member of my church who belonged to the Ku Klux Klan in the early sixties, it was as possible that I would have joined him as it was that I would be shocked. Sheer grace shocked me.

As imperfect as I am in my pursuit of racial and ethnic harmony, I am not where I was. This is owing to the gospel of Jesus Christ. I have no boast. Therefore, I am a glad debtor to Christians and non-Christians to bear witness to the grace of God in the gospel and how it frees from the slavery of racism.

THE BLOOD-BOUGHT PEOPLE NEED HELP

Third, as a pastor of a local church, I am responsible to shepherd the flock of God where he has made me an overseer. These are the people who are bought with Jesus's blood (Acts 20:28). Unbelievers cannot pursue Jesus-exalting racial diversity and harmony. They pursue another kind. It is better than race wars; but it is not what Jesus died to bring about. The church is the assembly of those in whom the gospel has taken root. Therefore, it is the group where the reconciling power of the gospel will be seen—or not.

On this issue, given our history, we are not as mature in America as we should be. God's word in Hebrews 5:12–14 rings true in this regard:

> Though by this time you ought to be teachers, you need someone to teach you again the basic principles of the oracles of God. You need milk, not solid food, for everyone who lives on milk is unskilled in the word of righteousness, since he is a child. But solid food is for the mature, for those who have their powers of discernment trained by constant practice to distinguish good from evil.

Maturity in the text is defined as having our powers of discernment trained by constant practice in distinguishing good from evil. Most Christians have not trained their powers of discernment in matters of racial and ethnic issues. Many of us shepherds have not done all that we could or should to help the sheep grow in the maturity—the wisdom—that comes with "constant practice to distinguish good from evil."

NEITHER OBLIVIOUS NOR IDOLATROUS

Churches sometimes swing between the extremes of painful obliviousness to ethnic concerns and idolizing the topic as the only thing that matters. An example of the obliviousness is cited by Soong-Chan Rah, senior pastor of Cambridge Community Fellowship Church (Massachusetts). He said in an interview in 2005:

> Last summer, [a major Christian publisher] distributed a vacation Bible school curriculum called *Far-out Far East Rickshaw Rally*. Sadly, the content played to every stereotype imaginable about Asian culture.

The theme song headlines like, "Wax on wax off, get your rickshaw ready"—stuff straight out of *The Karate Kid*. It had nothing to do with the reality of Asian culture. It showed images of little white girls in kimonos with chopsticks in their hair. Some activity suggestions are to have kids dress up in inflatable sumo outfits and wrestle each other. The stereotypes and caricatures are without shame. And this was not 1955 or 1971. It was 2004.

If you're a socially conscious, young Asian-American, why would you ever want to step foot in a church where you would encounter people with that kind of worldview? You'll want to stay with your own.[2]

On the other hand, in this same interview in 2005, Frank Reid, senior pastor of Bethel African Methodist Episcopal Church in Baltimore, pointed out the dangers of making the issue of race into an idol:

What the early Christians did not have to deal with to the same extent that we do today is how race has become an idol. On both sides of the racial divide, so much is twisted by the social constructs we've formed and cling to about race. . . .

We've made a sport of pointing out racism, when what we should be doing is focusing our prayers and actions toward creating congregations that proclaim Christ's lordship over his entire church.[3]

Some churches have never taken the first baby steps in thinking biblically about race and ethnicity. Others devote so much focus to it that people get sick of the issue, and backlash sets in. Neither of these extremes is helpful. The aim is biblical maturity—thoughtful, balanced, careful, informed, humble, experienced, wise, Jesus-exalting, God-centered, gospel-strengthened growth in the way we think and talk and act in regard to race and ethnicity—and in relation to real people different from ourselves.

THE ISSUE OF GLOBAL CREDIBILITY

The church is not called to be responsible for the way unbelievers run their lives. But we are called to be responsible, by the power of the Spirit and for the glory of Jesus, for the way believers live and the kind of relationships that are cultivated in the fellowship of the church. The credibility of the gospel around the world hangs in part on this dimension of our witness. Vinay Samuel, director of the Oxford Centre for Religion and Public Life, pointed to this credibility issue at the Lausanne II missions conference in Manila over twenty years ago. The relevance of these words remains:

> The most serious thing [concerning the credibility of our global witness] is the image around the world that evangelicals are soft on racial injustice. . . . One sign and wonder, biblically speaking, that alone can prove the power of the gospel is that of reconciliation. . . . [Hindus and Muslims] cannot duplicate the miracle of black and white together, of racial injustice being swept away by the power of the gospel. . . . Our credibility is at stake.[4]

We must not overstate this. The truth of the gospel does not depend on the assessments of fallen and fallible people in the world. And according to the book of Acts, the church grew in numbers even though "everywhere it is spoken against" (Acts 28:22). Outside the church there is no commitment to exalt Jesus and his cross through racial harmony. But that is the only kind of harmony that honors God and serves people longer than the vapor's breath of this life. So the world is not the final arbiter of our successes and failures. But what the world sees matters. We want to show we are Christians by the way we love (John 13:35), and we want to do the kinds of things that lead people to glorify our Father who is in heaven (Matt. 5:14–16).

"LOVE AND EVERYTHING ELSE"

Outside the church the motives for racial harmony range from noble to raunchy. For example, novelist and essayist Kurt Vonnegut said in the wake of the Rodney King verdict, "We can actually hate blacks if we want to so long as they have a fair shot at the American dream. To hell with love and everything else."[5] My pastoral colleague David Michael wrote in response, "The 'love and everything else' is what reconciliation is all about. It requires a change of heart, and therefore in the mind of my mentors, the only hope for reconciliation is at the foot of the cross."[6]

This is the main calling of the church—the "love and everything else." Above all this, everything includes the centrality of the cross and the glory of Jesus, bearing credible fruit in the works of love. And that love includes the humble pursuit of racial diversity and harmony. So, as a pastor, I feel a burden to help my people see these things and to lead them, as a sinful and forgiven pastor, into greater racial and ethnic maturity.

Therefore, the gospel that I love, and the happy debt that I owe my fellow sinners, and the needs of the church that I serve (and other needy churches like mine) move me to write this book. There are other reasons behind the writing of this book, such as the global shifts in population and church growth, and the peculiar status the black and white racial issue has in our land. These two I will take up in the following chapters.

Let the nations be glad and sing for joy,
    for you judge the peoples with equity
    and guide the nations upon earth.

PSALM 67:4

Many will come from east and west and recline at table with Abraham, Isaac, and Jacob in the kingdom of heaven, while the sons of the kingdom will be thrown into the outer darkness.

MATTHEW 8:11–12

CHAPTER THREE

GLOBAL SHIFTING AND THE NEW FACE OF THE CHURCH

One significant impulse behind this book is the fact that the necessity of relating to people racially and ethnically different from ourselves will only increase in the days ahead. This is true because of population trends around the world and because of the way the church is growing in the Global South.

DEMOGRAPHIC PROJECTIONS FOR THE UNITED STATES

Consider some projections for the United States made in 2008 by the Census Bureau.[1]

- Minorities, now roughly one-third of the US population, are expected to become the majority in 2042, with the nation projected to be 54 percent minority in 2050. By 2023, minorities will comprise more than half of all children.
- The non-Hispanic, single-race white population is projected to be only slightly larger in 2050 (203.3 million) than in 2008 (199.8 million). In fact, this group is projected to lose population in the 2030s and 2040s and comprise 46 percent of the total population in 2050, down from 66 percent in 2008.
- The Hispanic population is projected to nearly triple, from 46.7 million to 132.8 million during the 2008–2050 period. Its share of the nation's total population is projected to double, from 15 percent to 30 percent. Thus, nearly one in three US residents would be Hispanic.
- The black population is projected to increase from 41.1 million (14 percent of the population) in 2008 to 65.7 million (15 percent) in 2050.

- The Asian population is projected to climb from 15.5 million to 40.6 million. Its share of the nation's population is expected to rise from 5.1 percent to 9.2 percent.
- Among the remaining race groups, American Indians and Alaska Natives are projected to rise from 4.9 million to 8.6 million (or from 1.6 to 2.0 percent of the total population). The Native Hawaiian and Other Pacific Islander population is expected to more than double, from 1.1 million to 2.6 million. The number of people who identify themselves as being of two or more races is projected to more than triple, from 5.2 million to 16.2 million.

THE CHANGE IS ALREADY HERE

The present reality in America is already far more diverse in major parts of the country than many realize. As recently as 1970, the white non-Hispanic population of California was 80 percent.[2] In the year 2000, white non-Hispanics became a minority for the first time. Today that group is 43 percent of the population of California.[3]

Our major US cities, like urban centers around the world, are increasingly diverse, and there is no reason to believe the process of urbanization and diversification will not continue.

Through most of history, the human population has lived a rural lifestyle, dependent on agriculture and hunting for survival. In 1800, only 3 percent of the world's population lived in urban areas. By 1900, almost 14 percent were urbanites, although only 12 cities had 1 million or more inhabitants. In 1950, 30 percent of the world's population resided in urban centers. The number of cities with over 1 million people had grown to 83.

The world has experienced unprecedented urban growth in recent decades. In 2000, about 47 percent of the world's population lived in urban areas, about 2.8 billion. There are 411 cities over 1 million. More developed nations are about 76 percent urban, while 40 percent of residents of less developed countries live in urban areas. However, urbanization is occurring rapidly in many less developed countries. It is expected that 60 percent of the world population will be urban by 2030.[4]

With this urbanization comes increasing ethnic diversity. And that means people who are ethnically different are thrown closer together.

The urgency of racial and ethnic harmony amid increasing diversity increases year by year.

MY TOWN, THE TWIN CITIES

Here in my Midwestern hometown of Minneapolis/St. Paul, for example, a thousand miles from any ocean, there is a stunning array of ethnic diversity. John Mayer's *City View Report 2008* gives these remarkable facts:[5]

- The Twin Cities' Hispanic population more than doubled from 1990 to 2000. The Twin Cities was the eighth fastest growing Hispanic city in the United States during the 1990s.
- The Twin Cities was the ninth fastest growing Asian city in the US during 1990s.
- There are thirteen thousand international students in the Twin Cities (10,000 college students and 3,000 high school exchange students).
- There are two hundred different languages spoken in the Twin Cities area.
- The light rail system in the Twin Cities sells tickets in four languages: English, Spanish, Hmong, and Somali.
- The Phillips neighborhood [where I live] of South Minneapolis has become the most diverse single neighborhood in America with one-hundred-plus languages spoken there.
- In 2004, Minnesota ranked third in the nation for the most new refugees. Only California and Florida have more.
- The Twin Cities has the largest Hmong, Oromo (Ethiopian), Liberian, Karen (Burmese), Anuak (Ethiopian/Sudanese), and Somali populations in the US and is home to the second largest Tibetan population.

DISCOVERING THE "ETHNOBURB"

Our church established a new campus three years ago in Burnsville, Minnesota, sixteen miles south of our downtown campus in Minneapolis. Most people probably thought of this as an expansion to "the suburbs." In a sense, yes. But John Mayer calls Burnsville an "Ethnoburb." He describes it like this:

[Twenty-nine percent] of the kids in the Burnsville School District are non-white. Two blocks from my house is an Hispanic supermarket. One mile from my house is a Somali Muslim Halal Market. My next-door neighbor is from Cambodia. Next to them is a family from Belize. My wife's Indonesian. This is the new face of our city and our country.[6]

THE GLOBAL SOUTH

Not only is the population in general growing and moving in ways that throw us into more diverse relationships, but the Christian church is undergoing dramatic demographic shifts that will increasingly marginalize people who are not eager to be a part of something more diverse and less white.

Philip Jenkins, professor of history and religious studies at Pennsylvania State University, has clarified this development perhaps more than any one.[7] The new terminology that has been introduced into our vocabulary is the term *Global South*, a reference to the astonishing growth of the Christian church in Africa, Latin America, and Asia, while the formerly dominant centers of Christian influence in Europe are weakening. For example:

- At the beginning of the twentieth century, Europeans dominated the world church, with approximately 70.6 percent of the world's Christian population. By 1938, on the eve of World War II, the apparent European domination of Protestantism and Catholicism remained strong. Yet by the end of the twentieth century, the European percentage of world Christianity had shrunk to 28 percent of the total; Latin America and Africa combined provided 43 percent of the world's Christians.[8]
- In 1900, Africa had ten million Christians representing about 10 percent of the population; by 2000, this figure had grown to 360 million, representing about half the population. Quantitatively, this may well be the largest shift in religious affiliation that had ever occurred, anywhere.[9]
- The number of African Christians is growing at around 2.36 percent annually, which would lead us to project a doubling of the continent's Christian population in less than thirty years.[10]
- By 2050, Christianity will be chiefly the religion of Africa and the African diaspora. By then, there will be about three billion Christians in the world, and the population of those who will be white and non-Latino will be between one-fifth and one-sixth the total.[11]

- At the 1998 Lambeth Conference, the highest consultative body of the Anglican Communion, 224 of the 735 bishops were from Africa, compared with only 139 from the United Kingdom and Europe. Anglicans in Nigeria report seventeen million baptized members, compared with 2.8 million in the United States.[12]

WHAT'S THE POINT OF ALL THE STATISTICS?

The point of these statistics about the urbanization, diversification, and the changing global church is fourfold. First, I hope they humble those of us who are white and have assumed a kind of dominance for a long time. This is fading, and, if God would humble us under his wise and mighty hand, we would rejoice with tremendous joy.

Second, I hope this new ethnic reality inclines our hearts to know and love our Christian brothers and sisters who are ethnically different from ourselves and makes us eager and ready to be genuine partners with them in the great challenges of missions before us.

Third, I pray the reality of ever-nearer racial and ethnic diversity will make us go deeper into the grace of the gospel so that our roots are strong, when change seems overwhelming or even threatening. In that way, I pray we would increasingly bear the fruit of the gospel in the pursuit of Christ-exalting ethnic diversity and harmony. That's why I wrote the book.

SECTION TWO

BLACK AND WHITE AND
THE BLOOD OF JESUS

None is righteous, no, not one; no one understands; no one seeks for God. All have turned aside; together they have become worthless; no one does good, not even one.

ROMANS 3:10–12

CHAPTER FOUR

WHY THIS BOOK GIVES PROMINENCE TO BLACK-WHITE RELATIONSHIPS

It is unmistakable to the reader, and intentional by the writer, that this book is slanted toward the history and challenge of black-white relations. But I hope it is obvious that racial and ethnic diversity and harmony relate to thousands of ethnic people groups,[1] not just to two or three or five races. Depending on where one lives and travels, the situation will change from one kind of relational challenge to another. I mean for this book to take that into account.

But clearly the place of African Americans in the United States is foremost in my mind as I write. There are at least three reasons for this.

CLOSEST TO MY HISTORY

One is my history, which I narrated in chapter 1. Black and white is the interracial reality that has been closest to my experience and the one I feel the greatest burden to understand.

THE UNIQUENESS OF SLAVERY

The second reason for the prominence of black-white racial dynamics is that the black experience in America is unique. Among other reasons for this uniqueness, the main one is that African Americans are the only people group in our land who suffered centuries of race-based slavery at the hands of white masters. Adding to the weight of that experience is the fact that during most of that time this slavery was accompanied by, and often justified by, public conceptions of black inferiority.

African Americans cannot even look back to the Great Emancipator, Abraham Lincoln, without hearing him speak of their perceived inferiority. Two years before Lincoln became the sixteenth president of the United States, he debated Stephen Douglas in pursuit of the Illinois US Senate seat. Lincoln lost. He was too progressive on the issue of slavery for a state that made it a crime to bring into its boundaries "a person having in him one-fourth Negro blood, whether free or slave."[2]

But the debates did bring out the virtually universal racism of nineteenth-century America, including Abraham Lincoln's. For all his greatness—and it is extraordinary—Lincoln was in many ways a child of his time on matters of race (as we all are). He became the Republican candidate because his two main rivals (William Seward and Salmon Chase) were more progressive than he was.

In the 1858 Senate debates, Douglas baited Lincoln with the assertion that

> the signers of the Declaration of Independence had no reference to negroes at all when they declared all men to be created equal. They did not mean negro, nor the savage Indians, nor the Fiji Islanders, nor any other barbarous race. They were speaking of white men. . . . I hold that this government was established . . . for the benefit of white men and their posterity forever, and should be administered by white men, and none others.[3]

In response, Lincoln said he had "no purpose to introduce political and social equality between the white and black races." He was not in favor of "making voters or jurors of negroes, nor of qualifying them to hold office, nor to intermarry." He said there is a "physical difference between the two" that would "probably forever forbid their living together upon the footing of perfect equality."

Nevertheless, Lincoln argued,

> there is no reason in the world why the negro is not entitled to all the natural rights enumerated in the Declaration of Independence. . . . I agree with Judge Douglas he is not my equal in many respects—certainly not in color, perhaps not in moral and intellectual endowment.

> But in the right to eat the bread, without leave of anybody else, which his own hand earns, he is my equal and the equal of Judge Douglas, and the equal of every living man.[4]

Emancipation would come—over time, and most fully a century later—with the civil rights movement of the 1960s. Lincoln would be celebrated as a hero in that cause. But like every hero, his feet are made of clay. That is what fallen, human greatness is—flawed.[5]

Therefore, in my thinking about racial and ethnic diversity and harmony, there is an intentional prominence of the unique history and experience of African Americans in our country. It colors profoundly the way I think about racial and ethnic diversity.

THE SORROWS OF POST-CIVIL-RIGHTS DECLINE

The third reason for this prominence is the fact that almost fifty years since the civil rights movement, the racial situation in America is not as improved as many had hoped it would be—and some would even say it is worse. That's another reason for writing this book. I would like to be part of the solution, and not part of the problem.

BILL COSBY'S (IN)FAMOUS SPEECH

The heartbreaking reality is that since the decisive legal break-throughs of the civil rights movement, things have deteriorated for a huge segment of the black population in America. Bill Cosby has been praised and pilloried for his public lament over this situation. Juan Williams built an entire book around Cosby's famous—or infamous, depending on your point of view—speech on May 17, 2004, in Washington, DC, at Constitution Hall. Three thousand people were gathered to celebrate the golden anniversary of *Brown v. Board of Education* (1954), in which the Supreme Court ordered the integration of public schools.

The title of Juan Williams's book sums up Cosby's message: *Enough: The Phony Leaders, Dead-End Movements, and Culture of Failure That Are Undermining Black America—and What We Can Do About It.*[6] What we hear from Cosby and Williams is a cry, almost of desperation, that the world would take notice of the developments that Williams calls "a mortal threat to the race."[7] Since Williams's book was published, Cosby has written his own effort to sound the alarm and call his people to action. Cosby's book is titled *Come On People: On the Path from Victims to Victors.*[8]

MICHAEL DYSON'S WARNING

Before I let Cosby and Williams describe the heartache of decline since the civil rights era, I should make clear that other black voices find Cosby's and Williams's message to be misleading and unhelpful. Michael Eric Dyson wrote a *New York Times* bestseller called *Is Bill Cosby Right? Or Has the Black Middle Class Lost Its Mind?*[9] His primary criticism is that "Cosby's overemphasis on personal responsibility, not structural features, wrongly locates the source of poor black suffering—and by implication its remedy—in the lives of the poor."[10]

That is the issue we will take up in the next chapter. But it is important to realize at this point that there is more than one black perspective on the racial situation in America. In fact, Dyson goes so far as to say, "Cosby's remarks betray seething class warfare in black America that has finally boiled over to the general public."[11]

This boiling over into public is filled with potential harm. Dyson wants to make clear that there is a great danger in white people, like me, listening to Cosby and Williams's lamentation.

> It is that general public, especially white social critics and other prophets of black ethical erosion, that has been eager for Cosby's dispatches from the tortured front of black class war. Cosby's comments let many of these whites off the hook. . . . There's nothing like a formerly poor black multimillionaire bashing poor blacks to lend credence to the ancient assaults they've endured from the dominant culture.[12]

If I hope to move forward and be helpful in spreading Christ-exalting racial harmony in this situation, it is important that I know whether I should be on a "hook," and if so, which one, and how, from the position of that hook, I can best serve the cause of racial respect and peace and hope. It seems to me that, as painful and controversial as it is even to talk about the Crosby/Dyson perspectives, it would be utterly naïve to imagine the pursuit of racial diversity and harmony in America while being ignorant of the most explosive issues. That they are dangerous to deal with is obvious. The danger of ignoring them is greater. In fact, we will find in the next chapter that the gospel of Jesus has a bearing on these things that is not often probed. But first, we should hear the heart cry of Bill Cosby and Juan Williams.

BILL COSBY'S HEART CRY

Cosby describes the bleakness that has emerged since the civil rights movement:

> Obviously, many civil rights leaders had hoped that with the demise in the 1960s of officially sanctioned forms of segregation and discrimination, black males would have greater access to the mainstream of American society. They had fully expected that these young men would be in a better position in every way—financially, psychologically, legally—to sustain viable marriages and families. Instead, the overall situation has continued to go downhill among the poor who are mostly shut out from the mainstream of success.
>
> How is that possible?
>
> There is one statistic that captures the bleakness. In 1950, five out of six black children were born into a two-parent home. Today, that number is less than two out of six. In poor communities, that number is lower still. There are whole blocks with scarcely a married couple, whole neighborhoods in which little girls and boys come of age without seeing up close a committed partnership and perhaps never having attended a wedding.[13]

RACISM, YES—AND MORE

Cosby is not naïve. He knows there is racism and systemic obstruction to black progress. But what he sees is so appalling that he knows the problems must be attacked from every side. Blacks have always had to take responsibility when white people oppressed. Now is no time to stop.

> There is certainly institutional racism—particularly against black men—but racism doesn't explain everything. . . . The stereotype of the angry and potentially violent black male can lead to racial profiling by teachers in the early grades. This makes it doubly difficult for those

boys who are trying to behave and trying to get ahead to succeed. Soon the kids begin to stereotype themselves. These images lead to low expectations for achievement, which then becomes a self-fulfilling prophecy. Check the numbers:

- Homicide is the number one cause of death for black men between fifteen and twenty-nine years of age and has been for decades.
- Of the roughly sixteen thousand homicides in this country each year, more than half are committed by black men. A black man is seven times more likely to commit a murder (excluding military actions) than a white man, and six times more likely to be murdered. (Black mothers live with these numbers. We don't know how they sleep at night.)
- Ninety-four percent of all black people who are murdered are murdered by other black people.
- The life expectancy at birth of black men is sixty-nine years, compared to seventy-five years for white men, eighty for white women, and seventy-six for black women.
- In the past several decades, the suicide rate among young black men has increased more than 100 percent.
- In some cities black males have high school drop-out rates of more than 50 percent.
- Young black men are twice as likely to be unemployed as white, Hispanic, and Asian men.
- Although black people make up just 13 percent of the general population, they make up nearly 44 percent of the prison population.
- At any given time, as many as one in four of all young black men are in the criminal justice system—in prison or jail, on probation, or on parole.
- By the time they reach their midthirties, six out of ten black high school dropouts have spent time in prison.
- About one-third of the homeless are black men.

Cosby continues with his agonized response:

This is madness! Back in 1950, there were twice as many white people in prison as black. Today, there are more black people than white in prison. We're not saying there is no discrimination or racial profiling today, but there is less than there was in 1950. These are not "political" criminals. These are people selling drugs, stealing, or shooting their buddies over trivia.[14]

THE WHITE MASTERS ARE MIXED IN

There is plenty of blame to go around here. And Juan Williams spreads it widely, by way of illustration, when it comes to the culture-destroying effects of gangster rap.

> The emergence of the black gangster as a common hero in music and movies is more poison being injected into young black minds. Here is an open sewer throwing up the idea that black men are most genuine, most in touch with their power, when they are getting vengeance with a gun in hand. Yet no leader says anything.[15]

What is going on here? More than meets the eye. There is white mischief here—serious mischief. This is like the musical minstrel show familiar to nineteenth-century slave owners. The black faces are used to make the white people a pile of money by making blacks look foolish.

> In fact, there are similarities between the economics of slavery and the modern rap industry. Cheap labor, slaves, made it possible for the Southern plantation to make money. . . . In today's rap business, young musicians hungry for stardom are cheap labor, able to satisfy the white America's continuing desire to see Jim Crow jump in the black face minstrel shows. The problem is the white-owned corporations making big money off the music have to get past the risk of facing charges of promoting racial stereotypes.[16]

And what is that stereotype that white money-moguls exploit for millions of dollars, as rap surpassed country music in 2001 and became America's most popular music genre?[17] What is the stereotype in gangster rap that is purchased not mainly by black men, black women, and white women, but by "white men, mostly high-school- and college-age boys"? What is this stereotype that invites "immature white males to indulge their basest feelings about women and blacks"?[18] What is this white-funded, debasing stereotype of the black male?

> The rappers reinforce in the minds of those wild white frat boys—later to become our corporate captains and managers—that black women are sexually indiscriminate, stupid, greedy, and lazy. Young black men are thugs, and, in the words of music critic Stanley Crouch, "monkey-moving, gold-chain-wearing, illiteracy-spouting, penis-pulling, sullen, combative buffoons."[19]

HOW TO MAKE MONEY BY BEING RACIST

White corporate record company owners are not allowed to say such things about blacks openly. Instead, Williams says, they hire cheap labor, as it were, to say it for them. "Rap music allows the private sentiment of white males to come into public light with inoculation against any charges of racism. It is a money maker."[20]

How do white-run music companies get away with this?[21] It happens through a stunning perversion of black pride.

> Common sense was dismissed by rappers and their corporate partners as feeble protests from stuck-up white people and bourgeois black people who had lost touch with their ghetto roots. The defense of gangster rap, with its pride in guns and murder, was that it was all about "keepin' it real." In that stunning perversion of black culture, anyone who spoke against the self-destructive core of gangster rap was put down as acting white or selling out the ghetto. Violence, murder, and self-hatred were marketed as true blackness—authentic black identity.[22]

In this way Williams interweaves the white guilt of racial exploitation for big money with the black guilt of complicity in the perversion of the black experience that Martin Luther King Jr. died to make possible.

WHITE SIN

In the heartbreaking story of white and black sinfulness since the civil rights movement, there is a downward spiral *together*. It is not as though the white culture stood fast during these decades on some 1950s moral high ground. The white children of the flower children of the sixties have paid dearly for the abandonment of truth and moral absolutes.

Many studies have documented the collapse of moral clarity and virtue in the white church and mainstream white culture. David Wells is one such perceptive student of these things. In his book *Losing Our Virtue: Why the Church Must Recover Its Moral Vision*,[23] Wells sums up the disintegration of moral life in the American mainstream culture:

> While the great majority of Americans believe that they actually keep the Ten Commandments, only 13 percent think that each of these

66

commandments has moral validity. It is no surprise to learn that 74 percent say that they will steal without compunction; 64 percent say that they will lie if there is an advantage to be had in doing so; 53 percent say that, given a chance, they will commit adultery; 41 percent say that they intend to use recreational drugs; and 30 percent say that they will cheat on their taxes.

What may be the clearest indicator of the disappearance of a moral texture to society is the loss of guilt and embarrassment over moral lapses. While 86 percent admit to lying regularly to their parents, 75 percent to a friend, 73 percent to a lover, only 11 percent cited lying as having produced a serious level of guilt or embarrassment. While 74 percent will steal without compunction, only 9 percent register any moral disquiet.

While pornography has blossomed into a 4 billion dollar industry that accounts for a quarter of all the videos rented in shops, seen in the thriving hotel business or on cable, only 2 percent experience guilt about watching. And, not surprisingly, at the center of this slide into license and moral relativism is the disappearance of God. Only 17 percent define sin as a violation of God's will.[24]

In this progressing collapse of the last forty years, there can be no white or black finger-pointing. We have fallen together. And we who are white should be as keenly aware of the peculiarly white corruption. For example, in the months leading up to the writing of this book, the news has been full of several enormous financial fraud cases that have ruined hundreds of people and hurt thousands. The faces of these swindlers are white. In the last month, two more stories have been in the news of young killers mowing down students in school and random townspeople. What color do I expect to see on the television? A sullen, pale, white face in a dark coat.

And together with every other race, whites are killing their babies and wallowing in their porn and taking their illegal drugs and leaving their wives and having babies without marriage. The difference is that when you develop patterns of sin in the majority race, they have no racial connotation. Since majority people don't think of themselves in terms of race, none of our dysfunctions is viewed as a racial dysfunction. When you are the majority ethnicity, nothing you do is ethnic. It's just the way it's done. When you are a minority, everything you do has color.

WHERE DOES RACISM FIT IN?

There is one sin I have not mentioned in this closing list, namely, *racism*. Earlier we saw it woven into the white exploitation of rap perversions of black identity. But the question remains about the wider society and how the ongoing realities of racist attitudes and structures have affected the black sorrows that Bill Cosby and Juan Williams describe.

I have intentionally not raised the question of structural racism here so that I could deal with it in the next chapter more fully. What remains to be said here, and this foreshadows where we will go in the next chapter as well, is that there is no salvation or redemption on earth or in heaven that comes through blaming—whites blaming blacks or blacks blaming whites. There is overwhelming guilt in every human heart. We are sinners.

Our circumstances shape the form our sin takes. But before God we are guilty of infinite offense because we have scorned him. The seriousness of our sin is determined not mainly by the nature of our deed but the nature of the one we dishonor. A sin against an infinitely worthy God is an infinite sin. Color and ethnicity will count for nothing in the court of heaven.

ONE THING WILL COUNT IN THE COURT OF HEAVEN

One thing will count: the perfection of Jesus Christ. The question will be: are we "found in him, not having a righteousness of [our] own that comes from the law, but that which comes through faith in Christ, the righteousness from God that depends on faith" (Phil. 3:9)?

Which means that the root answer to moral disintegration—white and black—is not government help or self-help, but the gospel of Jesus Christ. This gospel is the power of God for salvation (Rom. 1:16). And this salvation is the power of "righteousness and peace and joy in the Holy Spirit" (Rom. 14:17). We will see the amazing relevance of this in the contemporary racial controversies of our day in the next two chapters.

Someone in the crowd said to him, "Teacher, tell my brother to divide the inheritance with me." But he said to him, "Man, who made me a judge or arbitrator over you?"

LUKE 12:13–14

CHAPTER FIVE

PERSONAL RESPONSIBILITY AND SYSTEMIC INTERVENTION

After the murder of the Cosbys' son Ennis on January 16, 1997, Bill Cosby's wife, Camille, said that racism is "omnipresent and eternalized in America's institutions, media and myriad entities."[1] John Hope Franklin, a distinguished African American historian who just died yesterday, as I am first writing this on March 26, 2009, said, "Every time people take a breath it's in terms of color."[2]

CONTINUING, PAINFUL, PERVASIVE

This deeply felt sense of race as a continuing, painful, and pervasive issue in America means that talking about race continues to be difficult. The feelings run very deep and very high. If your skin is thin, you had best hold your tongue. But holding our tongues does not usually advance understanding, deepen respect, warm the affections, or motivate action. So I speak and write. Not because I believe I have final answers to complex issues we face, but because I believe the gospel of Jesus is relevant and healing in more ways than most people realize.

In the previous chapter, I said that one of the reasons this book makes the relationships between black and white such a prominent issue is that the dream of the civil rights movement in the 1960s has not been realized in the way most of those involved had hoped. Which means that the situation we find ourselves in is not one of educational, economic, residential, political, or medical equality.[3] Nor is there a growing integration of our lives, but rather, for many, a retreat into greater separation.[4] In some ways, inequalities are greater, and segregation is on the rise.

For most African Americans, these realities shape their consciousness profoundly. The majority culture (which for a little while longer is still white) has the luxury of being oblivious to race (which would change in an instant, if we moved to Nigeria). But for minority peoples, race-related issues are a persistent part of consciousness. If these issues are silently ignored in our relationships, the resulting harmony will be shallow and fragile. That is why I am dealing with them in this book.

THERE HAS BEEN PROGRESS

Of course, in some ways there *has* been significant progress since the civil rights movement of the 1960s. For example, "In 1964 only one in five white Americans had any black neighbors; today the figure is three out of five, a national average that includes whites living in states like Utah and Vermont where black residents are rare."[5] Today, unlike forty years ago, black Americans form a massive block of voters, and the black middle class has swelled to about 50 percent.[6] "In 2000, 47 [percent] of African Americans owned their homes."[7]

"IT'S NOT WHAT WE HAD IN MIND AT ALL"

But the feelings run so high that even saying there has been progress runs the risk of sounding oblivious to the remaining struggles. William Raspberry wrote in the *Washington Post* that "when Stephan and Abigail Thernstrom write [in their 1997 book, *America in Black and White*] . . . that the black condition, white attitudes and race relations have all improved dramatically, it is taken as an assault on black America."[8]

I don't want to be oblivious to the racism and frustrations and structural obstructions that remain. I hear the deep disappointment in the voice of those who stood in the physical presence of Martin Luther King Jr. I hear it in the lament of the late Richard John Neuhaus, who wrote in 1996, "Thirty years of mostly well-intended policies that have turned upon us with a vengeance. It's not what we had in mind back then; it's not what we had in mind at all."[9]

But the question of how to explain the disillusioning outcomes of the last forty years has no single answer. Neither does the question of where the emphasis should fall in plotting a path forward. What I want to do in this chapter is bring to light the competing strategies for progress, and then in the next chapter bring the gospel of Jesus to bear on both sides of the controversy.

DYSON IS COSBY'S POPULAR CRITIC

We said in the previous chapter that the key popular-level criticism of Bill Cosby has come from Michael Dyson. His criticism reveals the two main racial strategies competing in our day. He said, "Cosby's over-emphasis on personal responsibility, not structural features, wrongly locates the source of poor black suffering—and by implication its remedy—in the lives of the poor."[10] The term *personal responsibility* sums up one cluster of strategies. The term *structural features* sums up the other. The question is, *Is the main problem today "structural (or systemic) racism" or is the main problem "personal responsibility"?*[11]

We should not be pressed to an either-or mentality here. None of the spokesmen for either of these views fails to see some of the truth in what the other side is saying. This is true at both the popular level and in the more academic literature. For example, Dyson concedes, "There are undoubtedly lethal circumstances afoot in black America, and we do indeed need the voices of the elders to ring out and the wisdom of the fathers and mothers to resonate loudly."[12] And Cosby concedes, "We're not saying there is no discrimination or racial profiling today."[13] But they disagree profoundly in where the emphasis is needed at the present time.

THERE IS ALSO AN ACADEMIC SIDE TO THIS DEBATE

A similar tension is found in the academic literature, with some empha-sizing cultural issues and personal responsibility, but most putting larger emphasis on the structural causes of racial inequities. Lawrence M. Mead teaches American politics and public policy at New York University. His academic focus is not race, per se, but poverty and wel-fare. Yet the issues are intertwined, and his work has direct bearing on how we think about the disadvantages of the urban poor both racially and economically.

He was one of the theoretical architects of the welfare reform of the 1990s. He does not discount institutional aspects of what he calls the "delimitation of life choices." "[There is] the need for both governmen-tal and private forms of intervention to reverse the delimitation of life choices that all too many African Americans face." But his burden is to defend the position that mandatory work requirements are essential to sound welfare policy. Thus his emphasis falls on public policies that call for individual responsibility.[14]

Similarly, Henry Louis Gates Jr., who serves as the Alphonse Fletcher University Professor at Harvard University, writes, "The causes of poverty within the Black community are both structural and behavioral." And he too accents the personal/cultural:

> Not to demand that each member of the Black community accept individual responsibility for their behavior—whether that behavior assumes the form of gang violence, unprotected sexual activity, you name it—is another way of selling out a beleaguered community.[15]

In *The Audacity of Hope*, Barack Obama acknowledges the personal and individual dimension of the problem but moves the emphasis more explicitly toward the institutional and structural side of the problem. "The responsibility to close the gap can't come from government alone; minorities, individually and corporately, have responsibilities as well," but in the end, the key will be public policy and structural reform that make "universal appeals around strategies that help all Americans . . . even if such strategies disproportionately help minorities."[16]

Elijah Anderson, who holds the William K. Lanman Jr. Professorship in Sociology at Yale University, puts the emphasis even more fully on structural solutions:

> Without a massive program of reconstruction, inner-city residents, especially young black men, will remain mired in hopeless circumstances, and the stereotype of the dangerous dark-skinned male will become increasingly entrenched. This stigma will afflict all young men of color, leading to an erosion of social capital even among the middle class and putting at risk the hard-won gains of the civil rights movement.[17]

Countering Anderson's emphasis, Orlando Patterson, who holds the John Cowles Chair in Sociology at Harvard University, asks why academic scholars have been "so allergic to cultural explanations" of racially imbalanced poverty. His own proposal for what hinders young blacks is not structural but the "cool-pose culture" of young black men [that is] simply too gratifying to give up . . . almost like a drug, hanging out on the street after school, shopping and dressing sharply, sexual conquests, party drugs, hip-hop music and culture, the fact that almost all the superstar athletes and a great many of the nation's best entertainers were black.[18]

In his 2009 book, *More than Just Race: Being Black and Poor in the Inner City*, William Julius Wilson, the Lewis P. and Linda L. Geyser University Professor at Harvard University, seeks for "a bold, new perspective" that incorporates concern for cultural factors into a framework that deals seriously with dominant structural issues:

> Conservatives tend to emphasize cultural factors, while liberals pay more attention to structural conditions, with most of the attention devoted to racialist structural factors such as discrimination and segregation. I hope in this discussion, however, to encourage the development of a framework for understanding the formation and maintenance of racial inequality and racial group outcomes that integrates cultural factors with two types of structural forces: those that directly reflect explicit racial bias and those that do not.
>
> Naturally, in this process I raise some warning flags about incorporating cultural arguments into our analysis of race and poverty that we should not ignore. Nevertheless, the long-standing problem of race in the United States calls for a bold, new perspective.[19]

What is clear from this brief glimpse into the more academic literature is that the tensions between Cosby and Dyson are not unique or isolated. They are deep and widespread. Most of the people who read this book will not be academic scholars. Nor am I competent to engage the breadth of the academic debate. So my hope is to let the debate between Dyson and Cosby illustrate the tensions that exist without glossing over the complexity of the issues at the academic level.

DYSON'S CRITICISM OF COSBY

Dyson criticizes Cosby for his "attack on the black poor."[20] His counterpoints to Cosby's pleas, for example, that young people stay in school and stay out of prison, have a sobering ring:

> If the rigidly segregated educational system continues to miserably fail poor blacks by failing to prepare their children for the world of work, then admonitions to "stay in school" may ring hollow. . . .
>
> Given the vicious way blacks have been targeted for incarceration, Cosby's comments about poor blacks who end up in jail are dangerously naïve and empirically wrong. Cosby's critique of criminal behavior among poor blacks neglects the massive body of work that catalogues the unjust imprisonment of young blacks. This is not to suggest an apologia for black thugs; instead, it suggests that a disproportionate number of black (men) are incarcerated for nonviolent drug offenses.[21]

Dyson would shift the emphasis from the *personal* to the *structural*, the institutional. "Cosby . . . slights the economic, social, political and other structural barriers that poor black parents are up against: welfare reform, dwindling resources, export of jobs and ongoing racial stigma."[22] "His discounting of structural forces and his exclusive focus on personal responsibility, and black self-help, ignore the persistence of the institutional racism."[23] Dyson concludes from his observation of the American scene that "structural barriers, much more than personal desire," shape the experiences of poor blacks.[24]

THE EVANGELICAL BLIND SPOT

Michael O. Emerson and Christian Smith, in their book *Divided by Faith: Evangelical Religion and the Problem of Race in America*,[25] argue that, for the main part, evangelical Christians[26] are blind to these structural dimensions of what they call the *racialization* of America.[27]

They give a good example of the difference between the merely personal and the structural approach toward racial change:

> Recall that in the Jim Crow era, "Most evangelicals, even in the North, did not think it their duty to oppose segregation; it was enough to treat blacks they knew personally with courtesy and fairness." The racialized system itself is not directly challenged. What is challenged is the treatment of individuals within the system.[28]

This same preference for personal relational efforts in racial harmony persists today, say Emerson and Smith:

White evangelical prescriptions do not address major issues of racialization. They do not solve such structural issues as inequality in health care, economic inequality, police mistreatment, unequal access to educational opportunities, racially imbalanced environmental degradation, unequal political power, residential segregation, job discrimination, or even congregational segregation. . . . In short, their prescriptions fail to render race inconsequential for life opportunities.[29]

They conclude that "such a perspective effectively reproduces racialization."[30] "As long as they do not see or acknowledge the structures of racialization they inadvertently contribute to them."[31]

Emerson and Smith, like Dyson, are right to point out the importance of structural obstacles that stand in the way of the fullest experience of freedom and virtue and productivity. But they seem to assume that if evangelicals would "see" and "challenge" the structures of our racialized society, the strategies would be obvious and the effect would be positive.

THE OTHER POINT OF VIEW: PERSONAL RESPONSIBILITY

Here is where the other viewpoint comes in. For many black thinkers, it is not at all obvious that this heavy focus on challenging the structures of institutional racism is where the emphasis should fall today. And even where it is still needed, the way to tackle the problem structurally is not transparent. Among these voices (besides Bill Cosby and Juan Williams) are Clarence Thomas,[32] Thomas Sowell,[33] Shelby Steele,[34] John McWhorter,[35] Ward Connerly,[36] and Dinesh D'Souza.[37]

The perspective that these writers bring suggests that not all structural intervention has been beneficial for race relations, and for black progress in particular. None of them is ignorant of the real problem of structural racism and its power to exclude from the fullness of life. Shelby Steele speaks for them when he says, "The great insight of structuralism was that an evil like racism could have an impersonal life in the structures of society (customs, manners, residential living patterns, folkways, even laws in the days of segregation). It could determine events apart from the will of individuals or even groups."[38]

Their point is not that there is no such thing as systemic racism but that there is no point waiting for it to change before radical individual and group action is taken, and there are aspects of legislative intervention and social engineering that can be counterproductive. We will see both of these concerns in what follows.

WHAT TO DO BEFORE THE LION LIES DOWN WITH THE LAMB

After hearing Cosby call parents to greater oversight of their children, Juan Williams said, "That is a call to arms . . . to stop waiting for the end of 'systemic racism' or for more money for schools. A black child born today will be old or dead long before the end of racism or before a time when every public school is successfully reformed."[39] He asks, "What are people who genuinely care about black poverty to do until the day that the lion lies down with the lamb, racism is ended, and here is a level playing field for all Americans on which the poor are given all the need to succeed?" And he answers: "The obvious answer is for people to take every step possible right now to take care of themselves and help their families. This is not letting government off the hook so much as dealing with real solutions to the immediate needs of real people."[40]

WHEN STRUCTURAL INTERVENTION IS COUNTERPRODUCTIVE

Not only do these writers emphasize personal and family and community action *alongside* political and structural intervention and *before* the dream of structural change arrives, but also they call some of that intervention as harmful to the very minorities they are meant to serve. I give some examples of their concern not because what they say points to obvious policy decisions, but because it shows how deeply personal and controversial structural intervention like affirmative action and welfare programs really are.

Shelby Steele, of the Hoover Institute at Stanford, describes one effect in his own case of government intervention to give minorities preference: "Yet, for me, it was precisely this virtuous interventionism that over time began to feel more and more humiliating. . . . Whether the determinism was bad . . . or intended to be good, as with interventionism, blacks were still seen as determined beings without will or agency, and therefore without full humanity."[41] In a word, Steele believes that in some kinds of preferential intervention, the effect is dehumanizing: "The most dehumanizing and defeating thing that can be done to black Americans, for example, is to lower a standard in the name of their race."[42]

THE MORAL SYMMETRY OF AFFIRMATIVE ACTION

Of course, the main structural intervention Steele has in mind is affirmative action. In education and business, the most harmful form, he says, is "the lowering of standards to increase black representation."[43] But he is not ignorant of the "moral symmetry" of this effort to redress years of discrimination:

> In America, many marginally competent or flatly incompetent whites are hired every day—some because their white skin suits the conscious or unconscious racial preference of their employer. The white children of alumni are often grandfathered into elite universities in what can only be seen as a residual benefit of historic white privilege. Worse, white incompetence is always an individual matter, while for blacks it is often confirmation of ugly stereotypes. . . . Given that unfairness cuts both ways, doesn't it only balance the scales of history that my children now receive a slight preference over whites? Doesn't this repay, in a small way, the systematic denial under which their grandfather lived out his days?
>
> So, in theory, affirmative action certainly has all the moral symmetry that fairness requires—the injustice of historical and even contemporary white advantage is offset with black advantage; preference replaces prejudice, inclusion answers exclusion.[44]

Add to this that ethnic diversity is a positive good, and not merely irrelevant in admitting students and hiring employees, and one sees a growing case for the moral and cultural wisdom of certain kinds of affirmative action.

THE DOWNSIDE OF AFFIRMATIVE ACTION

Nevertheless, Steele says, "I think affirmative action has shown itself to be more bad than good and that blacks . . . now stand to lose more from it than they gain."[45] He has four main concerns. First, he sees "the subtle ways that affirmative action revives rather than extinguishes the old rationalizations of racial discrimination."[46] Second, "One of the most troubling effects of racial preferences for blacks is a kind of demoralization, or put another way, an enlargement of self-doubt. Under affirmative action the quality that earns us preferential treatment is an implied inferiority."[47]

Third, racial preferences send us the message that there is "more power in our past suffering than our present achievements."[48] This leads to the deadly game of exploiting white guilt with the power of our victim status, which is alluring in the short run but consigns us forever to remain unequal. Fourth, "racial preferences allow society to leapfrog over the difficult problem of developing blacks to parity with whites and into a cosmetic diversity that covers the blemish of disparity—a full six years after admission, only about 26 [percent] of black students graduate from college."[49]

ANTI-INTELLECTUALISM A DEEPER PROBLEM

Steele and others would say that at the present time there is a deeper problem than discrimination in education, which is nevertheless rooted in centuries of demeaning discrimination. John McWhorter, formerly a professor of linguistics at the University of California, Berkeley, and now a senior fellow at the Manhattan Institute, describes it like this with an illustration from his own history:

> The belief that blacks and school don't go together has its roots in slavery's refusal to let blacks be educated. But it gained strength in the mid-1960s, when black separatism rejected traits associated with whites as alien, and black students, in this spirit, began teasing their fellows who strove to excel in school as "acting white," a much harsher taunt than merely dismissing them as nerds.
>
> When I was four—and this is my very first memory—a group of black kids in the neighborhood stopped me and asked me to spell a word. When I did, one of them directed his little sister to hit me repeatedly. I later watched a friend of mine treated similarly for answering such questions as, "How far is it from New Jersey to Florida," and I'll never forget being asked by one of his tormentors, "Are *you* smart?" in the menacing tone you'd use to ask, "Did you steal my money?"[50]

The heartbreaking irony is that the battle of the civil rights leaders of the 1960s was largely fought for the right of black children to go to school and be educated in schools that were not separate, underfunded, and inferior. Bill Cosby is passionate when he reminds parents that in 1957, black children had to endure violence from mobs, "being hit in the face with rocks and punched in the face," to get into Little Rock's Central High School. But then he cries out, "What the hell good is *Brown v. Board of Education* if nobody wants it?"[51]

"DROWNING SOUL AFTER SOUL"

Juan Williams sees the anti-school attitudes of many young blacks as part of an overwhelmingly destructive cycle:

> Rejecting the value of school has numerous consequences: children end up not learning standard English, not writing well, and, worst of all, accepting the idea of failure. . . . Cosby said nobody talks to teachers, but teachers tell him that the language spoken by black children coming into classrooms today is "horrible."
>
> This horror show—a refusal to master standard English, lack of interest in formal schooling, the acceptance of a culture of failure—is passed on to children and grandchildren as a legacy of being authentically black, when really it is a legacy of failure. And the tide of failure keeps rising, drowning soul after soul. The tragedy is blamed on white people, racism, or even abandonment by the black middle class.
>
> Yet there is no leadership speaking out to black parents and black students about the destructive cycle rooted in a crippling culture that sells disregard for education. No one is sounding the alarm to say the house is on fire. And black people, especially poor black people, are being left behind in a global competition for jobs that demands the highest level of academic achievement.[52]

The heart-wrenching issue is not only how to mobilize political and community will to create and fund better schools for the least advantaged children, but also how to transform homes and parents so that children are prepared for school when they are old enough to go and supported and celebrated in their progress as they study. What Williams and the writers with his perspective see is that sending children to school without preparation and support makes the jobs of the educators almost impossible:

The gap between black and white students already exists when the children are entering kindergarten. According to the National Center for Education Statistics, half of black children starting kindergarten scored in the bottom quarter on general knowledge; 40 percent of black kindergartners were in the bottom quarter on math; and one-third of black kindergartners were in the bottom quarter on reading.[53]

"THE GREATEST CIVIL RIGHTS ISSUE OF OUR TIME"

By many accounts, this issue is the most important civil rights issue of our time. Stephan and Abigail Thernstrom wrote in the 1999 preface to *America in Black and White*, "K-through-12 education must become *the* civil rights cause." Eight years later, Katherine Kerstine, columnist of the *Minneapolis Star Tribune*, said the same thing: "The racial achievement gap is . . . the greatest civil rights issue of our time."[54] The agonizing question is what to do.

As true as it is that such deadly cycles are rooted in centuries of slavery and white discrimination, the point of Williams and Cosby and the others is that damning whites doesn't save blacks. When the house is on fire, you holler for the kids to run, no matter who set the fire. Williams and the other writers who are sounding these alarms do not let whites off the hook from the obligation to work for better access for all to quality education. Shelby Steele puts it in a balanced way so that we who are white are sure to get our half of the message: "Blacks can have no real power without taking responsibility for their own educational and economic development. Whites can have no racial innocence without earning it by eradicating discrimination and helping the disadvantaged to develop."[55]

SEVEN FEELINGS RISE IN MY HEART

When I step back from this controversy over personal responsibility versus political and community engagement with systemic racism, I have at least seven different clusters of thoughts and feelings.

First, I feel *regret* for my own sinful contributions to the seemingly intractable problems of race relations between black and white in our land. Second, I feel *sorrow* over cycles of despair and hopelessness, and over the ruin of so many lives. Third, I feel *anger* at the sins I see on every part of the landscape of race relations and race discussions and racial intervention—all sides. None of us is righteous, no, not one (Rom.

3:10). Fourth, I feel *frustration* over the untold layers of complexity that make every proposal for improvement seem thanklessly embattled. I empathize with Harvard social scientist Nathan Glazer when he says that behind the racial troubles of our day are "factors in infinite regress."[56] Fifth, I feel *empathy* with the truth and the emotion of both sides of the controversy. Sixth, I feel a great *longing* to see the gospel of Jesus proclaimed, with the power of the Holy Spirit, into this situation and this controversy. And seventh, because of the power of the gospel, I feel *hope* that there are breakthroughs possible that human strategies from either side have not achieved.

THE GOSPEL CREATES NEW PEOPLE

The gospel of Jesus Christ touches this issue in more ways than any of us can see. It has a way of working that goes beyond what we can imagine or predict. It does not simply provide help to do what we think needs to be done, as though we were all-wise and just needed a little spiritual boost to carry out our plans. It goes over and under and around and through our imperfect plans. It destroys some and transforms others. Mainly, it deals explosively with us, not with our plans and strategies.

The gospel is not an ideology. It does not come in as one idea alongside some others and make its contribution. The good news that God sent his Son Jesus into the world to die in the place of sinners, and bear their punishment, and become their perfect righteousness, and absorb the wrath of God, and set us right with him through faith alone, and rise from the dead triumphant over every foe—that gospel does not come as an ideology but as supernatural power.

When this news of salvation from our sin and from God's wrath is proclaimed in the power of the Holy Spirit, it does not come with compelling ideas that create new thoughts; it comes with supernatural power that creates new people. The Bible calls this being born again. "You have been born again . . . through the living and abiding word of God . . . the good news that was preached to you" (1 Pet. 1:23–25). These new people will live forever with Jesus in the new heavens and the new earth when "the creation itself will be set free from its bondage to corruption and obtain the freedom of the glory of the children of God" (Rom. 8:21).

The power of the cross of Christ, applied by the Holy Spirit, is not a new philosophy or a new methodology or a new political persuasion, but "a new creation" (Gal. 6:15). Our old, unbelieving, insubordinate self dies, and a new, humble, believing, loving self is created by the power of the Holy Spirit, in the image of Jesus, through the gospel. "I have been crucified with Christ. It is no longer I who live, but Christ who lives in me. And the life I now live in the flesh I live by faith in the Son of God, who loved me and gave himself for me" (Gal. 2:20).

The gospel is not a heavenly demand of what we must do to be saved; it is a heavenly declaration of what God has done to save us. The added good news is that we cannot earn what he has done for us but only receive it as a gift. And even this receiving—this trust—is a gift of God. It is God's grace and God's power from start to finish. This is why it is in a class by itself. It does not fit alongside any politics or ideology or philosophy or culture. It is not one of them. It is God's breaking in with his own power to create a new spiritual reality—a new you.

This new you is united to Jesus Christ who has risen from the dead, so that your eternal life is secured and all that Christ is, he is for you. This is absolutely new. Before this, we were dead in sin. But now, we are alive in Christ Jesus. "Therefore, if anyone is in Christ, he is a new creation. The old has passed away; behold, the new has come" (2 Cor. 5:17). We have peace with God. Christ dwells within us. We are not our own. Jesus is our supreme treasure. And our highest joy is to extend the joy we have in his glorious grace to others.

THE GOSPEL IS NOT RIGHT WING OR LEFT WING

Because the gospel of Jesus is not an ideology or a philosophy or a methodology or a therapy but a supernatural in-breaking of God into our lives, I am concerned at how many Christians do not bring it to bear personally, critically, and explosively on the political right and left. It seems to me that too many Christians gravitate to right-wing Republican politics or left-wing Democratic politics because they see some parallel between a political plank and a part of the gospel. It's like saying that the party that uses candles must be the true one because they're shaped so much like sticks of gospel dynamite. The gospel was meant to explode with saving power in the lives of politicians and social activists, not help them decorate their social agenda.

Jesus did not come into the world to endorse anybody's platform. He doesn't fit in. He created the world. He holds it in being by his powerful word. He will return someday to judge the living and the dead. And he came the first time to die so that left-wing activists and right-wing talk-show hosts would be broken in pieces for their sin and put back together by the power of grace. He came so that from that day on Jesus himself would be the supreme treasure and authority in our lives. He came so that we would become radically devoted to the glory of God. He came so that the only kind of racial diversity and racial harmony we would pursue is Jesus-exalting, God-glorifying, and gospel-formed.

THE GOSPEL DOES NOT TAKE SIDES IN THIS CONTROVERSY

My concern is not that the political and social ideas of the right and the left are not often true, as far as they go. My concern is that these ideas are spiritually hollow and impotent. The gospel of Jesus does not come to the controversy between personal accountability and structural intervention and take sides. It calls both sides to repent and believe in Jesus and be born again and make the glory of Jesus the supreme issue in life. The gospel is not a political adviser standing to the side waiting to be asked for guidance. It is the arrival of God saving people from their sin and from the everlasting wrath of God, giving them the Holy Spirit, and bringing their lives progressively into conformity to Jesus.

For this reason, the impact of the gospel in race relations is unpredictable. It has potentials that no one can conceive. And, to our shame, there have been many contradictions between what the gospel is and what professing Christians have done. I will say more about that at the conclusion of this book. But the answer to those inconsistencies is not to domesticate the gospel into another ideological mule to help pull the wagon of social progress. If that's what it is, then we may safely set it aside, and eat, drink and be merry, for tomorrow we die.

In the next chapter, I will try to point to the kinds of ways the gospel can have an explosive effect in the racial issues of our times.

I am not ashamed of the gospel, for it is the power of God for salvation to everyone who believes, to the Jew first and also to the Greek.

ROMANS 1:16

You have been born again, not of perishable seed but of imperishable, through the living and abiding word of God. . . . And this word is the good news that was preached to you.

1 PETER 1:23–25

CHAPTER SIX

THE POWER OF THE GOSPEL AND THE ROOTS OF RACIAL STRIFE

The previous chapter ended with the claim that the gospel of Jesus does not enter controversy as another ideology or philosophy or methodology for social improvement. It enters like dynamite. It enters as the power of the Creator to reconcile people to himself and supernaturally make them new.

But lest we leave these claims hanging in the air with no examples of how explosive the gospel may be in the matter of race relations, consider how the gospel can create new possibilities of life when it is lodged like dynamite in the cracks of these nine destructive forces.

1) THE GOSPEL AND SATAN

Satan is called the god of this world. He is a real supernatural being who hates humans and is in diametric opposition to God. He comes to steal and to destroy. There is little doubt that where maddeningly hopeless, sinful, self-destructive behaviors and structures hold sway over large groups of people—white or black, left or right—the Devil is deeply at work. "The god of this world has blinded the minds of the unbelievers" (2 Cor. 4:4). "He was a murderer from the beginning, and has nothing to do with the truth, because there is no truth in him. When he lies, he speaks out of his own character, for he is a liar and the father of lies" (John 8:44).

What hope does a message of personal responsibility or structural intervention have against this supernatural power? None. *None.* They are like feathers in a hurricane. How shall any human stand against the deceitful, murderous power of Satan? There is only one answer: in the name of Jesus. Why is that? "The reason the Son of God appeared was to destroy the works of the devil" (1 John 3:8). How did he do that? By bearing our sin in his body so that "through death he might destroy the one who has the power of death, that is, the devil" (Heb. 2:14). When Jesus died, "he disarmed the rulers and authorities and put them to open shame, by triumphing over them in him" (Col. 2:15).

There is no other power in the world that can do this. The Devil is stronger than all humans, all armies, all politics, and all human morality put together. We have no chance against him except by one means, the power of Jesus Christ operating through us because he dwells within us. "He who is in you is greater than he who is in the world" (1 John 4:4).

The gospel of Christ conquers our hearts and brings us to repentance and faith in Christ. Christ enters our lives and dwells within us. All authority in heaven and on earth belongs to him. He commands the unclean spirits, and they obey him (Mark 1:27). Therefore, into the racial situation the gospel brings the only power that can set people and structures free from the bondage of the Devil. The Devil gives way to no other power than the power of Christ. And the power of Christ moves in the world through those who have believed the gospel and are indwelt by the Spirit of Christ. "Anyone who does not have the Spirit of Christ does not belong to him" (Rom. 8:9).

If Satan is to give way in his horrific influence on racist pride and paralyzing fears and feelings of hopeless inferiority, it will be through the gospel of Jesus or not at all. Who can imagine what a great awakening of faith in the gospel might look like as thousands of people resisted the Devil in Jesus's name and watched him flee from their white and black lives and families (James 4:7)?

2) THE GOSPEL AND GUILT

We are all guilty before God. "All, both Jews and Greeks, are under sin, as it is written: 'None is righteous, no, not one.' . . . Whatever the law says it speaks to those who are under the law, so that every mouth may be stopped, and the whole world may be held accountable to God"

(Rom. 3:9–10, 19). The gospel presupposes this. There is no gospel without this, because this is mainly what Christ came to save us from—the guilt of sin and the holy wrath of God against it.

Guilt is a huge player in the way blacks and whites relate to each other. It's huge and deadly when it is denied. It's huge and deadly when it is wallowed in. It's huge and deadly when it is exploited. There is no deliverance and no relief and no healing in any of those ways of dealing with guilt. Denial drives it below the surface where it creates endless illusions and self-justifications. Wallowing in it produces phony humility and obsequiousness and moral cowardice. Exploiting it gives a false sense of power that turns out to be only the weapon of weakness. If guilt is not dealt with more deeply, there will be no way forward.

What news does the gospel bring in regard to our guilt? "Christ died for our sins" (1 Cor. 15:3). "He himself bore our sins in his body on the tree" (1 Pet. 2:24). "Christ also suffered once for sins" (1 Pet. 3:18). "In Christ God was reconciling the world to himself, not counting their trespasses against them" (2 Cor. 5:19). "For our sake he made him to be sin who knew no sin, so that in him we might become the righteousness of God" (2 Cor. 5:21). Therefore, "everyone who believes in him receives forgiveness of sins through his name" (Acts 10:43).

There is no other savior from our guilt than Christ, because our guilt is ultimately guilt for sins against God. Only God can forgive those sins. And only Jesus was God in the flesh dying so that he could declare us righteous and remove our sin and guilt. "God put [Christ] forward as a propitiation by his blood . . . so that he might be just and the justifier of the one who has faith in Jesus" (Rom. 3:25–26). Only by believing in Jesus are we really and eternally freed from the real guilt that we all have before God.

Who can begin to calculate the effect of white and black from all persuasions and all parties suddenly delivered from the crushing burden of guilt? No more denial. No more wallowing. No more exploiting. What an unimaginable transformation would come. It is incalculable what the personal and relational dynamics would be in all our racial relations if we were set free with overflowing joy and gratitude that our guilt had been taken away.

3) THE GOSPEL AND PRIDE

God hates pride. "The LORD of hosts has a day against all that is proud and lofty, against all that is lifted up—and it shall be brought low. . . . And the haughtiness of man shall be humbled, and the lofty pride of men shall be brought low, and the LORD alone will be exalted in that day" (Isa. 2:12, 17). "Whoever exalts himself will be humbled, and whoever humbles himself will be exalted" (Matt. 23:12). "God chose what is low and despised in the world, even things that are not, to bring to nothing things that are, so that no human being might boast in the presence of God. . . . 'Let the one who boasts, boast in the Lord'" (1 Cor. 1:28–31).

Pride is a condition of the heart that does not submit to God. It does not delight in God having absolute power and authority. It presumes to rebel against God or negotiate with God. Therefore, it can be secular or religious. Pride loves to be made much of by men. It craves human approval. It may try to look cool in order to intimidate others. Or it may be meek and retiring for fear of offending others. It can look strong, and it can look weak. In either case, it is consumed with self and what a select group of others think.

Racial tensions are rife with pride—the pride of white supremacy, the pride of black power, the pride of intellectual analysis, the pride of anti-intellectual scorn, the pride of loud verbal attack, and the pride of despising silence, the pride that feels secure, and the pride that masks fear. Where pride holds sway, there is no hope for the kind of listening and patience and understanding and openness to correction that relationships require.

The gospel of Jesus breaks the power of pride by revealing the magnitude and the ugliness and the deadliness of it, even as it provides deliverance from it. The gospel makes plain that I am so hopelessly sinful and my debt before God was so huge that my salvation required the death of the Son of God in my place. This is devastating to the human ego. And God means it to be: "By grace you have been saved through faith. And this is not your own doing; it is the gift of God, not a result of works, so that no one may boast" (Eph. 2:8–9). He saves us by grace alone so that we would boast in him alone. Pride is shattered.

And not only are we saved by grace; we live moment by moment by grace. "But by the grace of God I am what I am, and his grace toward me was not in vain. On the contrary, I worked harder than any of them, though it was not I, but the grace of God that is with me" (1 Cor. 15:10). Therefore, Paul says, "I will not venture to speak of anything except what Christ has accomplished through me" (Rom. 15:18). His entire life is a gift of grace. This rules out all boasting in himself. "What do you have that you did not receive? If then you received it, why do you boast as if you did not receive it?" (1 Cor. 4:7).

There is no power on earth that can break the power of pride except the gospel of Christ. Until we are broken because of our sinfulness and delivered from the sin of rebellion and unbelief, we remain hard and resistant outlaws to God—no matter how meek we may seem to man. The sin of pride will subtly contaminate all our relationships, even where it is not recognized. A disease does not have to be diagnosed in order to infect and kill.

The cross of Christ is the key to killing pride and living in humility. "I have been crucified with Christ. It is no longer I who live, but Christ who lives in me. And the life I now live in the flesh I live by faith in the Son of God, who loved me and gave himself for me" (Gal. 2:20). Imagine what race relations and racial controversies would look like if the participants were all dead to pride and deeply humble before God and each other.

4) THE GOSPEL AND HOPELESSNESS

Countless dysfunctions and self-defeating behaviors are owing to a sense of hopelessness. This is true for white and black alike, though the typical behaviors vary largely along socioeconomic lines, not color lines. If a person cannot imagine a rewarding future, then there seems to be little reason for denying oneself any immediate pleasure now. Drug addiction, overeating, gambling, indolence, sexual promiscuity, lying, stealing—why wouldn't a person do these things if there is no hope? "If the dead are not raised, 'Let us eat and drink, for tomorrow we die'" (1 Cor. 15:32). It makes sense.

If there is no hope, then why would I bother myself with efforts in racial harmony? Why would I care about anybody? If there is no hope, why would I care about your civil rights? I have just a few short years to maximize my pleasure, then I will be eaten by worms, and that's that. Hopelessness destroys moral conviction by making it look ludicrous. And therefore it destroys almost everything that is beautiful and precious.

Without the gospel of Jesus, there is in fact no hope beyond the grave. "If Christ has not been raised, your faith is futile and you are still in your sins" (1 Cor. 15:17). When there is no hope beyond the grave, it is extremely difficult to talk yourself into the kind of self-denial required by justice movements such as civil rights. The energy it takes and the sacrifices one must make may seem heroic and admirable for a while, but the meaninglessness of it all will overtake you if you really feel hopeless about the moment of death.

It seems to me that we can call for personal responsibility till we are blue in the face, and the appeals will have no power at all without the awakening of hope. Juan Williams points out that statistically there is an almost foolproof way to stay out of poverty:

> The good news is that there is a formula for getting out of poverty today. The magical steps begin with finishing high school, but finishing college is much better. Step number two is taking a job and holding it. Step number three is marrying after finishing school and while you have a job. And the final step to give yourself the best chance to avoid poverty is to have children only after you are twenty-one and married. This formula applies to black people and white people alike.[1]

But what power can awaken hope and transform the heart so that these steps not only seem right but also doable, and not only right and doable but also a God-pleasing means of exalting Jesus as the Lord and Treasure of my life? The only answer is the gospel of Christ. It brings with it the gift of eternal life. And it comes with the assurance that God in Christ is for us and not against us. And if God is for us, no one can ultimately be successful against us (Rom. 8:31). We are "more than conquerors through him who loved us" (Rom. 8:37). Living in the power of this gospel "is of value in every way, as it holds promise for the present life and also for the life to come" (1 Tim. 4:8).

5) THE GOSPEL AND FEELINGS OF INFERIORITY AND SELF-DOUBT

Since all humans have a sinful craving to be seen as worthy or admirable in some way, we all fear being seen as inferior or unworthy or foolish. These fears are manifested, or masked, in very different ways ranging from the most pathological paralysis of depression, to self-hatred and self-destructive behaviors, to profound anxiety in the face of public opportunities, to sullen withdrawal from the world, to whining and complaining at how others make life difficult, to repeated pity parties in which we maneuver to get others to feel sorry for us, to constant put-downs of others so that our own flaws are minimized, to a cocky cloaking of our limitations that intimidates others with one kind of power to conceal another kind of weakness.

These sorrows and sins are not unique to any ethnic group. They are universal. But the history of a group shapes the way the fear is felt. Shelby Steele gives painful and penetrating expression to the effects of black history and black stereotypes on the black psyche.

> The condition of being black in America means that one will likely endure more wounds to one's self-esteem than others and that the capacity for self-doubt born of these wounds will be compounded and expanded by the black race's reputation of inferiority. . . .
>
> Black skin has more dehumanizing stereotypes associated with it than any other skin color in America, if not the world. When a black person presents himself in an integrated situation, he knows that his skin alone may bring these stereotypes to life in the mind of those he meets and that he, as an individual, may be diminished by his race before he has a chance to reveal a single aspect of his personality. . . . He will be vulnerable to the entire realm of his self-doubt before a single word is spoken. . . .
>
> Certainly in every self-avowed white racist, whether businessman or member of the Klan, there is a huge realm of self-contempt and doubt that hides behind the mythology of white skin. The mere need to pursue self-esteem through skin color suggests there is no faith that it can be pursued any other way. But if skin color offers whites a certain false esteem and impunity, it offers blacks vulnerability.
>
> This vulnerability begins for blacks with the recognition that we belong, quite simply, to the most despised race in the human community of races. To be a member of such a group in a society where all others gain an impunity by merely standing in relation to us is to live with a relentless openness to diminishment and shame.[2]

When I first read this, I felt a great heaviness. I feared to even open my mouth. In the face of such deep and pervasive effects of racism, most words will sound glib. Any claim to "know what it's like" will be untrue and naïve. In fact, it is this very moment of illumination for oblivious whites, who are just beginning to touch the nerve of interracial complexity, that paralyzes the relationship. It would sound superficial in the extreme to give "tips" at this point for what to say and what not to say.

What is needed is a miracle. I mean that literally. A supernatural in-breaking of God through the gospel of Christ. It is not even possible to describe the hope-filled relational dynamics that may happen when the gospel explodes in two hearts that bring such radically different experiences of sin and suffering to the relationship. "What is impossible with men is possible with God" (Luke 18:27).

This impossible hope for racial reconciliation and understanding and warm-hearted mutual joy is owing to the gospel of Jesus. He died on the cross not only to crucify pride and self-exaltation, but also to create new identity. Christ died so that no one would be puffed up with pride or paralyzed with weakness and inferiority—imagined or otherwise. How does the gospel do this?

Union with Christ is the key. When we trust Christ, we are united to him. His righteousness is counted as ours. Before God we are not guilty, not impure, not sinful. We are holy and righteous with the imputed righteousness of Christ. Not only that, but we are born into the very family of God. We are justified through faith, and we are sanctified through faith. We are counted as perfect in Christ, and we are put in the most magnificent family in the universe, God's family.

This is breathtaking. The apostle John is full of wonder as he says, "See what kind of love the Father has given to us, that we should be called children of God; and so we are. . . . Beloved, we are God's children now, and what we will be has not yet appeared; but we know that when he appears we shall be like him, because we shall see him as he is" (1 John 3:1–2). The gospel gives us a new identity that is so majestic that we would be the most arrogant people in the world—except that we know we don't deserve it, it cost Christ his life, and it is all a free gift of grace.

It is heartbreaking to see people of goodwill trying to patch up the damaged self-esteem of children in the hope that they will find it within them to be motivated for great achievements. It is a fool's errand. Even the shrewd analysis of Shelby Steele falls short of any real solution:

Educational reform for black students . . . [focuses] generally on identity enhancement and self-esteem. Its profound mistake is to assume that performance follows self-esteem, when in fact it is the other way around: performance follows high expectations; not high self-esteem. The proof of this is that Asian-American students routinely test lower on self-esteem measures than blacks, who routinely test higher than any other student group.[3]

But how do you break into this vicious cycle of self-doubt when all of us are sinners? We are torn—all of us—between the self-exalting pride of our hearts and our fearful, self-doubting sense of inferiority. What is the use of trying to build self-esteem for sinners without the gospel? It will only mask true weaknesses and sins while it feeds the inborn arrogance that we all have. Only the gospel can do two seemingly contradictory things: destroy pride and increase courage. Destroy self-exaltation and increase confidence. Destroy the pushiness of self-assertion and deliver from the paralysis of self-doubt.

A real Christian is a walking miracle. Supernatural power has entered his life. His arrogance has been shattered. His paralyzing or swagger-producing fear of failure has been replaced with the promises of God. He is forgiven, accepted, loved by God Almighty. He is secure enough in who he is not to be destroyed when, for Christ's sake, he is shamed. "They left the presence of the council, rejoicing that they were counted worthy to suffer dishonor for the name" (Acts 5:41). If he is knocked down in the quest for justice, he will get up—not with a swagger but with humble Christ-exalting courage to bear all things for the sake of Jesus's name.

6) THE GOSPEL AND GREED

A huge part of the corruption of white and black crime, and white and black racism, is energized by greed. The biblical word is *covetousness*. When we bought a duplex as our home in the poorest, most diverse neighborhood in Minneapolis thirty years ago, the wisdom on the street was, *This is not a good investment*. Housing values here are not going up. This is not where people move *to*; it's where people move *from*.

Our response was: *Money is not the issue; ministry is the issue*. We are not here to make money; we are here to make a name for Jesus. If greed were not part of the American landscape, race relations would be dramatically different. The desire to be rich is morally and socially catastrophic. Listen to this alarm God sounds in 1 Timothy 6:9–10: "Those who desire to be rich fall into temptation, into a snare, into many senseless and harmful desires that plunge people into ruin and destruction. For the love of money is a root of all kinds of evils. It is through this craving that some have wandered away from the faith and pierced themselves with many pangs."

Race relations in America were plunged into ruin and destruction the day the first slave arrived in America, kidnapped for white gain against God's law (Ex. 21:16; Deut. 24:7). And greed has driven the ruin and destruction of race relations ever since. And the greed in black hearts is no different from the greed in white hearts. Our shared sinfulness simply expresses itself in different ways according to our circumstances.

There is only one way to be free from greed for the glory of God— faith in the gospel of Christ. First, the gospel transfers our security from the power of money to the promises of God. When we trust Christ, our fear of the future is replaced by confidence in God. The mindset of the follower of Christ is this: "If God is for us, who can be against us? He who did not spare his own Son but gave him up for us all, how will he not also with him graciously give us all things?" (Rom. 8:31–32). God's giving of his Son guarantees, Paul says, that he will work all things together for our good. This may include "tribulation, or distress, or persecution, or famine, or nakedness, or danger, or sword" but even so, God is for us and we are more than conquerors (Rom. 8:31, 35, 37).

This position inside the sovereign care and guidance and provision of God creates a radical freedom from the love of money. God promises to work for us. We do not need to be anxious about tomorrow. Tomorrow will take care of itself. We are free to seek the kingdom first and let material things fall where they will (Matt. 6:33). This makes us servants of racial justice and harmony because that's what "the kingdom" looks like.

Second, the reason we can say with Martin Luther, "Let goods and kindred go, this mortal life also," is that Christ has become our supreme treasure. "I count everything as loss because of the surpassing worth of knowing Christ Jesus my Lord" (Phil. 3:8). If I lose everything and die, I still have Christ. Therefore, "to live is Christ, and to die is gain" (Phil. 1:21). Which means that I am not enslaved to the treasures of this world. I can use them freely for love, because I don't need them for my ego or my soul. I have the greatest treasure in the world—Christ.

Third, those who stake their lives on the gospel get the universe thrown in along with Christ. "Let no one boast in men. For all things are yours, whether Paul or Apollos or Cephas or the world or life or death or the present or the future—all are yours, and you are Christ's, and Christ is God's" (1 Cor. 3:21–23). The meek will inherit the earth (Matt. 5:5). Why would we covet this world when we already own it, and it is only a matter of time till we come into the fullness of our inheritance. "We are children of God, and if children, then heirs—heirs of God and fellow heirs with Christ" (Rom. 8:16–17). And Christ made and owns everything (Col. 1:16).

Therefore, the follower of Jesus, in the power of the promises of the gospel, does not lay up treasures on earth, but in heaven. How? By trusting Christ so fully that on earth we are driven by the joy of giving, not getting. We love being servants, not masters. We love meeting needs, not using people. Our Father will take care of us. "Fear not, little flock, for it is your Father's good pleasure to give you the kingdom. Sell your possessions, and give to the needy. Provide yourselves with moneybags that do not grow old, with a treasure in the heavens that does not fail, where no thief approaches and no moth destroys. For where your treasure is, there will your heart be also" (Luke 12:32–34).

The racial landscape in America, and the little patch of it where you live, will change in ways you cannot even imagine to the degree that you are freed from the desire to get rich and replace it with the desire to serve others.

7) THE GOSPEL AND HATE

The horrors of racial and ethnic hatred are indescribable. All over the world, through all of history, the slaughter of human life because of ethnic, tribal, and racial animosities is beyond imagination. If you could imagine it—in vivid color—you would not be able to bear it. From the Armenian genocide in Turkey in 1915, to the holocaust in Germany, to the Soviet Gulag, to the massacres in Rwanda in 1994, to the Japanese slaughter of six million Chinese, Indonesians, Koreans, Filipinos, and Indochinese—the litany of ethnic hatred goes on.

The gospel of Jesus cuts the nerve of hatred and anger and the bent to be a blaming person. It does so in many ways. I'll mention two that seem almost opposite but are both crucial in the quest for racial justice and harmony.

First, when we receive the gracious provision of God to forgive our sins through Christ, our bent to be unforgiving is broken. "Be kind to one another, tenderhearted, forgiving one another, *as God in Christ forgave you*. Therefore be imitators of God, as beloved children" (Eph. 4:32–5:1). Our kindness and forgiveness of others is empowered by our being forgiven. Our loving others is empowered by our being loved by God.

We know we are sinners. We know that the offense we have given to God is greater than any offense others have given to us, and if God was gracious to us, we must be gracious to others. You cannot authentically rejoice in being treated better than you deserve while treating others the way they deserve, or worse.

The gospel cuts the nerve of hatred by making us feel the broken-hearted gratitude that God's wrath was once on us and was removed, not because we deserved it but because of his absolutely free grace. Freely you have received; freely give. As the Father has sent me to love, Jesus said, so I send you. Love your enemies so that you may prove yourselves to be children of God, because that is the way he treated you. If you cherish grudges, you do not cherish God's grace. But the definition of a Christian is one who receives and cherishes the grace of God in Christ.

Second, the gospel overcomes vengeance by promising that justice will be done. One of the emotional boosters behind our judicial sense is that justice must be done, especially when *our* rights are denied. And when it looks like justice will not be done to us, we feel the need to take matters into our hands and exact vengeance.

To this impulse, the gospel comes with a double message. All wrongs in the world will be punished justly, either on the cross (for the wrongdoers who trust Christ) or in hell (for the wrongdoers who don't).

"Beloved, never avenge yourselves, but leave it to the wrath of God, for it is written, 'Vengeance is mine, I will repay, says the Lord.' To the contrary, 'if your enemy is hungry, feed him; if he is thirsty, give him something to drink; for by so doing you will heap burning coals on his head'" (Rom. 12:19–20).

What God is telling us is that forgiveness and love do not mean the perpetrators get away with their abuses and injustices. They don't. If they come to faith in Christ, their sins will be covered by his blood. But if they do not come to Christ, their sins will come on their own head, and God will see that justice is done. In this way, a life of love and forgiveness—a life of treating bad people better than they deserve—is not a foolish life. God's mercy and vengeance frees us from the soul-destroying bitterness of hatred and anger and blaming and vengeance. It makes us merciful without making us naïve about evil.

This effect of the gospel of Christ would transform the world of race and ethnicity more than we can imagine. Who can begin to describe the possibilities of reconciliation and harmony where the work of Christ replaces hatred with love, anger with patience, and blaming with forgiving, and all of this without surrendering a passion that justice must be done?

8) THE GOSPEL AND FEAR

No one escapes fear. It is a universal emotion. You even see it in the most courageous, because courage is not the absence of fear but the refusal to let it control you. One of the reasons that fear is a universal experience is that we know we are guilty before God and that we are not strong enough to save ourselves. Not everyone admits this, but the Bible makes clear that we all know God and we all know we have not measured up to his standards (Rom. 1:21; 2:15).

When this fear of death and judgment is not acknowledged and remedied with the gospel of Christ, it goes deeper into the subconscious where it produces multiple phobias and anxieties and disorders. In addition to the many fears of particular things that we know about, there is the even more common fear of the unknown. Therefore this root fear and its many manifestations have a pervasive effect on our relation to other races.

The Bible speaks of all humans as being in lifelong slavery to the fear of death until they are set free by the death of Christ and the defeat of Satan in their lives. "Since . . . the children share in flesh and blood [that is, since those for whom Christ came are all human], he himself likewise partook of the same things [became human], that through death he might destroy the one who has the power of death, that is, the devil, and deliver all those who through fear of death were subject to lifelong slavery" (Heb. 2:14–15).

We may not know who our slave master is. But God says it is the fear of death. Christ died to free us from this slavery. He did it by removing our guilt and taking our curse on himself (Gal. 3:13; Rom. 8:3). We are now reconciled to God. He is not against us, but for us. And he has given us his Spirit precisely to assure us that we do not need to be afraid. "For you did not receive the spirit of slavery to fall back into fear, but you have received the Spirit of adoption as sons, by whom we cry, 'Abba! Father!'" (Rom. 8:15).

Now that the biggest and deepest fear of death and judgment are gone, the minor fears of this life are as nothing by comparison. And our heavenly Father assures us that he cares for us so deeply and so thoroughly that we do not need to fear anything. "Do not fear those who kill the body but cannot kill the soul. Rather fear him who can destroy both soul and body in hell. Are not two sparrows sold for a penny? And not one of them will fall to the ground apart from your Father. But even the hairs of your head are all numbered. Fear not, therefore; you are of more value than many sparrows" (Matt. 10:28–31).

God will take meticulous care of us. When we face a racial situation that is unknown, we may enter it with the humble peace of Christ. "Peace I leave with you; my peace I give to you. Not as the world gives do I give to you. Let not your hearts be troubled, neither let them be afraid" (John 14:27). Because of the gospel of Christ, we may be sure that all the promises of God are ours. One of the most freeing as we walk into relational unknowns is, "Fear not, for I am with you; be not dismayed, for I am your God; I will strengthen you, I will help you, I will uphold you with my righteous right hand" (Isa. 41:10).

When all the self-protecting defenses that we put up because of our fears are removed, the possibilities for racial harmony are more than we can imagine.

9) THE GOSPEL AND APATHY

Apathy is passionless living. It is sitting in front of the television night after night and living your life from one moment of entertainment to the next. It is the inability to be shocked into action by the steady-state lostness and suffering of the world. It is the emptiness that comes from thinking of godliness as the avoidance of doing bad things instead of the aggressive pursuit of doing good things.

If that were God's intention for the godliness of his people, why would Paul say, "All who desire to live a godly life in Christ Jesus will be persecuted" (2 Tim. 3:12)? People who stay at home and watch clean videos don't get persecuted. Godliness must mean something more public, more aggressively good.

In fact, the aim of the gospel is the creation of people who are passionate for doing good rather than settling for the passionless avoidance of evil. "[Christ] gave himself for us . . . to purify for himself a people for his own possession who are zealous for good works" (Titus 2:14). The gospel produces people who are created for good works (Eph. 2:10), and have a reputation for good works (1 Tim. 5:10), and are rich in good works (1 Tim. 6:18), and present a model of good works (Titus 2:7), and devote themselves to good works (Titus 3:8, 14), and stir each other up to good works (Heb. 10:24).

And when they set about them, the word they hear from God is, "Do not be slothful in zeal, be fervent in spirit, serve the Lord" (Rom. 12:11). The gospel does not make us lazy. It makes us *fervent*. The Greek for *fervent* signifies boiling. The gospel opens our eyes to the eternal significance of things. Nothing is merely ordinary anymore.

Christ did not pursue us halfheartedly. Having loved his own who were in the world, he loved them to the uttermost (John 13:1). His death gives the deepest meaning to the word *passion*. Now he dwells in us. How will we not pray for the fullest experience of his zeal for the cause of justice and love? "So then, as we have opportunity, let us do good to everyone, and especially to those who are of the household of faith" (Gal. 6:10).

RETURNING TO THE CONTROVERSY

Which brings us back to the controversy between those who stress personal responsibility and those who stress structural intervention. God calls us to exalt his Son Jesus by doing good to everyone in reliance on the power of the Holy Spirit (Gal. 6:10). Surely, this means that, when it comes to the controversy over how to attack the racial inequalities and discrimination in this country, we will learn from both sides about the potentials and pitfalls of each. We will throw ourselves with the passion of Christ into the effort and make the gospel prominent in all our personal and structural action.

One example of a both-and person in this regard was Richard John Neuhaus, who died on January 8, 2009. He was called a voice of conscience in the civil rights and antiwar movements of the 1960s, marching side by side with Martin Luther King Jr. He had a word of tough love and hope at the personal-accountability level, and he had some clearheaded proposals at the structural level.

At the personal level he wrote:

> If we understand what is at stake, in every forum on every subject there will be zero tolerance of the abdication of personal responsibility. Nothing will do but a frankly moral condemnation of crime and vice, whether the vice be drug addiction or everyday sloth. The old excuses are out. Victim politics is finished. The American people have simply turned a deaf ear to all that. They've had enough, they've had more than enough. That seems harsh, and it is, unless joined to the hope that there is still a will to overcome the American dilemma, as in "we shall overcome."[4]

Neuhaus knew, in his heart, that the only hope for something more than a sentimental and nostalgic "we shall overcome" is the gospel of Jesus Christ.[5] But with that gospel and the power it brings, this kind of tough love is indeed full of hope.

At the structural level, Neuhaus gives us proposals, by way of example, on welfare reform and school choice. He is writing in 1996 but these particular suggestions, it seems to me, are still helpful:

> Welfare reform. Welfare reform is a moral imperative. . . . Hundreds of welfare experiments in all 50 states must get underway, and must

be carefully tested and not—or not chiefly—by whether they save money or cut down the size of government but by whether they help people take charge of their lives and enter the mainstream of American opportunity and responsibility.[6]

School choice. We can institute real school choice. Parental choice in education is a matter of simple justice and for many poor parents it is a matter of survival. Government monopoly school systems in New York and every other major city are an unmitigated disaster. They cannot be fixed, they must be replaced. The monopoly is defended by what is probably the most powerful political lobby in America, the teachers' unions. Whatever the noble intentions and heroic efforts of many teachers, these unions are the enemy of the children of the poor. With very few exceptions, nobody in these major cities who can afford an alternative sends their children to public school.

In New York, it is generously estimated that one out of 10 poor children beginning first grade will graduate from high school prepared for real college education. . . . The government school spends $9,000 per year per student, a parochial school considerably less than half that.[7] Middle-class and wealthy Americans have school choice. They pay tuition or move to where the schools are better. In opposing vouchers and other remedies the government school establishment invokes the separation of church and state. What we need, what the poor most particularly need, is the separation of school and state.[8]

THE GOSPEL IS ALWAYS RELEVANT

Whether Neuhaus is right about government involvement in school vouchers, we may be sure that the gospel of Christ is not irrelevant in the way Christians think about this issue. The gospel contains an undeniable impulse toward freedom. The reason is that the saving faith that it demands cannot be coerced. It is a free act of the soul under the sway of sovereign grace.

Therefore, the gospel will lean us away from structures that put the government in the position to demand or prohibit Christian faith. That leaves many questions unanswered, but it points to the fact that in this and dozens of other ways (some of which we have seen), the gospel of Christ is an explosive force in the matters of personal and structural engagement.

THE PERSONAL AND STRUCTURAL FORCE OF THE GOSPEL FOR WILLIAM WILBERFORCE

One of the best historical illustrations of the way the gospel of Christ transforms persons and sustains structural intervention is the life of William Wilberforce (1759–1833) and the Clapham Sect. One of the most important and least known facts about the battle to abolish the slave trade in Britain two hundred years ago is that it was sustained by a passion for the doctrine of justification by faith alone—which is at the center of the gospel of Christ.

Wilberforce was a spiritually exuberant and doctrinally rigorous evangelical. He had been personally transformed by the gospel and was carried along by a passion for the glory of Christ and the good of his fellow men. He battled tirelessly in Parliament for the outlawing of the British slave trade. And though most people do not know it, the particular doctrines of the gospel are the power that sustained him in the battle that ended the vicious trade.

The key to understanding Wilberforce is to read his own book *A Practical View of Christianity*.[9] There he argued that the fatal habit of his day was to separate Christian morals from Christian doctrines. His conviction was that there is "perfect harmony between the leading doctrines and the practical precepts of Christianity."[10] He had seen the devastating effects of denying this: "The peculiar doctrines of Christianity went more and more out of sight, and . . . the moral system itself also began to wither and decay, being robbed of that which should have supplied it with life and nutriment."[11] But Wilberforce knew that "the whole superstructure of Christian morals is grounded on their deep and ample basis."[12]

This "ample basis" and these "peculiar doctrines" that sustained Wilberforce in the battle against the slave trade were the doctrines of human depravity, divine judgment, the substitutionary work of Christ on the cross, justification by faith alone, regeneration by the Holy Spirit, and the practical necessity of fruit in a life devoted to good deeds. Wilberforce was not a political pragmatist. He was a radically God-centered, gospel-saturated Christian politician. And his zeal for Christ, rooted in this gospel, was the strength that sustained him in the battle.

THE CENTER OF THE GOSPEL AS THE KEY TO STRUCTURAL CHANGE

At the center of these essential "gigantic truths" was (and is) justification by faith alone. The indomitable joy that perseveres in the battle for justice is grounded in the experience of Jesus Christ as our righteousness. "If we would . . . rejoice," Wilberforce said, "as triumphantly as the first Christians did, we must learn, like them, to repose our entire trust in [Christ] and to adopt the language of the apostle, 'God forbid that I should glory, save in the cross of Jesus Christ,' 'who of God is made unto us wisdom and righteousness, and sanctification, and redemption' [Gal. 6:14; 1 Cor. 1:30]."[13]

In other words, the gospel of justification by faith alone is essential to right living—and that includes political living. Astonishingly, Wilberforce said that the spiritual and practical errors of his day that gave strength to the slave trade were owing to the failure to experience the truth of this doctrine:

> They consider not that Christianity is a scheme "for justifying the ungodly" by Christ's dying for them "when yet sinners"—a scheme "for reconciling us to God"—when enemies; and for making the fruits of holiness the effects, not the cause, of our being justified and reconciled.[14]

This was why he wrote *A Practical View of Christianity*. The "bulk" of Christians in his day, he observed, were "nominal"—that is, they pursued morality without first relying utterly on the free gift of justification by grace alone through faith alone on the basis of Christ alone. They got things backward: first they strived for moral uplift; then they appealed to God for approval. That is not the Christian gospel. And it will not transform a nation. It will not heal the racial wounds of a nation. It would not sustain a politician through eleven Parliamentary defeats over twenty years of vitriolic opposition.

The battle for abolition was sustained by getting the gospel right: "The true Christian . . . knows . . . that this holiness is not to precede his reconciliation to God, and be its cause; but to follow it, and be its effect. That, in short, it is by faith in Christ only that he is to be justified in the sight of God."[15] When Wilberforce put things in this order, he found invincible strength and courage to stand for the justice of abolition.

MAY THE GOSPEL RUN AND TRIUMPH

I pray that the gospel of Jesus Christ will have this kind of effect on many today. May it be spoken and lived by millions of true Christians in their daily lives. May it impel them into greater pursuits of racial diversity and harmony. May it awaken in some a passion for a public life of engagement in the community and the political arena. And may it conquer Satan, guilt, pride, hopelessness, paralyzing feelings of inferiority, greed, hate, fear, and apathy. In that triumph, may Christ be magnified and peoples of every race and ethnicity find harmony in him as their supreme treasure.

PART TWO

GOD'S WORD: THE POWER OF THE GOSPEL

WILLIAM WILBERFORCE
The Importance of Doctrine and "Coronary" Commitment

One of the lessons I have learned in six and a half decades of life is that very few good dreams should go on hold while you improve the shortcomings of your life. To be sure, the shortcomings should be opposed with Jesus's help in the power of his Word. The life of faith is war till our last breath (2 Tim. 4:7). To be sure, there are times you need to stop what you are doing and focus on conquering a flaw. But if you wait until all your shortcomings are remedied, your dreams will die. All our advances are with a limp.

If you wait till you are beyond criticism to pursue your dream, you will never do it. You won't marry or stay married. You won't decide to have children or raise them. You won't take your first job or keep it. You won't go into missions or stay there. You won't plant a church or stick with it for thirty years. Few things paralyze good people more than their own imperfections. And there are always people around to remind you of your flaws and suggest you can't go forward until you are better.

I'm thinking here specifically about pressing on in a ministry while racial and ethnic diversity and harmony are not what they could be or should be. Yes, there are many churches that are not concerned in the least with pursuing ethnic diversity and harmony. It's not even on the radar of their consciousness. They move forward with no thought about it at all. I hope this book changes some of those churches.

But I have in mind almost the opposite problem—the church that desperately wants to pursue deeper and wider ethnic diversity and harmony but is making little headway. Should they put all other things on hold indefinitely until they succeed? No. And the main reason is that issues of race and ethnic diversity and harmony are not a phase to be achieved but a lifelong quest. There is a good reason why Timothy George and Robert Smith called their book on racial reconciliation *A Mighty Long Journey*.[1] We resolve to work at it till we die, and then we make it part of all other pursuits.

If we are pastors or church leaders, we don't aim to grow or multiply or plant churches because we have perfection but because we have a dream. And part of that dream is that God might be pleased to so work that new churches in new places with new leaders may do some things a lot better than we do them, while drawn by the same biblical vision. It may be that the triumphs of Christ-exalting racial diversity and racial harmony will happen in the new work and then spill back onto the old.

LIVE FOR A GREAT CAUSE, NOT A GREAT COMFORT

One of the ways I think about the aim of this book, and the aim of my ministry, is that I labor to multiply a certain kind of person—persons who are committed to live for a great biblical *cause*, not a great earthly *comfort*. Over the years I have tried to wave this banner: *To be a Christian is to move toward need, not comfort*. Christian life means to get up in the morning and go to bed at night dreaming not about how to advance my comforts but how to advance some great God-centered cause. When we speak of multiplying and growing, we mean raising up a people who don't spend themselves day and night pursuing self-preservation and self-exaltation and self-recreation, but who pursue something bigger and greater than themselves or their family or their church.

What is the greater Cause *you* are living for? When I preach, for example, on the Martin Luther King holiday weekend and on the following Sanctity of Life Sunday, what I am asking, whether I say it every time or not, is: Are there some of you—hundreds of you—who will say, "It is the grand cause of my life to magnify Jesus Christ through God-centered, Christ-exalting, Bible-saturated racial justice, racial diversity, and racial harmony"? Or who say, "It is the grand cause of my life to magnify Jesus Christ through God-centered, Christ-exalting, Bible-saturated justice for the unborn."

Oh, that God would raise up, against all self-centeredness and flimsy loyalties and undisciplined devotion, men and women who sustain a great cause, not the way adrenaline does but the way the heart does!

Adrenaline produces a spurt of needed energy, then lets the body drop. But the heart keeps on pumping life into the body in good times and hard times, winter and summer, sad and happy, strong and weak, sick and well! Oh, for more *coronary* Christians in the cause of racial justice, not just *adrenaline* Christians!

WE NEED WILLIAM WILBERFORCES

I want to mention William Wilberforce here again at the beginning of part 2 of this book because the reason he was such a remarkable coronary Christian in the cause of slave-trade abolition was his intensely doctrinal biblical foundations.

Part 2 of this book is designed to provide the biblical foundation for the main point of part 1, namely, that the gospel—the good news of Christ, crucified in our place to remove the wrath of God and provide forgiveness of sins and power for sacrificial love—is our only hope for the kind of racial diversity and harmony that ultimately matters. The flow of chapters moves from the objective accomplishments of Christ on the cross, to the more personal application of that accomplishment in our conversion and way of life, to the ultimate goal of the gospel, to some specific issues that trouble our time.

The conviction underlying this half of the book is that the more difficult a way of life is—the more it demands coronary commitment, not adrenaline commitment—the more deep and strong the doctrinal foundations need to be in the Word of God. Religious tradition and human opinion are powerless to create and sustain a life of Christ-exalting ethnic diversity and harmony. Only a deeply rooted grasp of what God has achieved through the gospel of Jesus can do this.

William Wilberforce believed this with all his heart and showed it in his life. He was an evangelical member of Parliament in England who lived from 1759 to 1833. He is best known for his extraordinary perseverance in the cause of abolishing the British slave trade. What most people don't know is how deeply doctrinal were the foundations of his public life.

As I mentioned at the end of part 1, he published only one book, *A Practical View of Christianity*,[2] and the central thesis is that the public morality of Britain depends on evangelical Christianity recovering the doctrine of justification by faith alone. In particular he was jealous to maintain the right relationship between good works and justification. He wrote that "Christianity is a scheme for 'justifying *the ungodly*' [Rom. 4:5], by Christ's dying for them *'when yet sinners'* [Rom. 5:6–8] . . . [and] 'for reconciling us to God' while we were still enemies [Rom. 5:10]." And he believed the nation was in particular need of recovering the truth that Christianity was a scheme "for making the fruits of holiness *the effects, not the cause*, of our being justified and reconciled."[3]

In other words, Wilberforce's unwavering, lifelong commitment to justice for the African slaves was built on the deep foundations of biblical doctrine. That is what part 2 of this book aims to provide for the cause of racial harmony.

Who among you are the William Wilberforces for our time? He was deeply Christian, vibrantly evangelical, and passionate over the long haul for a cause far greater than himself. On October 28, 1787, he wrote in his diary at the age of twenty-eight, "God Almighty has set before me two great objects, the suppression of the Slave Trade and the Reformation of [morals]."[4]

Battle after battle in Parliament he was defeated because the African slave trade was woven too deeply into the financial interests of the nation. But he never gave up and never sat down. He was not an *adrenaline* Christian, but a *coronary* Christian. On February 24, 1807, at 4:00 a.m., twenty years after he wrote in his journal, the decisive vote was cast and the slave trade became illegal.

Still the work was not done after twenty years of perseverance. What about slave-*holding*? On July 26, 1833, sixteen years later, and three days before he died, the vote was cast and *slavery itself*—not just *slave-trading*—became illegal in England and her colonies.

So when I dream about the outcomes of this book, or of my ministry in general, I think mainly of breeding this kind of person—this kind of passion, coronary-like passion, not adrenaline-like passion. God-centered, Christ-exalting, Bible-saturated, justice-pursuing, never-say-die commitment to a great cause, not a great comfort. To that end, we turn to the kinds of biblical foundations that awakened and sustained William Wilberforce.

SECTION ONE

THE ACCOMPLISHMENT
OF THE GOSPEL

And he came to Nazareth, where he had been brought up. And as was his custom, he went to the synagogue on the Sabbath day, and he stood up to read. And the scroll of the prophet Isaiah was given to him. He unrolled the scroll and found the place where it was written, "The Spirit of the Lord is upon me, because he has anointed me to proclaim good news to the poor. He has sent me to proclaim liberty to the captives and recovering of sight to the blind, to set at liberty those who are oppressed, to proclaim the year of the Lord's favor." And he rolled up the scroll and gave it back to the attendant and sat down. And the eyes of all in the synagogue were fixed on him. And he began to say to them, "Today this Scripture has been fulfilled in your hearing." And all spoke well of him and marveled at the gracious words that were coming from his mouth. And they said, "Is not this Joseph's son?" And he said to them, "Doubtless you will quote to me this proverb, 'Physician, heal yourself.' What we have heard you did at Capernaum, do here in your hometown as well." And he said, "Truly, I say to you, no prophet is acceptable in his hometown. But in truth, I tell you, there were many widows in Israel in the days of Elijah, when the heavens were shut up three years and six months, and a great famine came over all the land, and Elijah was sent to none of them but only to Zarephath, in the land of Sidon, to a woman who was a widow. And there were many lepers in Israel in the time of the prophet Elisha, and none of them was cleansed, but only Naaman the Syrian." When they heard these things, all in the synagogue were filled with wrath. And they rose up and drove him out of the town and brought him to the brow of the hill on which their town was built, so that they could throw him down the cliff. But passing through their midst, he went away.

LUKE 4:16–30

CHAPTER SEVEN

THE MISSION OF JESUS AND THE END OF ETHNOCENTRISM

We turn first to the beginning of Jesus's public ministry. It is simply amazing how in-your-face he was in his first hometown sermon concerning the issue of ethnocentrism. He almost got himself thrown off a cliff for this—for undermining ethnocentrism. What I mean by *ethnocentrism* is the conviction or the feeling that one's own ethnic group should be treated as superior or privileged. The aim of Jesus in this incident is to make clear that the new people of God—the new Israel—that he has come to gather and to save is not ethnically defined. It is defined by attachment to him, the Messiah.

CLAIMING TO BE THE MESSIAH DOESN'T CAUSE THE RIOT

The story is found in Luke 4:16–30. Here is a local young man coming back to his hometown, Nazareth, after making a name for himself in Capernaum. He goes to the synagogue on the Sabbath, and a crowd comes to hear him. What he does in this message is almost incredible. He virtually incites a riot. And he does it intentionally.

First, they give him the scroll of Isaiah the prophet to read from, and he chooses chapter 61. It's about the coming redeemer who will set free the oppressed and proclaim the favorable year of the Lord (vv. 18–19)—and he claims that it is being fulfilled in their hearing. Luke 4:21: "And he began to say to them, 'Today this Scripture has been fulfilled in your hearing.'"

Now that was astonishing. Headline: "Homegrown boy claims to be the Messiah." But this did not cause the riot. So far they were positive: "And all spoke well of him and marveled at the gracious words that were coming from his mouth" (v. 22). So far, so good.

But what he says next is utterly unexpected. Inexplicable, it seems, if what you want is a following. Inexplicable if you only want "church growth." He chooses to tell two stories from the Old Testament that fly right in the face of the ethnocentrism of his own hometown. He could hardly have been more offensive.

He knows what their response is going to be, because he says in verse 24, "Truly, I say to you, no prophet is acceptable in his hometown." This is *before* they get riled up. In other words, *Yes, you are speaking well of me now* (v. 22) *while you have your own conception of what the Messiah will do, and what his kingdom will be like. But wait till I tell you what I am about to do and what my kingdom will be like.*

TWO STORIES OUT OF THE BLUE—AND IN YOUR FACE

Then he tells story number one. Verses 25–26 are taken from 1 Kings 17: "But in truth, I tell you, there were many widows in Israel in the days of Elijah, when the heavens were shut up three years and six months, and a great famine came over all the land, and Elijah was sent to none of them but only to Zarephath, in the land of Sidon [Phoenicia], to a woman who was a widow."

Out of the blue, he tells a story about God's passing over all the ethnic Jews to bring a miraculous blessing to an ethnic and political foreigner—a Gentile from the land of Sidon (Phoenicia). And he does this blatantly and forcefully and without softening or explanation: *There were many widows in Israel, and God blessed a foreigner.* That's what he said.

And if that were not enough, he tells a second story in Luke 4:27 from 2 Kings 5: "And there were many lepers in Israel in the time of the prophet Elisha, and none of them was cleansed, but only Naaman the Syrian." Again the point is: of all the people that God might have chosen to heal of leprosy, he chose a foreigner—a Syrian, not a Jew. These two stories were not lost on the ethnocentrism of Nazareth. Luke 4:28–29: "When they heard these things, all in the synagogue were filled with wrath. And they rose up and drove him out of the town and brought him to the brow of the hill on which their town was built, so that they could throw him down the cliff." They got it, and they didn't like it.

ETHNICALLY AND RACIALLY—THE KINGDOM IS NOT WHAT YOU THINK

Now what is the point of this story? The point is: *The kingdom I am bringing*, Jesus says, *is ethnically different from what you think.* Your chosen place as Israel has not produced humility and compassion, but pride and scorn. Jesus is the end of ethnocentrism. *Look to me*, he says. *Learn from me. I have come to redeem a people from every ethnic group, not just one, or a few. Woe to you for your failure to see, in the justice and mercy of God, his zeal to gather from all the peoples a kingdom of priests and friends.*

FAITH IN JESUS REPLACES JEWISH ETHNICITY

Have I been too hard on the people of Nazareth? You decide as you consider another story, this time from Matthew 8:5–13. Jesus finishes the Sermon on the Mount in Matthew 5–7 and then, in Matthew 8:1–4, he touches a leper, one of the most despised and ostracized of all people in Israel, and heals him. Then, in the next verse, he enters Capernaum and meets another despised and offensive kind of person—a Roman centurion. Jesus's behavior is like a US Marine caring for a Taliban freedom fighter.

The fact that this particular centurion has some popularity among the Jews (Luke 7:3–5) is passed over by Matthew. It is not relevant for his point. The man is a foreigner, a non-Jew. Matthew's point turns on that.

What will be the point of this story? The centurion begs Jesus, saying, "Lord, my servant is lying paralyzed at home, suffering terribly." Without the slightest query or hesitation, Jesus says in verse 7, "I will come and heal him." Then the centurion says something Jesus finds astonishing. Verse 8: "Lord, I am not worthy to have you come under my roof, but only say the word, and my servant will be healed. For I too am a man under authority, with soldiers under me. And I say to one, 'Go,' and he goes, and to another, 'Come,' and he comes, and to my servant, 'Do this,' and he does it."

When Jesus hears this, he marvels (v. 10). Then he takes this whole situation, which everyone thought was about healing and power and authority, and he turns it into something utterly different, namely, a situation about the composition of the kingdom out of foreigners and about the dangers of banking on ethnic identity for blessing.

Jesus says in verses 10–11: "Truly, I tell you, with no one in Israel have I found such faith. I tell you, many will come from east and west . . . " East and west! What's he getting at? That is Phoenicia (the Gaza Strip)! So who is from east and west? Egypt, Greece, Arabia, Persia, and—if I may be permitted a bit of anachronism—Jordan, Iran, Iraq, Afghanistan, Pakistan, India, China?

And what will happen when they come—these foreigners with their uncircumcised, non-kosher, foreign ways and foreign features? Verses 11–12 give the answer: "And [they will] recline at table with Abraham, Isaac, and Jacob in the kingdom of heaven, while the sons of the kingdom will be thrown into the outer darkness. In that place there will be weeping and gnashing of teeth."

A SHOCKING VIEW OF ETHNIC DE-PRIORITIZATION

Now this is utterly shocking! Feel the force of this. Here is Jesus saying to the chosen people of Israel that first Romans, such as this believing centurion, and then all kinds of unclean, ethnically and racially different Gentiles, will enter the kingdom of heaven, but the Jews, the "sons of the kingdom," will be cast into outer darkness. This is almost unheard of to speak of the chosen race this way. What is he saying? He is saying: *I am the end of ethnocentrism.*

Or to put it more positively: Jesus is saying that with his coming, a radically new way of defining the people of God is here, namely, faith in *him*. Faith in Jesus trumps ethnicity. Over and over in the Gospels this happens:

- The story of the Good *Samaritan*: a foreigner is the hero of compassion (Luke 10:33).
- The healing of the ten lepers, and only one returns—and what is he? A *Samaritan*. A foreigner shines with humble gratitude (Luke 17:16).
- The healing of the *Syrophoenician's* daughter (Mark 7:26).

- The worshiping of the wise men *from the east*, probably Persia or Arabia (Matt. 2:1).
- When he drove the moneychangers out of the temple, he said "My house shall be called a house of prayer *for all the nations*" (Mark 11:17).
- Even though during his earthly ministry Jesus focused his ministry on "the lost sheep of the house of Israel" (Matt. 10:6; 15:24); nevertheless, a decisive shift happens with the death and resurrection of Jesus: "Go therefore and make disciples of *all nations*" (Matt. 28:19).
- And Jesus gives an interpretation of his death and resurrection in the parable of the tenants in Matthew 21:33–43. The owner of the vineyard (representing the God of Israel) sends his son (representing Jesus the Messiah) to gather fruit from his people (representing worshipful obedience). Instead of giving him fruit, they kill him. Jesus asks, "What will [the owner] do?" That is, what will God do when his Son is rejected by the Jewish people? Verse 43 gives the answer: "Therefore I tell you, the kingdom of God will be taken away from you and given to *a people producing its fruits*"—that is, the new people of God transformed by the Messiah.

In other words, over and over, Jesus shows that the people of God will no longer be defined in an ethnic way—which had been largely the case since the call of Abraham. The new people that he is calling into existence is defined not by race or ethnicity or political ties, but by "producing the fruit of the kingdom" (Matt. 21:43). These are the people who follow Jesus and are transformed by who he is and what he did in dying for sinners and rising again (as we will see).

NOT COLOR, BUT FAITH IN CHRIST

This will mean a new global family made up of believers in Christ from every ethnic group on the planet. And it will mean that those who love that vision will work toward local manifestations of that ethnic diversity. Jesus is the end of ethnocentrism—globally and locally. Not color but faith in Christ is the mark of the kingdom. But it is a mighty long journey. And the price is high. Jesus was on the Calvary road every step of the way. He knew what it would finally cost him. It would cost him his life. But his heart was in it. To the end. That is what we turn to in the next chapter.

Therefore remember that at one time you Gentiles in the flesh, called "the uncircumcision" by what is called the circumcision, which is made in the flesh by hands—remember that you were at that time separated from Christ, alienated from the commonwealth of Israel and strangers to the covenants of promise, having no hope and without God in the world. But now in Christ Jesus you who once were far off have been brought near by the blood of Christ. For he himself is our peace, who has made us both one and has broken down in his flesh the dividing wall of hostility by abolishing the law of commandments expressed in ordinances, that he might create in himself one new man in place of the two, so making peace, and might reconcile us both to God in one body through the cross, thereby killing the hostility. And he came and preached peace to you who were far off and peace to those who were near. For through him we both have access in one Spirit to the Father. So then you are no longer strangers and aliens, but you are fellow citizens with the saints and members of the household of God, built on the foundation of the apostles and prophets, Christ Jesus himself being the cornerstone, in whom the whole structure, being joined together, grows into a holy temple in the Lord. In him you also are being built together into a dwelling place for God by the Spirit.

EPHESIANS 2:11–22

CHAPTER EIGHT

THE CREATION OF ONE NEW HUMANITY BY THE BLOOD OF CHRIST

How did Jesus accomplish his mission to end ethnocentrism? How did he create the new people of God who would be defined not by ethnic features but by faith in Christ? He did it through his death. That is what we will focus on in the next three chapters.

Probably no passage of Scripture is clearer than Ephesians 2:11–22 that horizontal reconciliation between alienated peoples happens through vertical reconciliation with God through the blood of Christ. The enemies in this text "have been brought near *by the blood of Christ*" (v. 13)—near to God and near to each other.

The peoples in view here are Jew and Gentile. But we will see shortly that this alienation was no less deep and intransigent than any we may experience today. It is an astonishing passage of Scripture as it uncovers what Paul calls the "mystery of Christ" (Eph. 3:4). Few passages in all the Bible have greater implications not only for racial harmony, but also for how we understand the plan of God in history for the one people of God.

NO LONGER STRANGERS AND ALIENS

First, notice how this Ephesians 2 text begins and ends. It *begins* in verses 11–12 with a description of the alienation that exists between God and all the non-Jewish ethnic groups in the world (Gentiles). And therefore, since God's redeeming work had focused so long on Israel, this alienation with God also produced an alienation between Jew and Gentile:

Remember that at one time you Gentiles in the flesh, called "the uncircumcision" by what is called the circumcision, which is made in the flesh by hands—remember that you were at that time separated from Christ, alienated from the commonwealth of Israel and strangers to the covenants of promise, having no hope and without God in the world.

Then in verses 19–22, the text *ends* with a description of the conciliation between Jewish Christians and Gentile Christians:

So then you are no longer strangers and aliens, but you are fellow citizens with the saints and members of the household of God, built on the foundation of the apostles and prophets, Christ Jesus himself being the cornerstone, in whom the whole structure, being joined together, grows into a holy temple in the Lord. In him you also are being built together into a dwelling place for God by the Spirit.

Consider the amazing changes that have happened between the beginning and the ending of this text. First, in verse 19, two negatives and two positives: (1) The Gentiles are no longer strangers. (2) And they are no longer aliens. Rather, positively, (3) they are fellow citizens with the saints; and (4) they are part of the same household of God.

Once we Gentiles were separated from Christ; now Christ himself has drawn near to us. Once we were excluded from the commonwealth of Israel; now we are fellow citizens in Israel. Once we were strangers to the covenants of promise; now we are fellow partakers of the promise. Once we were without hope; now we are fellow heirs of all God has to give. Once we were without God in the world; now we are members of God's household.

And here's the crucial thing for our present purpose: the whole picture here is not that we (Jew and Gentile) move into these blessings on separate, parallel tracks—Jews without Jesus, and Gentiles with Jesus—but that we move into them together on *one* track—through one Savior, one cross, one body, one new man, and one Spirit to one Father. The picture here is that the true Israel becomes the church of Christ and the church of Christ emerges as the true Israel. And what unites this new people is Jesus, by the blood of his cross.

THE RABBI SAW THINGS VERY DIFFERENTLY

Not everyone sees it this way. Some years ago I called on the phone the main rabbi at Temple Israel, a synagogue a few miles from our church, and invited him to lunch. We went to a restaurant together and had a very frank, and sometimes tense, talk about Jews and Christians.

The conclusion of that talk was that the rabbi solved the problem of Jews and Christians like this: God has two plans to bless people. One is the Jewish covenant, and the other is the Christian covenant. Jews do not have to be Christians to be accepted by God, and Christians do not have to be Jews in order to be accepted by God. Both can get to God their own way—with Jesus (for Christians) or without Jesus (for Jews).

Now that is the opposite of what Ephesians 2:11–22 is saying. But to see this more clearly we need to be more specific. Walk with me through verses 13–18 to see what happened between the alienation of verses 1–12 and the reconciliation of verses 19–22.

BY THE BLOOD OF CHRIST

Ephesians 2:13 trumpets the foundational note with the word *blood*. "But now in Christ Jesus you who once were far off have been brought near *by the blood* of Christ." The "nearness" Paul has in mind is nearness to God and to Jews. Gentiles find reconciliation with God and with Jews "by the blood" of Christ. We watch this unfold as we move through the following verses.

Paul says in verse 14 that Christ "himself is our peace, who has made us both one." In other words, Christ did not come to open a second, alternative way to God. He came to shed his blood for sinners, both Jew and Gentile, and by his sacrifice to give Jew and Gentile a common access to God through faith.

Then Paul adds in verse 15 that the aim of Christ was "that he might create in himself *one new man* in place of the two, so making peace." Here he pictures the church as a single person. Once there was a Jewish people, and there were Gentile peoples. Then Christ came, and by his blood united them to himself so that "in himself" there would be only one new person, namely, Christ. He is their common identity. Which leads us naturally to verse 16 where Jew and Gentile are the one *body* of the one new man Jesus Christ.

Verse 16: "[Christ reconciled] us both [Jew and Gentile] to God *in one body* through the cross, thereby killing the hostility." The reconciling work of Christ brings people to God not in two alien bodies, one rejecting him (Jewish) and one trusting him (Christian). Christ brings Jew and Gentile to God in one body, the church redeemed by his one sacrifice.

And not only in one body, but also in one Spirit. Verse 18: "For through him we both have access *in one Spirit* to the Father." So Paul sums up this great unified work of salvation in 4:4–6, "There is one body and one Spirit—just as you were called to the one hope that belongs to your call—one Lord, one faith, one baptism, one God and Father of all, who is over all and through all and in all."

UNVEILING THE MYSTERY OF CHRIST

What Paul is doing in these verses is describing how the great "mystery of Christ" is grounded in the work of Christ on the cross. The "mystery of Christ" is the mystery that Jew and Gentile are now one people in the Messiah. Paul defines this "mystery" as clearly as possible in Ephesians 3:4–6:

> When you read this, you can perceive my insight into the *mystery of Christ*, which was not made known to the sons of men in other generations as it has now been revealed to his holy apostles and prophets by the Spirit. This mystery is *that the Gentiles are fellow heirs, members of the same body, and partakers of the promise in Christ Jesus through the gospel.*

There had always been a faithful remnant of believing Jews in physical, ethnic Israel. These were the *true* Israel. Not all Israel was true Israel (Rom. 9:6). But some were. And when Jesus the Messiah came, the proof of whether a Jew was part of the true Israel was whether he confessed Jesus as the Son of God or denied him.

John said, "No one who denies the Son has the Father. Whoever confesses the Son has the Father also" (1 John 2:23). And Jesus said, "Whoever does not honor the Son does not honor the Father who sent him" (John 5:23). If you reject Jesus, you reject God; and if you reject God, you are not part of true Israel.

Jesus is the point in redemptive history where the true Israel becomes the church of Christ and the church (Jew and Gentile) emerges as the true Israel. This is the mystery of Christ, now revealed, and it is possible because of the cross.

THE RABBI WAS MISTAKEN

There are not two saving covenants. There are not two saved peoples. And the reason is that there are not two ways of salvation. There are not two Saviors or two crosses. What could be clearer than this: "[Christ] has broken down in his flesh the dividing wall of hostility . . . that he . . . *might reconcile us both to God in one body through the cross*" (Eph. 2:14–16). Jew and Gentile are reconciled to each other by being reconciled to God "through the cross." One way to God for both of us, not two ways. And we go together, or not at all.

So there is one saving covenant, the new covenant in the blood of Christ. In believing on Christ, we are reconciled to God. And in being both reconciled to God through Christ, we are reconciled to each other.

There is no clearer text in the Bible, it seems to me, than verse 16, concerning the indivisibility of reconciliation *to God* through the death of Christ and reconciliation *to each other* of all people groups who come to God through Christ. Vertical and horizontal reconciliation happen together and inseparably through faith in Christ.

Jews needed the cross, and Gentiles needed the cross. After centuries of animal sacrifices that pointed forward to the True Sacrifice, Jews needed to be reconciled to God, and Gentiles needed to be reconciled to God. There was enmity not only between Jew and Gentile, but at root there was enmity between Jews and God, and Gentiles and God, that needed to be overcome by the peacemaking, propitiating work of Christ. "Are we Jews any better off? No, not at all. For we have already charged that all, both Jews and Greeks, are under sin" (Rom. 3:9).

So there was one great work of salvation on the cross when Jesus died to remove the enmity between God and Jew and between God and Gentile. And he did this reconciling work not separately but in one body, the church. That is why there cannot be two peoples of God and two tracks to heaven. For there is one way to be reconciled to God:

Christ reconciles us to God by uniting us to himself. And that means we become one body, Jew and Gentile, in Christ.

BRINGING IT UP TO OUR TIME

Keep in mind that the divide between Jews and Gentiles was not small or simple or shallow. It was huge and complex and deep. It was as intractable as any ethnic hostilities we experience today.

It was, first, religious. The Jews knew the one true God, and Christian Jews knew his Son, Jesus the Messiah. And for many the Gentiles seemed utterly outside religiously; they were pagan and did not know God.

The divide was also cultural or social with many ceremonies and practices like circumcision and dietary regulations and rules of cleanliness and holy days, and so on. These were all designed to set the Jews apart from the nations for a period of redemptive history to make clear the radical holiness of God.

And the divide was racial. This was a bloodline going back to Jacob, not Esau, and Isaac, not Ishmael, and Abraham, not any other father. So the divide here was as big, or bigger, than any divide that we face today among Anglo-, African-, Latino-, Asian-, or Native-American.

LIVING TO GLORIFY THE AIM OF THE CROSS

May we never lose sight of this one phrase: "Brought near by the blood of Christ" (Eph. 2:13). Brought near to God and therefore brought near to each other. By the blood. By the cross.

Ponder this implication of "by the blood." Paul says in Galatians 6:14—and I hope we say with him—"Far be it from me to boast except in the cross of our Lord Jesus Christ." Boast only in the cross. Does this not mean, among other things, that we want the meaning and the worth and the beauty and the power of the cross of Christ to be seen and loved because of the way we live?

And if one design of the cross of Christ is to reconcile alienated ethnic groups to each other by reconciling them to God in Christ, then will we not display and magnify the cross of Christ better by more and deeper and sweeter ethnic diversity and harmony in our corporate and personal lives? If Christ died—mark this, *died!*—to make the church a diverse, reconciled body of Jew and Gentile—"red and yellow, black and white," and every shade and shape in between—then to glory in the cross is to glory in the display of the fruit of that cross.

The riches of God's wisdom in the way he achieved this great work through Christ are bottomless in their depth. I don't want us to pass too quickly from the depths of this foundation to the superstructure of human reconciliation. So we turn in the next chapter to dig down more deeply into the ways of God in what he accomplished through the cross of Christ.

And they sang a new song, saying, "Worthy are you to take the scroll and to open its seals, for you were slain, and by your blood you ransomed people for God from every tribe and language and people and nation, and you have made them a kingdom and priests to our God, and they shall reign on the earth."

REVELATION 5:9–10

CHAPTER NINE

RANSOMED FOR GOD
FROM EVERY TRIBE

We have seen (in chapter 7) that it was the explicit aim of Jesus, in his earthly ministry, to save and gather a people of God not defined by any one race or ethnicity, or any political banner, but rather defined decisively by faith in himself as the only Savior, absolute Lord, and supreme Treasure. Thus his mission was, among other glorious things, the end of ethnocentrism.

Then we saw that the way Jesus accomplished this mission was through his death (chapter 8). The religiously, ethnically, and racially divided groups who were hostile to each other "have been brought near *by the blood of Christ*" (Eph. 2:13)—that is, brought near to God and near to each other. He has done it by his blood—his death, as a substitution in the place of hostile sinners.

Now, what I am eager to do is to show from Scripture more specifically how God accomplished this reconciling work through the death of Jesus. Sometimes we are content to see the fact but then neglect the riches of the foundations. The Bible reveals stupendous foundations for our faith in the reconciling work of Christ. I would like to go as deep as the Bible goes in grasping how God achieves racial and ethnic harmony.

PUTTING MY THEOLOGICAL CARDS ON THE TABLE

I will put my theological cards on the table. I am a lover of the Reformed faith—the legacy of the Protestant Reformation expressed broadly in the writings of John Calvin and John Owen and Jonathan Edwards and Charles Spurgeon, and contemporaries such as R. C. Sproul and J. I. Packer and John Frame.

I speak of love for this legacy the way I speak of loving a cherished photo of my wife. I say, "I love that picture." You won't surprise me if you point out, "But that's not your wife; that's a picture." Yes. Yes. I know it's only a picture. I don't love the picture *instead of* her; I love the picture *because of* her. She is precious *in herself*. The picture is not precious in itself but because it reveals her. That's the way theology is precious. God is valuable in himself. The theology is not valuable in itself. It is valuable as a picture. That's what I mean when I say, "I love Reformed theology." It's the best composite, Bible-distilled picture of God that I have.

The point of bringing up Reformed theology is not that its representatives have always been the best examples in its history of how to pursue racial harmony. I gave up looking for perfect heroes a long time ago. Everyone but Jesus lets you down. There have been good models of racial reconciliation among those who do not embrace all of the Reformed faith. And there have been many who embraced much of the Reformed faith who have fallen short. And, yes, there have been beautiful examples of Reformed believers who have lived well for the cause of ethnic diversity and harmony.[1]

My point is that the truths themselves, when rightly understood and embraced and cherished with a good heart, cut the legs out from under racist attitudes. That I am chosen for salvation in spite of all my ugly and deadening sinfulness, that the infinitely precious Son of God secured my eternal life through his own infinite suffering, that my rebellious and resistant heart was conquered by sovereign grace, and that I am kept by the power of God forever—if these truths do not make me a humble servant of racial diversity and harmony, then I have not seen them or loved them as I ought.

One of the things that excites me about this picture of God—this Reformed faith—is first that it is a faithful summary of what the Bible really teaches. In the end, what matters is not whether we are Reformed or not. Labels don't matter much. What matters in the end is whether we are humbly submissive to all the Bible teaches. Another thing that excites me about this Reformed faith is the way it brings to light the foundations of the work of Christ in shattering racial pride and ethnocentrism. That is what I want to show.

REFORMED IN THE BROAD SENSE

Notice that I included the Baptist Charles Spurgeon as part of the Reformed legacy. Some folks in the tradition don't like that, since they see the implications of Reformed theology as excluding the Baptist viewpoint. But the way I am using the term "Reformed faith" and "Reformed theology" does include Baptists. I have two defining clusters of beliefs in mind when I speak of the Reformed faith.

One cluster is the commitment to the great "*solas*" of the Reformation—that God's justification of sinners is by *grace* alone, through *faith* alone, because of *Christ* alone, to the *glory of God* alone, on the authority of *Scripture* alone. The other cluster is sometimes called "Reformed soteriology," or "the five points of Calvinism," and is summed up in these five beliefs: (1) pervasive, disabling human depravity, (2) unconditional election, (3) extending the atonement beyond its power to make the offer of eternal life valid for all people to its actual effect in the particular purchase of the bride of Christ, (4) the power of God's sovereign grace to overcome all human resistance, and (5) the purpose of God to preserve the faith and salvation of all his saints. My point will be that all five of these truths are meant to advance racial and ethnic diversity and harmony.

From the standpoint of the Reformed faith, every aspect of the way God views and saves sinners is designed to undermine racism and lead to a new reconciled and redeemed humanity from every people group in the world. The fact that these implications of the Reformed faith have not always been seen, and that there is a legacy of racism in the Reformed tradition (as in all traditions), does not change the fact that the implications are there.

Kenneth J. Stewart, in his book *Ten Myths About Calvinism: Recovering the Breadth of the Reformed Tradition*, tackles the issue head-on in a chapter titled "Myth Ten: Calvinism Fosters Racial Inequality." He addresses the heavily Presbyterian and Reformed Christianity that coexisted with American slavery and the Dutch Reformed church that coexisted with South African apartheid. These two historical realities have tarnished the Reformed Faith.

And rightly so. But not uniquely so. That is, virtually all branches of Christianity—indeed all faiths, and all nonfaiths—are tarnished, if not by collusion with racism then with some other evil. The human race, including the partially redeemed Christian part of it, are sinners still.

But Kenneth Stewart is helpful in honestly admitting the stain but distinguishing between causation and association.[2] He shows that the European, American, and South African forms of slavery were not produced or caused by the Christian faith nor by the Reformed branch in particular. Rather, the sin lay in tolerating and coexisting and even endorsing. But in every case, the day came when the very Bible, and the very faith, that had once been used to condone slavery was finally seen to undo it.[3]

This was certainly the case in my own experience. It was not Reformed theology that in any way spurred or strengthened my adolescent racism. In those days I was as much against theological predestination as I was against racial integration. For me, at least, Reformed theology was not the reason for my racism but the remedy for it. My deliverance from man-centered, free-will-thumping, rationalistic piety went hand in hand with my deliverance from demeaning views of other races. I'm not saying that the embrace of Calvinism and the abandonment of racist views go together for everyone. But they did for me.

And, not surprisingly, for centuries there have been African Americans who have found in the Reformed view of God not an oppressive truth but a liberating and empowering one. In our own day there is a kind of awakening among many black Christians to the truth and beauty of this God of the Bible. Anthony Carter has served us well with his groundbreaking book *On Being Black and Reformed: A New Perspective on the African-American Christian Experience*.[4] And he has joined nine other African Americans in describing their theological journeys in *Glory Road: The Journeys of 10 African Americans into Reformed Christianity*.[5]

The question of why the church is not more quick and successful in exposing and overcoming sin corporately is very much connected to the question of why we as individuals are not more quick and successful in exposing and overcoming sin personally. It is a hard and sad question. I have wrestled with it in *Spectacular Sins and Their Global Purpose in the Glory of Christ*. Why didn't God simply destroy Satan at the beginning, and all sin with him?

The ultimate answer . . . is that "all things were created through Christ and for Christ" (Colossians 1:16). God foresaw all that Satan would do if he created Satan and permitted him to rebel. In choosing to create him, he was choosing to fold all of that evil into his purpose for creation.

That purpose for creation was the glory of his Son. All things, including Satan and all his followers, were created with this in view. They were created knowing what they would do, and that knowledge was taken into account in God's decision to create them. Therefore, the evil that they do in the world is part of how the greatest purpose of God will be accomplished.

Satan's fall and ongoing existence is for the glory of Christ. The Son of God, Jesus Christ, will be more highly honored and more deeply appreciated and loved in the end because he defeats Satan not the moment after he fell, but through millennia of longsuffering, patience, humility, servanthood, suffering, and eventually his own death. A single, sudden, and infinitely holy display of power to destroy Satan immediately after his fall would have been a glorious display of power and righteousness. But it would not have been the fullest possible display of all the glories in the Son and the Father. God chose an infinitely wise way of displaying the full array of divine glories in letting Satan fall and do his work for millennia.

The glory of Christ reaches its highest point in the obedient sacrifice of the cross where Jesus triumphed over the devil (Colossians 2:15). Jesus said in that final hour of his own sacrifice, "Now is the Son of Man glorified, and God is glorified in him" (John 13:31). Paul said that the crucifixion of Christ is the point where we see his wisdom and power most gloriously displayed: "We preach Christ crucified . . . the power of God and the wisdom of God" (1 Corinthians 1:23–24).

Jesus said to Paul about Satan's thorn in Paul's side, "My power is made perfect in weakness" (2 Corinthians 12:9). Satan, and all his pain, serves in the end to magnify the power and wisdom and love and grace and mercy and patience and wrath of Jesus Christ. We would not know Christ in the fullness of his glory if he had not defeated Satan in the way he did.[6]

The work of sin and Satan go on in our day. God permits this, within bounds, to expose the exceeding sinfulness of sin and to magnify the greatness of his mercy in saving sinners like us. None of us is in a position to claim that our theology is the right one *because of the quality of our lives*. Truth is grounded in God's Word, not our works.

And, while it is true that "you will recognize them by their fruits" (Matt. 7:16), it is not true that you can know their theology by their fruits. Man's capacity for hypocrisy is great. And Jesus can say even of the Pharisees, "Practice and observe whatever they tell you—but not what they do" (Matt. 23:3). And Paul can say of the preaching of some heartless, pretentious evangelists, "What then? Only that in every way, whether in pretense or in truth, Christ is proclaimed, and in that I rejoice" (Phil. 1:18).

One generation is blind to some implications of their faith. Other generations are blind to others. One ethnic group is blind to one thing. Another ethnic group is blind to another. My aim is not to whitewash the Reformed tradition but to show what it really implies.

THE DOCTRINE OF DEPRAVITY

The fact that "Christ Jesus came into the world to save sinners" (1 Tim. 1:15)—to reconcile them to God and to each other—assumes that something terrible had gone wrong in creation. The death of the Son of God is as drastic an act of rescue as can be imagined. The fact that it had to take place so that God would be just in the justification of sinners (Rom. 3:25–26) implies that we humans were in a miserable condition and could not save ourselves.

What the Reformed faith has seen in Scripture is that all human beings, since Adam and Eve, are pervasively depraved—so depraved that not only are we unable to atone for our sins (Ps. 49:7, 15), but we are also unable to humble ourselves and trust in a redeemer.

The Bible teaches that since the original sin of Adam, all humans are spiritually dead and morally incapable of submitting to God in faith and obedience. By nature we have a mindset that cannot submit to God. "The mind that is set on the flesh is hostile to God, for it does not submit to God's law; indeed, it cannot. Those who are in the flesh cannot please God" (Rom. 8:7–8). The reason for this moral inability is given in Ephesians 2:1—"You were dead in the trespasses and sins in which you once walked." And therefore, we are "sons of disobedience" and "children of wrath" (vv. 2–3).

The "natural" person—the way we are in our sinful nature—apart from the work of the Holy Spirit, does not see the truth as true and desirable. Instead, we consider the truth of the gospel to be foolishness. So we cannot embrace it as true and precious. So Paul says in 1 Corinthians 2:14, "The natural person does not accept the things of the Spirit of God, for they are folly to him, and he is not able to understand them because they are spiritually discerned." So when the Reformed tradition refers to "total depravity," it does not mean that we do as many bad acts as we possibly could. It means that we are *totally unable* to trust Christ and do the "work of faith" (1 Thess. 1:3; 2 Thess. 1:11) without the decisive intervention of God's enabling grace.

The implications of this doctrine for racial harmony are huge. Most often Christians celebrate the great positive common denominator among races, namely, that we are all created equally in the image of God (Gen. 1:27; 5:1; 9:6; James 3:9). That is true, powerful, relevant, and wonderful. But there is a problem if we treat that doctrine in isolation. The problem is: we are not good enough to hear it and make good use of it.

If you only convince a sinful, depraved, unrepentant, unregenerate person that he is created in the image of God, you will probably fuel his innate pride. And that pride may so distort a person's view of reality that he easily convinces himself that he is above others. That's how irrational sin can make us.

What is desperately needed is another conviction—no less strong but even more shattering to pride—namely, the conviction that all human beings, including me and you, are corrupt, depraved, guilty, and condemned. We are all under the just sentence of hell where there will be weeping and gnashing of teeth. And the racial diversity of hell will be as great as it is in heaven, but there will be no harmony there.

The ethnic diversity of hell is a crucial doctrine. Paul put it like this: "There will be tribulation and distress for every human being who does evil, the Jew first and also the Greek" (Rom. 2:9). God is no respecter of persons in salvation or in damnation. The human race—and every ethnic group in it—is united in this great reality: we are all depraved and condemned. We are all lost in the woods together, sinking on the same boat, dying of the same disease.

If we saw this more clearly, two things would happen. We would be humbled and frightened and made desperate, like a little child who desperately wants to find Mommy when he is lost in the store. We would be broken and humbled. I have never seen a white-hooded Klansman or a Farrakhan follower who was brokenhearted for his sin, humble, and desperate for a savior.

The other thing that would happen if we saw how united we are in sin is that the sins of others would look like the out-workings of *our own* hearts, and we would be slower to judge and quicker to show mercy. The doctrine of total depravity has a huge role to play in humbling all ethnic groups and giving us a desperate camaraderie of condemnation leading to the one and only Savior, Jesus Christ.

GOD'S PURCHASE OF HIS PEOPLE

Hand in glove with the doctrine of our disabling depravity is the doctrine of God's effective purchase of his people on the cross. The reason it's like hand and glove is that our inability because of sin calls for a kind of redemption that does more than offer us a forgiveness we don't have the ability to receive. Rather, it calls for a redemption that effectively purchases not only our forgiveness but also our willingness to receive it. In other words, the unwilling glove of depravity calls for the insertion of a powerful hand of ability-giving redemption.

Sometimes this doctrine is called "limited atonement." It's not a helpful term. Better would be the terms *definite atonement* or *particular redemption*. The reason *limited atonement* isn't helpful is that, in fact, the doctrine affirms *more*, not less, about Christ's work in redemption than its rival view called "unlimited atonement."[7]

The view of unlimited atonement takes all the passages that say the death of Christ is "for us" (Rom. 5:8; 1 Thess. 5:10), or for his own "sheep" (John 10:11, 15), or for "the church" (Acts 20:28; Eph. 5:25), or for "the children of God" (John 11:52), or for "those who are being sanctified" (Heb. 10:14) and makes them refer to all human beings. In this "unlimited atonement" view, the sentence "Christ died for you" means: Christ died for *all sinners*, so that if you will repent and believe in Christ, then the death of Jesus will become effective in your case and will take away your sins.

Now as far as it goes, this seems to me to be biblical teaching—salvation is offered to all because of Christ. But then this view *denies* something that I think the Bible teaches. It denies that Christ died *for his church*—his bride (Eph. 5:25)—in any way different from the way he died for unbelievers who never come to faith.

There is no dispute that Christ died to obtain great saving benefits for all who believe. Moreover, I have no dispute with saying that Christ died so that we might say to all persons everywhere without exception: "God gave his only begotten Son to die for sin so that if you believe on him you will have eternal life."

The dispute rather is whether God intended for the death of Christ to obtain *more* than these two things—more than (1) saving benefits after faith, and (2) a bona fide offer of blood-bought salvation to every person on the planet. Specifically, did God intend for the death of Christ to obtain the free gift of faith (Eph. 2:8) and repentance (2 Tim. 2:25)? Did the blood of Jesus obtain not only the benefits that come *after* faith but also the gift of *faith itself*?

We want to be biblical. Does the unlimited atonement interpretation of any of the "universal" texts on the atonement necessarily contradict this *more* that I am affirming about God's intention for the death of Christ—texts like John 1:29; 2 Corinthians 5:19; 1 Timothy 2:6; Hebrews 2:9; 2 Peter 2:1; and 1 John 2:1–2?

I don't think so. The historic view of definite atonement is just as eager as I am to avoid saying that these texts teach "universal salvation." It does not teach that the death of Christ "for all" means that all will be saved. Rather, definite atonement says, in the words of Millard Erickson, "God intended the atonement to make salvation *possible* for all persons. Christ died for all persons, but this atoning death becomes *effective* only when accepted by the individual."[8]

What has become clearer to me as I have pondered these things is that those who believe in definite atonement do *not* say that in the death of Christ God intends to *effectively* save all for whom Christ died. They only say that God intends to *make possible* the salvation of all for whom Christ died. But that view of these "universal" texts does *not* contradict the Reformed view I am affirming. The fact that God makes salvation possible for all through the blood of Christ does not contradict the view that God does *more* than that through the death of Christ. I don't affirm that God does less but that he does more. He actually secures the salvation of his chosen people. He secures all the grace needed for their salvation, including the grace of regeneration and faith.

Paul says in Ephesians 5:25, "Christ loved the church and gave himself up for her." This was a particular redemption. Christ had his bride in view differently than he had all in view. He knew his bride, and he wanted his bride, and he bought his bride. Jesus says, "I lay down my life for the sheep" (John 10:15). He said, "I am praying for them. I am not praying for the world but for those whom you [Father] have given me, for they are yours" (John 17:9). He said, "And for their sake I consecrate myself [to die], that they also may be sanctified in truth" (John 17:19). In other words, Christ had a specific design in his death for the sake of his people—the cross would be *sufficient* for the salvation of the world, but *efficient* for his sheep, his bride.

And Paul carried through this understanding of Christ's work when he said in Romans 8:32–33, "He who did not spare his own Son but gave him up for us all, how will he not also with him graciously give us all things? Who shall bring any charge against God's elect?" God's elect in verse 33 are the same as the "us all" in verse 32. This group, he says, will most surely receive "all things." God will see to it. And the reason Paul gives is that Christ did not spare his own Son but gave him up "for us all." That means that the giving of the Son guarantees all the blessings of the elect.

This does not limit the extent of what the atonement offers. The benefits of the atonement are offered to everyone. If you believe on Christ, they are all yours. But "the Lord knows those who are his" (2 Tim. 2:19). For them, for his bride, he is securing something that cannot fail—their faith and their justification and their glorification. Those for whom he died, in this fullest sense, will most certainly obtain all things—they will finally inherit the kingdom of God. His death is infallibly effective for the elect.

Definite Atonement—the Great Leveler

This is enormously important for racial and ethnic diversity and harmony. It means that no person, no matter what ethnic group, ever made any contribution to the ransom that frees him from the slavery of sin. We have seen above that because of our common depravity, we are all equally slaves to sin, corruption, futility, death, and condemnation. That is our common slavery. But now we also see that the payment for our liberation—the blood and righteousness of Christ—is so complete that we could not and did not make any contribution to it, whether by our willing, or running (Rom. 9:16), or any ethnic distinctives. When Christ died in our place and for our sins, the whole ransom was paid. So fully paid, in fact, that our freedom was not just offered but secured, guaranteed.

The cross of Christ is a great leveler of human beings, not only because it shows that we are all desperate sinners, and not just because it can only be received by faith, but also because it is such a full and effective ransom for the elect that no child of God dare ever think that we made any contribution to the purchase. Even our new birth and faith were secured by the blood of Jesus. No color, no ethnicity, no intelligence, no skill, no human wealth or power can add anything to the all-sufficient, all-effective sacrifice of Christ. The redeemed of every race and ethnicity are one in our utter dependence on his effective blood and righteousness.

An Illustration of Particular Redemption and Racial Harmony

Perhaps the text in all of Scripture that displays the connection most clearly between the particular redemption of God's people and the ethnic diversity and harmony of that people is Revelation 5:9. The inhabitants of heaven are singing to the risen Christ. "And they sang a new song, saying, 'Worthy are you to take the scroll and to open its seals, for you were slain, and by your blood *you ransomed people for God from every tribe and language and people and nation.*"

Notice that it does *not* say that Christ purchased all individuals in every tribe and tongue and people and nation. It says that Christ purchased people "*from* every tribe and language and people and nation." In fact, in the original Greek, there is no direct object for the verb *purchased*, and so the emphasis falls very hard on *every tribe*. It's as though I said, "I paid a huge amount to purchase from every booth in the market." In that sentence, I don't mention what I purchased. The emphasis falls not on what I purchased but on the fact that I bought whatever it was *from every booth*. That's the way Revelation 5:9 reads—Jesus ransomed "from every tribe and language and people and nation."

I know it is possible to interpret this text loosely, as though the purchase of particular people, with a particular composition from every tribe, was not designed by God—that it just happened that way because people in all the tribes simply choose to believe. And so the composition of God's people (what kind of ethnic groups are in it) is by human chance and not a certain divine design.

If this were another kind of book, I would point to all the texts in the other writings of John besides this one—his Gospel and epistles—to show why I don't think he means it that way (for example, John 6:44, 65; 6:37; 10:16; 11:51–52).[9] But for now, I will simply appeal to the fact that when you purchase something (as Christ did his people), you generally purchase something particular. You choose it, and you buy it.

So when it says in Revelation 5:9 that Christ was slain, and by his blood purchased people "from every tribe," it is not likely that it is a coincidence or merely by chance that those he bought do come from every tribe. In fact, Jesus said, "I have other sheep that are not of this fold. I must bring them also, and they will listen to my voice" (John 10:16). And John said that Jesus died "to gather into one the children of God who are scattered abroad" (John 11:52).

This was the design of his death. He bought a people who were scattered all over the earth *among all the peoples of the world*. By his blood he obtained them for himself, and he "must bring them also." That is what world missions is for. Christ gathers his sheep through his ambassadors.[10]

If the purchase of a people—a bride, a church, a kingdom, a priesthood—"*from every tribe*" is intentional, designed, and purposeful, and not a coincidence, not by human chance, then the implications for racial and ethnic diversity and harmony among Christ's people are huge.

First, God intends to have a people not just from three or four ethnic groups ("red and yellow, white and black"), but from *all ethnic groups*. All shades, all shapes, all cultures. This is underlined by the four words "people," "tribe," "language," and "nation" (Greek *ethnos*). This covers the whole range of ethnic diversity in the world.[11] God intentionally pursued a people that is extraordinarily diverse.

Second, God intends for these people to be in profound God-centered harmony. You can see this in the words of Revelation 5:10: "You have made them a kingdom and priests to our God, and they shall reign on the earth." All of them will be priests, and all of them will reign. Now this would be utter chaos and religious anarchy if the single priesthood and the single reign of all these ethnic groups were not profoundly unified. You can't have priests who hate each other and refuse to serve together in one temple, or live together in one neighborhood, or hang out together after hours.

If all those who are purchased from every tribe are priests to God and fellow rulers with God, who worship God and reign with God, then they must have a deep unity in the truth and in love. The kind of divisions and hostilities and prejudice and mistreatment and ridicule and suspicion that has existed in the church among races is unthinkable in view of what Christ is pursuing in this text.

The third implication is that this aim of ethnic diversity and harmony in the people of God (the one priesthood and kingdom) was pursued by God at infinite cost. The cost of diversity was the blood and life of the Son of God. This is not an overstatement. Consider the wording of Revelation 5:9 very closely: "You were slain, and by your blood you ransomed people for God from every tribe and language and people and nation." God paid the infinite price of his own Son's life to obtain a priesthood of believers and a kingdom of fellow rulers from every race and every ethnic group on earth. Think on it. He paid this price particularly. It was for this particular people. He ransomed people "*from* the nations." The issue of racial and ethnic diversity and harmony in the church is not small, because the price God paid precisely for *it* was not small. It was infinite.

Fourth, the final implication from the text is that this infinite price was paid and this racial and ethnic diversity and harmony were pursued by Christ "*for God.*" Don't miss those little words in verse 9: "You were slain, and by your blood you ransomed people *for God* from every tribe and language and people and nation." Racial diversity and racial harmony in the blood-bought church of God is "for God"—for God's delight and for God's glory.[12]

What do we see this people doing who are gathered from every race and tribe? They were praising God and the Lamb of God and falling on their faces before him. They were saying, "'To him who sits on the throne and to the Lamb be blessing and honor and glory and might forever and ever!' And the four living creatures said, 'Amen!' and the elders fell down and worshiped" (Rev. 5:13–14). Blood-bought ethnic and racial diversity and harmony is for the glory of God through Christ. It is all aiming at the all-satisfying, everlasting, God-centered, Christ-exalting experience of many-colored, many-cultured worship, an aroma that delights the heart of God.

Implications for Us

And if it cost the Father and the Son such a price, should we expect that it will cost us nothing? That it will be easy? That the Devil, who hates the glory of God and despises the aims of the cross, will relent without a battle? No. To join God in pursuing racial diversity and racial harmony will be costly. So costly that many simply try for a while and then give up and walk away from the effort to easier things.

But if you love God—if you live to spread a passion for his supremacy in all things for the joy of all peoples through Jesus Christ—you will trust him and seek his help and pursue with your life what cost Jesus his.

UNCONDITIONAL ELECTION

I mentioned earlier that one of the things I love about the Reformed faith is that it so deeply undermines the ethnocentrism and racism that Jesus came to destroy. We have seen this first in regard to our human depravity and the camaraderie of condemnation it creates. And we have seen it in the particularity of God's purpose in the death of Jesus. Very closely connected with this divine design in the death of Jesus is the truth of God's unconditional election. What an amazing explosive under the boulders of pride in human racial and ethnic differences!

What this doctrine teaches is that God chooses his people before the foundation of the world apart from any conditions in them. It is unconditional. "He chose us in him before the foundation of the world" (Eph.

1:4). This does not mean we don't have to believe on Christ to be saved. Nor does it mean people will be condemned apart from real sin and guilt. We are saved by faith. And we are condemned because of sin and unbelief.

What it does mean is this: who it is that believes and is saved, and who it is that rebels and is not saved, is ultimately decided by God. This is mysterious, and I do not claim to have all the answers to the questions it raises. I believe it because it is so clearly taught in the Bible.[13]

Taught in the Bible

For example, Acts 13:48 puts it like this after Paul's sermon in Antioch of Pisidia: "When the Gentiles heard this, they began rejoicing and glorifying the word of the Lord, and *as many as were appointed to eternal life believed.*" Faith does not come first, and then God's decision to ordain to life. It's the other way around. First comes God's choice, and that determines who will believe. "As many as were appointed to eternal life believed."

First comes God's sovereign "purpose of election," as Paul says in Romans 9:11; then comes faith. Faith and repentance are a gift (Eph. 2:8; 2 Tim. 2:25). Therefore, the condition of who gets the gift cannot be that one has the gift already. God chooses for reasons that are wise and mysterious and shattering to human self-exaltation. So the "purpose of election" is not conditional on faith or any other human decision or feeling or behavior or distinctive. It is unconditional. God is free and unconstrained by anything outside his own will when he elects his people.

He makes his appointments before we were "born and had done nothing either good or bad" (Rom. 9:11), so that "it depends not on human will or exertion, but on God, who has mercy" (Rom. 9:16). Thus Paul says of his own salvation and calling, "He . . . set me apart before I was born, and . . . called me by his grace" (Gal. 1:15).

Unconditional Election Severs the Root of Racism

This means that God does not choose his people on the basis of skin color or any other ethnic distinctive. No ethnic group can say they are chosen because of God's preference for their physical or psychological or intellectual qualities. And no ethnic group can say that they are *not* chosen because of their qualities—not even the worse moral and spiritual qualities.

God's choice to set his favor on us is unconditional. It is not based on anything in us. He is absolutely free and unconstrained. This is his glory, his name. "I . . . will proclaim before you my name 'The LORD.' And *I will be gracious to whom I will be gracious, and will show mercy on whom I will show mercy*" (Ex. 33:19; Rom. 9:15). *God is God* means *God is free.*

Therefore, the doctrine of unconditional election severs the deepest root of all racism and all ethnocentrism. If I am among God's elect, it is owing entirely to God's free grace, not to my distinctives. Therefore, there is no ground in God's election for pride. And there is no ground in God's election for despair. If you are a believer in Jesus, nothing in you caused God to choose you. And if you are not yet a believer, nothing in you made you be among the elect, and nothing evil in your past—no matter how horrible—can be brought forward as an argument that you are not among the elect. To know if we are chosen, we simply come to Christ as the Savior and Lord and Treasure of our lives. If we believe in Jesus like that, this is the evidence that we are his. He chose us. He brought us to himself.

When it comes to election, every race, every ethnic group, is on the absolutely level field of unconditional mercy: "I will have mercy on whom I have mercy, and I will have compassion on whom I have compassion" (Rom. 9:15). Divine election, understood and embraced and cherished as utterly undeserved—as it is in the Bible—destroys racism and ethnocentrism.

Before turning to the racial implications of the remaining two doctrines of the "five points" (irresistible grace and perseverance of the saints), it will be helpful at this point to dig down into the racial out-workings of the doctrine of justification by faith. The Reformed understanding of the Bible puts this doctrine at the core of what the Christian gospel is. When we understand that God's act of justifying the ungodly (Rom. 4:5) is by grace alone, through faith alone, on the basis of Christ alone, for the glory of God alone, we begin to see how shattering it is to ethnocentrism and racial pride. That is what we focus on in the next chapter.

Then what becomes of our boasting? It is excluded. By what kind of law? By a law of works? No, but by the law of faith. For we hold that one is justified by faith apart from works of the law. Or is God the God of Jews only? Is he not the God of Gentiles also? Yes, of Gentiles also, since God is one—who will justify the circumcised by faith and the uncircumcised through faith.

ROMANS 3:27–30

CHAPTER TEN

EVERY PEOPLE JUSTIFIED THE SAME WAY

I have been arguing in the last two chapters that the biblical portrait of God and his work called "Reformed theology" is devastating to racism and ethnocentrism. I said that I have two defining clusters of beliefs in mind when I speak of the Reformed faith. One is sometimes called the "five points of Calvinism." We have now worked our way through three of those (disabling depravity, particular redemption, and unconditional election) and will return to the last two "points" (irresistible grace and perseverance of the saints) in chapters 11 and 12.

The other cluster of beliefs is summed up in the "*solas*." It's important to see that all of these *solas* relate most immediately to the great doctrine of justification. Hence, God's justification of sinners is by *grace* alone, through *faith* alone, because of *Christ* alone, to the *glory of God* alone, on the authority of *Scripture* alone.

What I want to do now is dig down into this doctrine of justification to show how profoundly it undermines racism and ethnocentrism and advances the cause of racial and ethnic diversity and harmony. We are still answering the question, *How does the death of Christ do its reconciling work between God and man, and between man and man?* What are the deeper foundations of Ephesians 2:13, which says that alienated groups have been "brought near [to God and each other] by the blood of Christ"?

Romans 3:27–31, especially verses 29–30, deals with gigantic theological realities. Not surprisingly Paul applies these realities to ethnic relationships. Let me use a couple of really big words to underline the bigness of the realities. The *metaphysical* oneness of God and the *soteriological* act of justification are brought into connection with the reconciliation of ethnically alienated peoples.

PAUL'S LINE OF THOUGHT

Focus first on Romans 3:29–30. Paul has just said that we are justified by faith apart from works of the Jewish law. Now he asks, "Or is God the God of Jews only? Is he not the God of Gentiles also? Yes, of Gentiles also, since God is one—who will justify the circumcised by faith and the uncircumcised through faith." There are three steps in Paul's order of thought here. I will state the three steps in reverse order, and then take them one at a time and try to show how Paul relates them to the issue of ethnic relations.

First, there is the great affirmation in verse 30: "God is one." Second, there is the inference that since he is one, therefore he justifies Jews and Gentiles in the same way, not in two different ways. He "will justify the circumcised by faith and the uncircumcised through faith." Third, since he is one, and justifies all peoples in the same way, not in different ways, he is not the God of the Jews only but the God of the nations as well—all ethnic groups, not just Jews. That's the gist of the passage. And you can see immediately why this way of talking about justification is so relevant to the burden of this book. Let's take it a step at a time.

GOD IS ONE

First, from verse 30, let's consider the oneness of God: ". . . since God is one—who will justify the circumcised by faith and the uncircumcised through faith." God is one. What does this mean?

1) There Is One True God

Paul's statement that "God is one" has several implications. It means, first of all, that there is only one true God, not many gods. That is the way the NIV translates it: "There is only one God." This is an absolutely necessary belief, in view of what it means to be God.

Paul says in Romans 11:36, "From him and through him and to him are all things. To him be glory forever." If that is what it means to be God, there cannot be two of them. If the very meaning of being God is that he is the ultimate source of all that is, there can be only one. Two competing gods cannot both be the ultimate source of all things. One would be the ultimate source of the other, and so only one would be God; or both would be equally ultimate and neither would be the source of all things, and so neither would be God, by Paul's definition. There is only one God, the Creator and Sustainer of all that is outside of God.

2) God's Unity and Coherence

Which leads us to a second implication of the statement that "God is one." For Paul, the oneness of God is not simply a statement that there is only one true God but also a statement that this God has a unity and coherence to his identity. That is, he is what he is and not what we make of him. He is what he is and not something else. He has identity in himself. He has fixed attributes. He does not change. He is not inconsistent or schizophrenic. He does not have contradictory personalities. All his characteristics cohere in one unified Being. He makes himself known as who he is. He is one.

This has tremendous implications for religious pluralism, and religious pluralism, as we will see shortly, is closely connected with ethnic diversity. Paul's statement about God's unity implies, for example, that not all religions are true and lead to heaven. It also implies that those who know the true God because of his gracious revelation should try to persuade others to know and trust the one true God. And it implies that, since the true God of the Bible is a God who is known only by authentic, voluntary faith and not coerced words or deeds, therefore no violence or force will be used to demand or restrict religious belief.

Which means, interestingly, that the uniqueness and singleness of the one true God of the Bible are both a threat and protection for religious pluralism. Keep in mind that religious pluralism is inextricably connected to ethnic diversity. Paul is dealing with Jews and Gentiles, whose racial, ethnic, cultural, and religious differences were so great and so interwoven that they could not be easily separated. As Paul deals here with *religious* pluralism, he is laying the foundation for *racial* and *ethnic* reconciliation.

So I repeat, the oneness of God is a threat *and* a protection of religious pluralism. The absolute claim of the singular, unified God of the

Bible on all persons and all religions is a spiritual *threat to religious pluralism* in that it does call for repentance from all false religion (Acts 17:30). It calls for personal faith in the one true God through his one and only Son, Jesus Christ (John 3:36; 5:23; 1 John 5:12).

But this single, true God of the Bible is a *protection for religious pluralism* until Jesus returns, because he forbids that his cause be advanced by the sword or by external coercion. Jesus said to Pilate, "My kingdom is not of this world. If my kingdom were of this world, my servants would have been fighting, that I might not be delivered over to the Jews. But my kingdom is not from the world" (John 18:36). We Christians are called to love our enemies and to suffer injustice rather than return evil for evil (Matt. 5:43–48; Rom. 12:14).

Therefore, true Christianity is both a threat and a support for religious pluralism. It is a *spiritual* threat and a *political* support. True Christianity will not endorse ethnic cleansing against Muslims, or pogroms against Jews, or hostilities against Hindus (legalized or otherwise). True Christianity does not advance by the sword or the gun. It advances by proclamation and persuasion and prayer and love, and by being persecuted, not by persecuting.

3) Not Three Gods, but One

There is a third implication of Paul's words "God is one," namely, that the deity of Christ and of the Holy Spirit do not turn Christians into polytheists. We do not worship three Gods, but one God. The mystery of the Trinity is a stumbling block for Muslims and Hindus and Jews and secularists. It always has been, and it always will be. But it is not surprising that the one true God would exist from all eternity in a way that pushes our little minds to the breaking point. Suffice it to say that the revelation of God through Jesus Christ is that Jesus is God, the Spirit is God, the Father is God, and there is one God.[1]

That is the first step in Paul's argument in verse 30: God is one.

GOD HAS ONE WAY OF JUSTIFYING PEOPLE

Now the second step in Paul's train of thought is that this one God has one way of saving people, namely, justification by faith in Jesus Christ. Verse 30: ". . . since God is one—who will justify the circumcised by faith and the uncircumcised through faith." The oneness of God is connected to the oneness of the way he makes people right with himself—justification.

One way to say this would be that God threatens religious pluralism with the glorious freeness of grace. He sends us as his ambassadors to every religion and every ethnic group with this message: There is good news for you! God declares to you that, even though you have sinned against him and are under his wrath, you may be counted righteous and forgiven all your sins and be reconciled to your Creator and have everlasting life. The way to be justified before God is by grace alone through faith alone in his Son Jesus Christ, who already acted in history once for all to pay for sin and provide righteousness. If you believe in Christ, you will be "justified by his grace as a gift, through the redemption that is in Christ Jesus" (Rom. 3:24). He will take away your guilt. He will give you eternal life. If you do not turn to him by faith alone for grace alone on the basis of Christ alone, you remain under his wrath (John 3:36).

Some will say that this universal demand for repentance and faith in Jesus Christ is arrogance and presumption. But a better name for it is *love*. Yes, it undermines religious pluralism and ethnic pride. Christianity does not come to other religious systems and try to replace one way to work for God with another way to work for God. It comes with a declaration of amnesty. The one true God has made a truce at the cost of his Son's life. He offers pardon to every person freely and offers everlasting joy to those who will trust his Son.

The oneness of God means that there is one way to be justified before God—not the way of works, but the way of grace alone through faith alone. Works is the fruit of justification, not the cause (Eph. 2:9–10). And because justification comes only by way of faith, it cuts across all ethnic and political and language and cultural barriers. Verse 30: God "will justify the circumcised by faith and the uncircumcised through faith." "Circumcision" stands for any religious or ethnic trait that you might think would commend you to God. And "uncircumcision" stands for any trait, or missing trait, that you think might keep you from God.

The gospel of Jesus Christ comes and says, "Justification (getting right with God by being counted as righteous) is by faith, not works." Therefore, *having* certain ethnic or religious advantages proves to be of no advantage. And *not* having certain ethnic or religious advantages proves to be of no disadvantage. The reason is that faith in Christ, by its very nature, looks away from distinctives (positive or negative) that you have in yourself and looks to God's free grace in order to be justified and have eternal life.

God's oneness means that there is one way of justification for all. And, because this one God is the great sovereign, self-sufficient God who can't be worked for but overflows in grace, the one way of justification is by grace through faith, and that is not of ourselves; it is the gift of God, not of works, lest anyone—any culture or race or ethnic group—should boast (Eph. 2:8–9).

That's the second step: since God is one, he justifies Jews and Gentiles in the same way, not in two different ways. He justifies the circumcised (Jews) by faith and the uncircumcised (Gentiles) through faith.

HE IS THE GOD OF ALL PEOPLES

Finally, the third step: since God is one and justifies all peoples in the same way—through faith alone on the basis of Christ alone, not in different ways—therefore, *he is not the God of the Jews only, but the God of the nations as well.* Verse 29: "Is God the God of Jews only? Is he not the God of Gentiles also? Yes, of Gentiles also." And, of course, "Gentiles" refers to all kinds of racial and ethnic groups.

So what does it mean for us today to say that God is the God of the nations, the God of every ethnic group that you will ever see in the most diverse urban centers in the world? It means four things, at least.

Every Member of Every Ethnic Group Created in God's Image

First, that God is the God of the nations means that God created all the nations. More specifically, he created all the people in those nations in his own image. This is not Paul's explicit focus in Romans 3:29–30, but it is implied in what he says here.

He makes this focus explicit in Acts 17:26: "He made from one man every nation [Greek *ethnos*] of mankind to live on all the face of the earth." Notice two things from this text. First, God is the maker of ethnic groups. "God *made* from one man every nation." Ethnic groups do not come about by meaningless, random genetic change. They come about by God's design and purpose. The text says plainly, "*God* made every *ethnos*."

Also, God made all the ethnic groups from one human ancestor. Paul says, "He made *from one* man every *ethnos*." This has a special wallop when you ponder why he chose to say just this to these Athenians on the Areopagus. The Athenians were fond of boasting that they were *autochthones*, which means that they sprang from their native soil and were not immigrants from some other place or people group.[2]

Paul chooses to confront this ethnic pride head-on. God made all the ethnic groups—Athenians *and* barbarians—and he made them out of one common stock. So you Athenians are cut from the same cloth as those despised barbarians.

When you put this teaching of Acts 17:26 together with Genesis 1:27 ("God created man in his own image, in the image of God he created him; male and female he created them") what emerges is that all members of all ethnic groups are made in the image of God.

No matter what the skin color or facial features or hair texture or other genetic or cultural traits, every human being in every ethnic group has an immortal soul in the image of God: a mind with unique, God-like reasoning powers, a heart with capacities for moral judgments and spiritual affections, and a potential for relationship with God that transforms us into the image of his Son, Jesus Christ. This "image of God" sets every person utterly apart from all the animals, which God has made. Every human being—whatever color, shape, age, gender, intelligence, health, or social class—is made in the image of God.

This is true of all human beings in every ethnic group. And all those groups are by God's design. So we are put on alert to beware of our prejudices. If we find in our hearts a distaste for the ethnic diversity of the world with all its many physical, linguistic, and cultural dimensions, we should fly to God for his justifying and transforming grace.

He Will Redeem from Every Ethnic Group

Second, that God is the God of all the nations means that he will redeem a people for himself out of every nation. The election of Israel, from the very first moment, was aiming ultimately at the inclusion of all the peoples in the blessing of Abraham: "In you all the families of the earth shall be blessed" (Gen. 12:3; cf. 18:18; 22:18; 26:4; 28:14; Jer. 4:2; Acts 3:25; Gal. 3:8, 16).

So when the Messiah came, his death was designed to ransom people from all the different ethnic peoples of the world. We saw this when we unpacked the meaning of Revelation 5:9: "You were slain, and by your blood you ransomed people for God from every tribe and language and people and nation." God means to have a redeemed people from every ethnic group. Therefore, none is to be despised, but welcomed in Christ Jesus.

One Way of Justification in Every Group

Third, that God is the God of the nations means he is ready to justify anyone, anywhere, from any ethnic group through faith in Jesus Christ alone. There is one way of justification for all the nations. God is the God of the nations because he has made a way for them all—the same way—and it is a way to be counted righteous by grace alone, through faith alone, on the basis of Christ alone to the glory of God alone.

God Will Be Known in Every Group

Fourth, that God is the God of the nations means that God aims to be known by all the nations. Psalm 96:1–4:

> Oh sing to the LORD a new song;
>   sing to the LORD, *all the earth!*
> Sing to the LORD, bless his name;
>   tell of his salvation from day to day.
> Declare his glory *among the nations,*
>   his marvelous works among *all the peoples!*
> For great is the LORD, and greatly to be praised;
>   he is to be feared above all gods.

ETHNIC DIVERSITY HAS THE DEEPEST ROOTS IMAGINABLE

We should pause and let all this sink in. God's concern to include all the ethnic peoples of the world in his saving purposes—in his final, eternal family—is unbreakably linked with the two greatest realities in the universe: God's very being as one God and the way God has ordained to put sinners in the right with himself through justification in Christ. Ethnic diversity is not connected to God marginally. It's connected at the center—his infinite being and his single, glorious way of justifying sinners.

As this sinks into our minds and hearts, the effect it should have is to change the way we think and feel about the racial and ethnic diversity of the world and the church. We are constantly in danger of feeling (even when we are not thinking this way) that God is partial to our tribe—that he has a special liking for our ethnicity and cultural norms.

This danger is especially present and unseen among majority cultures and majority ethnic groups. When we are in a very large majority, we do not even operate with the category of our own ethnicity. We are just *human*, so we are prone to think. *Others* have ethnicity. This makes us very vulnerable to the assumption that God is our God in a way that minimizes his being the God of other ethnic groups.

May the astonishing way that Paul speaks in Romans 3:29–30 of justification by faith alone awaken us from this deadly assumption. And may it fill us with a sense of amazement at God's passion in the pursuit of all the ethnic groups of the world. May we never forget that this pursuit is rooted in God's being one infinite God and in his justifying sinners in one glorious way through faith alone in the blood and righteousness of his Son, Jesus Christ.

In the next three chapters (section 2) we turn from what the gospel *accomplished* for us in history through the death and resurrection of Christ to the *application* of the gospel in our lives.[3] We will take up the meaning of *conversion* and then complete our treatment of the "five points of Calvinism," which we left behind in chapter 8, namely, the truths of *irresistible grace* and the *perseverance of the saints*. Without these sovereign "applications" of the gospel, the glorious "accomplishment" of it through the cross would not come to pass. The total fabric of God's salvation cannot be torn apart. It is all woven together.

SECTION TWO

THE APPLICATION OF THE GOSPEL

If then you have been raised with Christ, seek the things that are above, where Christ is, seated at the right hand of God. Set your minds on things that are above, not on things that are on earth. For you have died, and your life is hidden with Christ in God. When Christ who is your life appears, then you also will appear with him in glory. Put to death therefore what is earthly in you: sexual immorality, impurity, passion, evil desire, and covetousness, which is idolatry. On account of these the wrath of God is coming. In these you too once walked, when you were living in them. But now you must put them all away: anger, wrath, malice, slander, and obscene talk from your mouth. Do not lie to one another, seeing that you have put off the old self with its practices and have put on the new self, which is being renewed in knowledge after the image of its creator. Here there is not Greek and Jew, circumcised and uncircumcised, barbarian, Scythian, slave, free; but Christ is all, and in all. Put on then, as God's chosen ones, holy and beloved, compassionate hearts, kindness, humility, meekness, and patience.

COLOSSIANS 3:1–12

CHAPTER ELEVEN

DYING WITH CHRIST FOR THE SAKE OF CHRIST-EXALTING DIVERSITY

So far in part 2 of this book, we have seen that one crucial aim of Jesus in coming to earth was to put to death the pride of ethnocentrism (chapter 7). Then we saw in chapter 8 that the way he did this was by a historical act of (vertical and horizontal) reconciliation "by the blood of Christ" (Eph. 2:13). Then I put my theological cards on the table and began to celebrate how the Reformed faith undermines racism and ethnocentrism. The first focus of that Reformed faith was on depravity, atonement, and election (chapter 8). The next focus was on justification (chapter 9). At every point, we are drawing out the implications for our lives in reconciled racial and ethnic diversity.

Now, in this chapter and the next, we move toward the reality of conversion and living the Christian life. And we complete our focus on the "five points of Calvinism" by taking up the last two: irresistible grace and the perseverance of the saints. In spite of our depravity in God's eyes, he chose a people for himself and predestined us in love for adoption before the foundation of the world (Eph. 1:5). He sent his Son Jesus Christ into the world to purchase that bride for his Son from every tribe and people and language and nation (Rev. 5:9). By his grace, God provided a way of justification for the ungodly from all nations (Rom. 3:29–30). Now the question is: *How do people who are depraved and unbelieving and rebellious and alienated from God and each other take part in that great justification and reconciliation?* That question leads us to the sovereignty of grace and the keeping power of God.

Of course, the answer at one level is "by faith alone." We have already seen that in chapter 10. But now we are asking about the experience itself. Someone is unbelieving and guilty and alienated. Then they are believing and justified and reconciled. What happened? What do we mean by *conversion*?

RACISM AND THE REDUCTION OF CONVERSION

I think that one of the reasons some Christians have a hard time relating their Christianity to issues like racial and ethnic harmony and justice is that their view of what happens in conversion to Christ is superficial.[1] Let me illustrate with the way the apostle Paul handled a misuse of his gospel message.

Somewhere along the way, Paul's gospel of justification by grace alone through faith alone was distorted like this: "Well, if we are saved by grace alone through faith alone, then let's just sin all the more that grace may abound. The more sins we commit, the more grace God shows in forgiving—and the more glory he gets for his wonderful grace." We see that distortion in Romans 6:1: "What shall we say then? Are we to continue in sin that grace may abound?"

Given the way some professing Christians think and feel and act today toward people of other races, it seems that this distortion is alive and well. Salvation is by grace through faith, so there is no necessity for a change in how we feel or think or act toward people on the basis of race or ethnicity. God forgives and gets more glory for being more gracious. They don't say this out loud. But their actions show that they live by this superficial view of conversion. I became a Christian by some earlier choice to believe certain things, and there is no reason to think my attitude toward races has to change because of it. I'm saved by faith, not works. So they say.

DEAD PEOPLE ARE NOT DOMINATED BY SIN

So how does Paul answer this distortion of his gospel of justification by grace alone through faith alone? The answer is devastating to a superficial view of Christian conversion that reduces it merely to a "decision for Christ." Here is what he says: "What shall we say then? Are we to continue in sin that grace may abound? By no means! How can we who died to sin still live in it?" (Rom. 6:1–2). The point is that when we put our faith in Jesus, we are united with him so that his death becomes our death and his perfect life becomes our perfect life. His death and righteousness are counted as being ours before God.

Paul says that in baptism, which happens "through faith" (Col. 2:12), "we have been united with [Jesus] in a death like his" (Rom. 6:5). This union with Christ is how we experience death. "You have died, and your life is hidden with Christ in God" (Col. 3:3). "I have been crucified with Christ. It is no longer I who live, but Christ who lives in me" (Gal. 2:20).

So two kinds of things happen when we trust in Christ and are united to him by the work of the Spirit. One is that we are counted as having died with Christ so that we received the punishment of our sin in his punishment. God condemned *our* sin in *his* flesh (Rom. 8:3). The other kind of thing that happens is that our old unbelieving, sin-loving, Christ-neglecting self really dies. That is, we are not just forgiven for our sins, but we are given a new identity.

This is how Paul responds to the question: *Shall we sin that grace may abound?* No. The self that loves sin has died. The new self is not yet perfect. It sins. But it does not make peace with sin. It hates sin. It confesses sin and makes war on sin. That is the background of Paul's question, *How shall we who died to sin still live in it?*

"How shall we who died to racism still live in it?" "How shall we who died to the pride of ethnocentrism still live in it?" "How shall we who died to unkindness and cruelty and meanness and injustice and ugliness and hardheartedness and bitterness and hostility and anger still live in it?"

Paul is saying: If we condone ongoing sin on the basis of abounding grace—if we minimize the seriousness of sin in our lives—we don't know what conversion to Christ means. It means death. Death to sin. "Shall we continue in sin—in hating or mistreating or demeaning other races—because grace abounds? God forbid! How can we who died to sin still live in it?"

RACISM AND DEATH WITH CHRIST

Now I ask, is there biblical warrant for dealing with racism on these terms? Is this the way to think about racism? The answer is yes. We see it in Colossians 3. Let's put Paul's reference to race and ethnicity into the flow of the passage. First, consider Colossians 3:2–3: "Set your minds on things that are above, not on things that are on earth. For you have died, and your life is hidden with Christ in God." There is Paul's bold statement of what it means to be a Christian.

You have died. No exceptions. If you haven't died, you are not a Christian. To be converted to Christ is to be united by the Spirit of God to Christ in such a way that we die with him (Rom. 6:5). In this sense, the convictions and impulses and drives and values and affections and passions that governed our lives as unbelievers and gave us identity are dealt a mortal blow (a deathblow) by the Spirit of God as we turn to Christ.

Paul said the same thing in Galatians 6:14: "Far be it from me to boast except in the cross of our Lord Jesus Christ, by which the world has been crucified to me, and I to the world." What the world meant to Paul, before he met Christ, died on that day. And the old Paul that loved the world more than Christ died on that day. A new Paul—believing Christ, trusting Christ, loving Christ, treasuring Christ, honoring Christ—was born (created) on that day. That is what it means to become a Christian.

DEAD PEOPLE PUT SIN TO DEATH

What it means to *be* (not just *become*) a Christian is to go on affirming by our behavior that a death has happened and a new life has been created. The death and new creation are decisive and once for all. But the living out of this reality is a daily work of faith.

Consider Colossians 3:5: "Put to death therefore what is earthly in you." Similarly in Romans 6:11, Paul says, "You also must consider yourselves dead to sin and alive to God in Christ Jesus." In other words, your old unbelieving, sin-loving self really did die with Christ. Now live in the reality that God has worked in you. *Consider* your old self dead. Treat it as dead. You have died. Believe this, and live out the implications of this death.

THE LIAR DIED

Before looking at the way Paul connects this with race, consider what he says about lying. In Colossians 3:9–10 he says, "Do not lie to one another, seeing that you have put off the old self with its practices and have put on the new self, which is being renewed in knowledge after the image of its creator." The imagery changes here, but only superficially. The same reality is in view. A death has happened. The old self that needed to lie, and depended on lying, died. A new creation that loves truth has come into being. Except here Paul speaks of it in this way: we have decisively, once for all, "put off the old self" (Col. 3:9). The old self died, and you laid it aside like a garment—really, like a corpse.

But the positive side is given in verse 10: you "have put on the new self." That is a decisive thing that has happened in conversion. And where did it come from? Who made this new self that came into being when the old self died? The answer is given at the end of verse 10. God did. "You . . . have put on the new self, which is being renewed in knowledge *after the image of its creator*" (Col. 3:9–10). God created the new self that comes into being at conversion. In conversion, our old self died and was laid aside with its impulses and drives and values and loves and convictions. And a new self was created by God. This is called in other places *the new birth* or *being born again* (John 3:3; 1 Pet. 1:3).[2]

Lest we be discouraged by a perfectionistic view of conversion, notice that even though this death and new creation are decisive, past acts of God in the life of every believer, they do not mean that we live perfect lives in this world. This is why we are told to put the old self to death (Col. 3:5) and to put on the new self (Col. 3:12). This is also why, in verse 10, Paul says that the new self "*is being renewed* in knowledge after the image of its creator."

In other words, we are becoming in behavior what we have become in the eyes of God in Christ. We are working out our decisively assured salvation by God's enabling grace (Phil. 2:12–13). Or, as Paul says in 1 Corinthians 5:7, "Cleanse out the old leaven that you may be a new lump, as *you really are unleavened*." The evidence of *being* "unleavened" is that we hate the old leaven of sin and "cleanse it out" again and again.

THE ETHNIC AND CULTURAL CANYON DID NOT STOP LOVE AND FELLOWSHIP

Now just at this point, the issues of class and culture and race are raised by the apostle in Colossians 3:11. He says that, in these converted hearts and in this community of Christian believers, "there is not Greek and

Jew, circumcised and uncircumcised, barbarian, Scythian, slave, free; but Christ is all, and in all."

This was an absolutely staggering statement in his day. Greek and Jew, as we have seen, were divided by ethnicity, religion, and culture. The canyon between them was immense. But Paul says: where people have died with Christ and been created as new selves in the image of God, this canyon will not stop love and fellowship.

The reference to *barbarians* and *Scythians* is a reference to the way the cultured Romans and Greeks viewed anyone whose speech or manners or habits were foreign and seemingly uncouth and unrefined. If you have died with Christ and been created as a new self in the image of God, these kinds of differences will not stop love and fellowship. The reference to *slave* and *free* is a reference to the deepest divisions of class.

This text gives some of the seeds of the end of slavery. Paul didn't attack the institution directly. He undermined it among Christians—those who have died and risen with Christ. *Brother* and *sister* are the terms that replace *slave* and *free*. This was the way Paul spoke to Philemon about his slave Onesimus: "That you might have him back forever, no longer as a slave but more than a slave, as a beloved *brother*" (Philem. 15–16).

THE END OF RACISM WHEN "CHRIST IS ALL, AND IN ALL"

But the crucial, final word for us in Colossians 3 is at the end of the verse 11. In the heart of the one who has died with Christ and is being renewed as a new creature in Christ, "there is not Greek and Jew, circumcised and uncircumcised, barbarian, Scythian, slave, free; but *Christ is all, and in all.*"

Here is the living effect of dying to sin when you turn to Christ. Here too is the great power to destroy racism in the church. "Christ is all and in all." It has two parts.

First, let's focus on the second half of the phrase. "Christ is *in* all." When you die to sin, Christ moves *in*. "I have been crucified with Christ. It is no longer I who live, but Christ who lives *in* me" (Gal. 2:20). When you are crucified with Christ in union with Christ, you die and Christ lives in you. The new self we spoke of above is the self that welcomes Christ with joy as the Savior, Lord, and Treasure of our lives.

Every true Christian, of every class and culture and race, is indwelt by the living Son of God who loved us and gave himself for us. "Anyone who does not have the Spirit of Christ does not belong to him" (Rom. 8:9). It is impossible to really believe and revel in that truth and yet mistreat a believer of a different race—at least, we can't do it without some redemptive witness in our conscience that we must repent.

Second, let's focus on the first half of the phrase, "Christ is all." Here is the death knell to racism. Why do we despise? Or hate? Or shun? Or avoid? Or disparage? Or distort? Is it not because we are weak and fearful and insecure and proud and angry and without deep peace and love in our souls? Do those ugly things come from people who say (and mean), "Christ is everything to me"—people whose treasure is an all-satisfying fellowship with Christ?

BECAUSE JESUS IS ALL THE WORLD TO ME

Therefore, what we need is to reckon ourselves dead to all but Christ as the satisfaction of our souls. We need to love him so much and find in his fellowship such completeness that we speak like the psalmists: "I say to the LORD, 'You are my Lord; I have no good apart from you'" (Ps. 16:2). And: "Whom have I in heaven but you? And there is nothing on earth that I desire besides you. My flesh and my heart may fail, but God is the strength of my heart and my portion forever" (Ps. 73:25–26). Or like the old hymn writer: "Jesus is all the world to me, my life, my joy, my all."

Oh, that our churches would be full of people who sing that, and mean that, and live that! Jesus is all the world to me—my life, my joy, my all. Christ is in all. And Christ is all! In that fellowship, Paul says, "there is not Greek and Jew, circumcised and uncircumcised, barbarian, Scythian, slave, free." Lord, grant that, through our faith in Christ and through our profound union with him, we might so die and so live that Christ will be all and in all. That would be the end of ethnocentrism and racism in our churches.

IRRESISTIBLE GRACE

Jesus came on a mission to create a new people for whom he is the supreme treasure, and among whom racism and ethnocentrism are unthinkable. How is it possible that such a deep and dramatic change could happen to humans like us, who are enslaved to disabling depravity? I raise this question here to draw out another magnificent mark of the Reformed faith and how it so effectively undermines racism and ethnocentrism.

We have seen this in regard to our humanity-wide depravity (point one of Calvinism), and in regard to Christ's atonement of a people from every race and tribe (point three of Calvinism), and in regard to God's gracious, unconditional election of a people out of this depravity and through this atonement (point two of Calvinism). And we have seen that the way we participate in that salvation is through justification by faith alone. This faith comes into being through conversion—that is, through being united with Jesus by faith so that we die with him and rise with him to a new life of faith and love.

Now I raise the question of how such faith in Christ is possible for depraved rebels like us. The answer of the Reformed faith is that God overcomes our depravity and our rebellion and grants us the gift of faith and repentance. This is often called *irresistible grace*. We believe that when Christ died to obtain his church (Eph. 5:25), he obtained for her not only the grace that results from faith (like forgiveness and justification and sanctification and eternal life), but also the grace that produced the faith in the first place.

This grace is called "irresistible" not because we can't resist it, but because God overcomes this resistance at the point of our conversion. He overcomes our unbelief and grants that we see Christ for the irresistibly glorious Savior that he is. He makes Christ look compelling—as he really is—so that we follow him. In the moment of our coming to Christ we are decisively drawn by God and more free than we have ever been (John 6:44; 8:32).

God may allow resistance for a long time (Acts 7:51). For example, even though Paul said that God set him apart before he was born (Gal. 1:15), nevertheless, between Paul's birth and conversion he was in total rebellion against God. He was "breathing threats and murder against the disciples of the Lord" (Acts 9:1). All this God tolerated in Paul before the appointed time came for God to take Paul captive on the Damascus Road (Acts 9:1–20).

Irresistible grace means that since no human being can submit to

God because of our hardness of heart and rebellion and spiritual deadness (Rom. 8:7; 1 Cor. 2:14), the only way any of us is saved is by sovereign, irresistible grace. Jesus said, "No one can come to me unless the Father . . . draws him" (John 6:44). "No one can come to me unless it is granted him by the Father" (v. 65). We are saved by grace through faith, Paul said, and that is not of ourselves; it is the gift of God (Eph. 2:8–9; cf. Phil. 1:29). Our faith is a gift from God. And so is repentance, as Paul says in 2 Timothy 2:25: "God may perhaps grant them repentance."

This means that not only did our ethnic distinctives contribute nothing to our election, and nothing to our ransom by the cross, but our ethnic distinctives also contributed nothing to the rise of our faith and the emergence of our repentance. We are all equally dependent on irresistible grace to be called and to believe and to be saved.

Not only that, but irresistible grace also means that there is no scoundrel—no racist, no white or black or brown or red or yellow arrogance—that God cannot overcome and subdue and bring to humble repentance and faith and everlasting holiness and joy. We were not only comrades in condemnation, but now, more gloriously, we are comrades in utter dependence on irresistible grace.

Which means that we are comrades in hope that none of us is too far gone in our racial sins to be saved. And when we are saved, none of us can make the claim that we had the slightest hand in raising ourselves from the dead. Every ethnic group is equally incompetent to raise itself from the dead. And every group stands on the same ground of humble gratitude that only grace opened our eyes and caused us to see the Savior and come.

In the next chapter we turn from our focus on the application of the gospel in conversion to its application in the way we live *after* conversion. The gospel goes on undoing racism and ethnocentrism in the lives of those who have been converted to Christ. Finally, in this next chapter, we will take up the fifth point of Calvinism, the perseverance of the saints, and see how relevant it is to our pressing on in the battle for ethnic diversity and harmony in Christ.

When Cephas came to Antioch, I opposed him to his face, because he stood condemned. For before certain men came from James, he was eating with the Gentiles; but when they came he drew back and separated himself, fearing the circumcision party. And the rest of the Jews acted hypocritically along with him, so that even Barnabas was led astray by their hypocrisy. But when I saw that their conduct was not in step with the truth of the gospel, I said to Cephas before them all, "If you, though a Jew, live like a Gentile and not like a Jew, how can you force the Gentiles to live like Jews?" We ourselves are Jews by birth and not Gentile sinners; yet we know that a person is not justified by works of the law but through faith in Jesus Christ, so we also have believed in Christ Jesus, in order to be justified by faith in Christ and not by works of the law, because by works of the law no one will be justified.

GALATIANS 2:11–16

CHAPTER TWELVE

LIVING IN SYNC WITH GOSPEL FREEDOM

It is a good and beautiful thing when Christians of different ethnic origins (not just black and white) live and work and worship and relax and eat together in joyful, Christ-exalting peace. There may be situations where living with all one ethnic group is inevitable. If so, I don't condemn it. But there are solid biblical, historical, and cultural reasons why ethnically diverse Christians living, working, worshiping, relaxing, and eating together is a Christ-exalting and beautiful thing—and therefore worth pursuing.

What we are doing in part 2 of this book is pointing to the biblical foundations for the claim of part 1 that the gospel of Christ is the only hope for Christ-exalting racial and ethnic diversity and harmony. We saw in chapter 7 how Christ came on a mission to form a new people not defined by ethnic distinctives but by faith in him. Then we saw in chapter 8 that the crucial way he accomplished this was "by the blood of Christ" (Eph. 2:13).

In chapter 9 we probed into the nature of the atonement that the blood of Christ worked for us and saw the connection between that atonement and our depravity and God's election. In chapter 10 we looked at the ethnic implications of justification by faith in order to see how the atonement actually works for us. And in chapter 11 we focused on how we, as helpless sinners, are made part of this great reconciling work of Christ, namely, through the irresistible grace of God leading to our death and resurrection with Christ called "conversion."

Now what we will see in this chapter and the next is the way the gospel governs not only the way we are converted but also the way we live after conversion. Just as the gospel shattered ethnocentrism and racism in the way it saved us and in the standing it gave us, so it keeps on shattering them by the kind of life it brings about. One of the clearest texts to show how the gospel goes on exerting this effect is Galatians 2:11–16:

> But when Cephas came to Antioch, I opposed him to his face, because he stood condemned. For before certain men came from James, he was eating with the Gentiles; but when they came he drew back and separated himself, fearing the circumcision party. And the rest of the Jews acted hypocritically along with him, so that even Barnabas was led astray by their hypocrisy. But when I saw that their conduct was not in step with the truth of the gospel, I said to Cephas before them all, "If you, though a Jew, live like a Gentile and not like a Jew, how can you force the Gentiles to live like Jews?" We ourselves are Jews by birth and not Gentile sinners; yet we know that a person is not justified by works of the law but through faith in Jesus Christ, so we also have believed in Christ Jesus, in order to be justified by faith in Christ and not by works of the law, because by works of the law no one will be justified.

NOT IN STEP WITH THE TRUTH OF THE GOSPEL

The key statement in this passage is in verse 14: "But when I saw that their conduct was not in step with the truth of the gospel, I said to Cephas before them all, 'If you, though a Jew, live like a Gentile and not like a Jew, how can you force the Gentiles to live like Jews?'" The statement is: "Their conduct is not in step with the truth of the gospel." What this implies is that there is conduct—behavior, action, things you do—that may be out of step with the truth of the gospel. Or to put it another way: the gospel governs not just our beliefs but also our actions. There is gospel belief, and there is gospel behavior. Some beliefs contradict the gospel, and some actions contradict the gospel. Peter's action here was contradicting the gospel.

This is the most important question we can ask about any habit or action or behavior: Does it contradict the gospel? Is it in step with the truth of the gospel? Does our action say true things about the gospel? Does it reflect the gospel? Is it the kind of action that would flow from the gospel?

AT THE HEART OF THE GOSPEL

Now Paul leaves little doubt in the book of Galatians what is at the heart of the gospel. We don't have to go any farther than Galatians 2:16 to see it: "We know that a person is not justified by works of the law but through faith in Jesus Christ, so we also have believed in Christ Jesus, in order to be justified by faith in Christ and not by works of the law, because by works of the law no one will be justified."

At the heart of the gospel is justification by faith alone apart from works of the law. We focused on justification by faith in chapter 10. But we did not exhaust its riches or its implications for racial and ethnic diversity and harmony. There is more. Justification is what a judge does in a courtroom. It is a declaration that a defendant is found innocent. And the declaration is made because the judge (or jury) presumes there is real innocence—real righteousness. So for an infallible judge, there are no mistakes. No innocent people are punished. And no guilty go free. In the courtroom of an infallible judge, the only time there is justification is when there is real innocence—real righteousness. The defendant is *declared* to be just, because he is found to *be* just.

FAITH ALONE, NOT WORKS OF LAW

Of course, that is a huge problem for us, because none of us is righteous—no, not one (Rom. 3:10). We have all sinned. We are guilty as charged. We deserve God's full sentence of condemnation. Works of the law cannot save us. We have broken God's law. Now the law condemns us. So how can we be justified? How can God, the judge, declare us righteous and innocent?

The answer is that Jesus Christ lived and died to provide our righteousness and bear our punishment. That's the point the following texts show. The first group shows that Christ provided our righteousness, and the second shows that he bore our punishment.

> "For as by the one man's disobedience the many were made sinners, so by the one man's obedience the many will be made righteous" (Rom. 5:19). "For our sake he made him to be sin who knew no sin, so that in him we might become the righteousness of God" (2 Cor. 5:21). "You are in Christ Jesus, who became to us . . . righteousness . . . " (1 Cor. 1:30). "[I am] found in him, not having

a righteousness of my own that comes from the law, but that which comes through faith in Christ, the righteousness from God that depends on faith" (Phil. 3:9).

"Christ died for our sins in accordance with the Scriptures" (1 Cor. 15:3). "Christ redeemed us from the curse of the law by becoming a curse for us—for it is written, 'Cursed is everyone who is hanged on a tree'" (Gal. 3:13). "By sending his own Son in the likeness of sinful flesh and for sin, [God] condemned sin in the flesh" (Rom. 8:3). "Everyone who believes in him receives forgiveness of sins through his name" (Acts 10:43).

It is by trusting Christ that his righteousness is imputed to us and his death is counted as ours. Faith alone, not works, unites us to Christ. "By grace you have been saved *through faith*. And this is not your own doing; it is the gift of God, *not a result of works*, so that no one may boast" (Eph. 2:8–9). "Since we have been justified *by faith*, we have peace with God through our Lord Jesus Christ" (Rom. 5:1).

No works of any kind connect us with Christ and his righteousness and atonement. Good works are the result, not the cause, of God's being 100 percent for us. If he were not for us because of faith alone, owing to Christ alone, we would be hopelessly unable to do good works, because our works would not magnify his grace but our resolve. Instead, we look away from ourselves. We despair of measuring up. We cast ourselves utterly on him—his righteousness, his blood. And for his sake alone, God counts us righteous and accepts us and welcomes us into his fellowship for our joy forever.[1]

A CENTRAL CADENCE OF THE GOSPEL WALK

That is the heart of the gospel—the good news. And, oh, how many new, sweet, tender, deep, strong, beautiful, noble, humble, kind, wise, patient, caring, serving attitudes and behaviors flow from this gospel. Read the second half of most of Paul's letters to see how he describes life when it is lived "in step with the truth of the gospel." That is what we are focusing on in this chapter. The gospel governs Christian conversion, and it governs Christian living. There is a way to live that is "in step with the truth of the gospel."

One of the central cadences of the gospel walk is the breaking down of ethnic hostilities and suspicions, and the impulse of unity and harmony. We saw this in our discussion of Romans 3:29–30 in chapter 10. "Is he not the God of Gentiles also? Yes, of Gentiles also, since God is one—who will justify the circumcised by faith and the uncircumcised through faith."

In other words, since there is only one way for all people in the world to get right with God and to be God's children—namely, by faith in Jesus Christ—therefore, no ethnic distinctives can any longer be compelling separators of those who trust Christ. Justification by faith alone puts all of us on a level ground of utter dependence on grace.

PETER WAS RUNNING WELL

Now consider how Peter failed in this and how Paul rebuked him.

> But when Cephas came to Antioch, I opposed him to his face, because he stood condemned. For before certain men came from James, he was eating with the Gentiles; but when they came he drew back and separated himself, fearing the circumcision party. And the rest of the Jews acted hypocritically along with him, so that even Barnabas was led astray by their hypocrisy. (Gal. 2:11–13)

Paul says in the next verse (14) that this behavior is "not in step with the truth of the gospel." Peter had been experiencing the freedom of the gospel as a Jew and was crossing the ethnic and religious barriers to eat with Gentiles. He was *eating* with them—simply hanging out doing the most ordinary thing, eating together. In spite of all the food laws that might be jeopardized, it was still a good thing, because Jesus "declared all foods clean" (Mark 7:19). That was a good thing.

That is what we want to happen across ethnic lines in our churches and neighborhoods and schools. It's not staged. It's not artificial or programmed. These are simple, free, natural relationships. They were eating together. There should be huge amounts of eating together in Christian relationships.[2] And in the process, we should enjoy gospel freedom in forgetting all ethnic limitations. There can be and should be a natural, joyful, spontaneous mixing of ethnic groups in our table fellowship.

PETER'S SERIOUS MISSTEP

What happened to Peter? It says in verse 12 that certain men came from James. They reported to Peter that there were Jerusalem conservatives who believed that Gentiles—because of their uncircumcision and their non-kosher dietary habits and failure to keep the holy days—were off-limits, even as Christians. Religious and ethnic issues were inseparable.

But for Paul, justification by faith alone had overcome all that. "In Christ Jesus you are all sons of God, through faith. . . . There is neither Jew nor Greek, there is neither slave nor free, there is no male and female, for you are all one in Christ Jesus" (Gal. 3:26, 28). But at the end of Galatians 2:12, we see that Peter was governed by fear, not by the gospel.

It is remarkable that in both Philippians and Galatians, life that accords with the gospel is described as fearlessness and unity. Philippians 1:27–28 says, "Let your manner of life be worthy of the gospel of Christ . . . standing firm in *one* spirit, with *one* mind striving *side by side* for the faith of the gospel, and *not frightened* in anything by your opponents." Unity and fearlessness. Galatians 2 confirms this fruit of the gospel by showing what happens when it is missing. Peter "feared," and Peter withdrew from unified fellowship with Gentiles. Fearful disunity is not the fruit of the gospel.

What was Peter afraid of? He wasn't afraid of the Gentiles. He was afraid of his own ethnic group, the Jews. Why?

WHY WAS HE AFRAID?

Here are some possibilities.

1) He was afraid of conflict. "The Jerusalem conservatives are going to cause a scene. It's going to be very awkward. Maybe we can just avoid a scene, and they will be satisfied that we don't hang out together and go home, and we can return to normal." Paul calls that fearful behavior *hypocrisy* and says it is not in step with the gospel. Beware of living a life governed by the fear of controversy. It may drive you to hypocritical behaviors.

2) Or maybe Peter was afraid that his convictions were not well-founded and that the Jerusalem conservatives might get the best of him in an argument based on the Mosaic law. His faith was weak, and his

gospel intuitions faltered. Beware of embracing justification by faith alone without knowing what you are doing. Your gospel behavior will be challenged someday. And only clear, firm faith in all that Christ has done for you will stand.

3) Or maybe Peter was afraid of being called a Paul groupie. He can hear the intimidating Jewish people from Jerusalem saying, "What a wimp! As soon as you leave your cozy hometown in Jerusalem, you just start copying the compromiser Paul. Everybody copies Paul. Paul, the big shot. Not even Peter can stand up to the great Paul." Are you afraid of doing something in the cause of racial harmony because of whom you will be associated with?

I'm not sure precisely what Peter was afraid of. Maybe a mixture of all three. But what's clear is that his fear ruined practical gospel faithfulness. He had been free. He was eating with brothers across ethnic lines. And fear (for a moment) destroyed the diversity and the harmony.

PETER'S WITHDRAWAL DISTORTED THE GOSPEL

But what is clear is that Paul's response to Peter's unwillingness to eat with those who were ethnically different took him straight to the gospel. There was no sentimental talk about how hurtful it is when you snub someone. That's true. It is hurtful. But Paul didn't go there. He had something much deeper and more serious to do. The remedy for Peter's fear and his hypocrisy was to see more clearly and love more dearly and follow more nearly *the gospel*.

So Paul publicly rebukes Peter. "When I saw that their conduct was not in step with the truth of the gospel, I said to Cephas *before them all* . . ." (Gal. 2:14). Basically what Paul says is, "Your behavior communicates that faith in Christ is not a sufficient means of being justified before God. Your abandonment of the Gentile brothers and your lining up with the works of the law is saying to those brothers: justification—real complete acceptance with God—comes about not through faith alone, but through faith plus works. So your behavior is contradicting the gospel." Here's the way Paul actually put it:

> "If you, though a Jew, live like a Gentile [that is, enjoy table fellowship with Gentiles] and not like a Jew, how can you force the Gentiles to live like Jews?" [This was the message Peter was in essence delivering

to the Gentiles.] We ourselves are Jews by birth and not Gentile sinners [meaning those who live outside the Jewish code]; yet we know that a person is not justified by works of the law but through faith in Jesus Christ, so we also have believed in Christ Jesus, in order to be justified by faith in Christ and not by works of the law, because by works of the law no one will be justified. (Gal. 2:14–16)

In other words, "Even we Jews who are Christians have come to Christ to be justified by faith alone. Even though we are not 'Gentile sinners,' we are sinners. We need a basis for our justification outside ourselves. None of our law keeping can suffice to justify us. That, Peter, is what you are not communicating to the Gentiles with your fearful, hypocritical withdrawal from them."

FALL IN LOVE AGAIN WITH THE GOSPEL

The implication of this for our day, among other things, is that any kind of racially or ethnically based exclusion will send the wrong message about the basis of our acceptance with God. It will subtly suggest that something about our race or our ethnicity or our works or our natural distinctives is the means of our justification. But if faith in Christ alone is that means, then Christ becomes the sole foundation of our justification, and everyone who trusts him is on the same footing of acceptance with God.

Far more important in the long run than any particular strategy of racial reconciliation and harmony is that more and more Christians glory in the grace of the gospel of justification by faith alone. When we are thrilled by the unspeakable freedom of being right with God in spite of the magnitude of our sinful corruption—and that others of every race and ethnicity enjoy the same freedom with us—there will be a humility and a love and a zeal to magnify grace that dissolves ethnic hostilities.

Don't let fear ruin your joyful freedom in living and working and worshiping and relaxing and eating with brothers and sisters who are ethnically or racially different from you. Or to put it positively, fall in love again with the gospel. Rejoice all over again that, even though your sin is great, you are justified by faith alone. And then wake up to the gospel truth that justification by faith alone means that this faith is the great, eternal unifier of all the peoples of the world who trust in Christ.

PERSEVERANCE OF THE SAINTS

But the question arises: *How can weak and sinful people like us be assured that we will keep on trusting Christ and walking in step with the gospel—even imperfectly?* In the previous chapter I raised a similar question: *How did depraved, rebellious sinners, like we were, become willing to put our faith in Christ in the first place?* The answer was irresistible grace. And the answer here is God's sovereign keeping power to preserve us in what is sometimes called "the perseverance of the saints."

In other words, I want to draw out the implications for racial harmony from another great truth of the Reformed faith, namely, the perseverance of the saints. And I want us to see how relevant it is to ethnic relations. So I am asking: *How can we be sure we will endure to the end, believing the gospel and walking in step with it?* I answer: God guarantees the perseverance of all his people.

Perseverance simply means that *those whom God calls, he keeps.* If you are a true believer, you will persevere in faith and (imperfect) obedience to the end and be saved. God will see to it. "Those whom he predestined he also called, and those whom he called he also justified, and those whom he justified he also glorified" (Rom. 8:30). Between justification and glorification, no one drops out. All persevere from justification to glorification.

Jesus said, "My sheep hear my voice, and I know them, and they follow me. I give them eternal life, and they will never perish, and no one will snatch them out of my hand" (John 10:27–29). Paul said, "I am sure of this, that he who began a good work in you will bring it to completion at the day of Jesus Christ" (Phil. 1:6; see 1 Cor. 1:8; 1 Thess. 5:23). If someone leaves the faith, it was because they never truly belonged to Christ. This is the way the apostle John described that situation in his day: "They went out from us, but they were not of us; for if they had been of us, they would have continued with us. But they went out, that it might become plain that they all are not of us" (1 John 2:19).

IT KEEPS US ON THE ROAD OF RACIAL HARMONY

What does perseverance of the saints mean for racial and ethnic harmony? I pick out one implication. If the kind of love that pursues racial harmony is woven into the very fabric of God's sovereign, sanctifying grace, and if therefore loving like that is part of what it means to be a Christian, then the promise of perseverance is a promise to keep us pursuing racial harmony till we die or till Jesus comes.

This is utterly crucial. Of all the moral issues that challenge the church from decade to decade, this one we are tempted to abandon more often, because in this battle we get more quickly and deeply wounded along the way. If you have thin skin, or if you have a bigger sense of rights you are owed than mercies you need, or if you have small faith in God's preserving grace, you will set out on the road of racial harmony and then quit. Because you are going to be criticized. You will try to say something or do something that you thought was helpful, and the first thing you hear is: you said it wrong, or you should have said it a long time ago, or you should have also said such and such, or it was not the time to say anything.

What will you do when that happens? I pray that you will persevere. Tom Skinner, one of the soul-doctors of "racial reconciliation" till his death in 1994, used another image for sticking it out in these moments of discouragement or anger. He said, "Racial reconciliation is whites and blacks holding on to each other, not letting go, and doing surgery on each other."[3] In their book *More Than Equals*, Chris Rice and Spencer Perkins pick up this note of perseverance from Skinner and add, "Reconciliation requires exposing our vital organs to the truth that we speak to each other. . . . When we build trust and *stay on the table to the end of the surgery*, there is hope for healing in the most delicate and vital places of our racial residue."[4]

Will we "stay on the table"? Stay on the road? That is what the doctrine of perseverance is for—to keep us faithful in the kind of obedience that is sustained by the foretastes of heaven and leads to the glory of heaven. Christ has purchased our perseverance. The Holy Spirit applies the purchase. None of us will persevere perfectly. But getting up when you are knocked down is a mark of Christ's followers. We know life is short and eternity is long. This eternal perspective does not take us out of the world. It gives us freedom from self-pity. We are about to inherit the earth (Matt. 5:5). We don't need to have it now, or the ease and comfort that go with it. We can work at this till we drop. For our labor is not in vain in the Lord.

I pray that you will ponder your own sin, your own undeserved and unconditional election, your triumphant ransom by the blood of Christ, your own miraculous and merciful awakening to faith, and the promise of God to complete the work that he has begun—and then press on in what you know is right and show that Christ is your comfort in life and death.

SOME HAVE STAYED ON THE ROAD A LONG TIME

Take heart and inspiration from people like John Perkins, who left Mississippi when he was seventeen after his brother was murdered, vowing never to return. But after he was converted to Christ in 1960, he went back and has been working for racial harmony for over forty years. He wrote in the foreword to Dwight Perry's book *Building Unity in the Church of the New Millennium*[5] that he had seen in this book what he wanted to see and said, "I can almost say as Simeon said when he saw the child Jesus, 'Now may this old man depart in peace.'"[6]

But until he or we depart in peace, there is much to be done. And the thrust of this chapter on living in sync with the freedom of the gospel leads us to an even fuller exposition of gospel life. Gospel freedom is called "the law of liberty" in James 1:25 and 2:12. We will do well to stop over there and hear how James relates such living to the issue of partiality.

If anyone thinks he is religious and does not bridle his tongue but deceives his heart, this person's religion is worthless. Religion that is pure and undefiled before God, the Father, is this: to visit orphans and widows in their affliction, and to keep oneself unstained from the world. My brothers, show no partiality as you hold the faith in our Lord Jesus Christ, the Lord of glory. For if a man wearing a gold ring and fine clothing comes into your assembly, and a poor man in shabby clothing also comes in, and if you pay attention to the one who wears the fine clothing and say, "You sit here in a good place," while you say to the poor man, "You stand over there," or, "Sit down at my feet," have you not then made distinctions among yourselves and become judges with evil thoughts? Listen, my beloved brothers, has not God chosen those who are poor in the world to be rich in faith and heirs of the kingdom, which he has promised to those who love him? But you have dishonored the poor man. Are not the rich the ones who oppress you, and the ones who drag you into court? Are they not the ones who blaspheme the honorable name by which you were called? If you really fulfill the royal law according to the Scripture, "You shall love your neighbor as yourself," you are doing well. But if you show partiality, you are committing sin and are convicted by the law as transgressors. For whoever keeps the whole law but fails in one point has become accountable for all of it. For he who said, "Do not commit adultery," also said, "Do not murder." If you do not commit adultery but do murder, you have become a transgressor of the law. So speak and so act as those who are to be judged under the law of liberty. For judgment is without mercy to one who has shown no mercy. Mercy triumphs over judgment.

JAMES 1:26–2:13

CHAPTER THIRTEEN

THE LAW OF LIBERTY AND THE PERIL OF PARTIALITY

This chapter is an extension of the theme in the previous one. The point there was that the gospel of God's justifying grace governs not only how we are converted to Christ but also how we live afterward—especially in relation to ethnic diversity in Christ. It will be helpful, I believe, to focus on one more passage of Scripture in this regard. In James 1:26–2:13 the main point is: *Don't show partiality because of riches or rank, but live under the law of liberty; that is, love your neighbor as you love yourself.* The text is not explicitly about race or ethnicity. But I will try to make the case that partiality in regard to riches and rank has a common root with partiality in regard to race and ethnicity—whether rich or poor. And what is at stake again is living in sync with the gospel—which is brought under the "law of liberty."

SETTING THE STAGE

The last two verses of James 1 set the stage for the main point about partiality (and racial harmony)—first with a word about *worthless* religion, then with a word about *true* religion.

1) Worthless Religion (James 1:26)

First, verse 26 speaks of worthless religion: "If anyone thinks he is religious and does not bridle his tongue but deceives his heart, this person's religion is worthless." That's astonishing! If you don't bridle your tongue, your Christianity is a sham. Why? Because Jesus said, "Out of the abundance of the heart the mouth speaks" (Matt. 12:34). Your tongue tells the truth about your heart.

James tells us the kind of thing he has in mind. He says, in James 3:8–9, that the tongue "is a restless evil, full of deadly poison. With it we bless our Lord and Father, and with it we curse people who are made in the likeness of God." He has in mind how we speak about people made in the image of God. That's his central concern with the tongue—how we talk about people. That's what needs to be bridled. That's one of the reasons we can see the common root of partiality based on riches and partiality based on race. Both involve a demeaning attitude toward another human being—the poor or the ethnically different.

So here the stage is set for our thinking about racial and ethnic harmony: bridle your tongue when talking about white people, black people, Asian people, Hispanic people, Jewish people, Native American people, Muslim people. Behold the image of God in man, and bridle your tongue by the mercy of God. Make the mule of your tongue serve the mercy of your heart.

2) True Religion (James 1:27)

Again James sets the stage of racial harmony for us in verse 27 with a word about *true religion*. He is not talking directly about race or ethnicity here. But, if you stay with me, I think you will see the relevance. "Religion that is pure and undefiled before God, the Father, is this: to visit orphans and widows in their affliction, and to keep oneself unstained from the world." When the God-given, Christ-shaped mercy of your heart has put your tongue in the bridle of obedience, then it puts your legs on the path to the poor. In one way or another, every true Christian cares about the poor.

And, James adds at the end of verse 27, every true Christian cares about being pure and unstained from the world. True religion visits orphans and widows, *and* true religion "keep[s] oneself unstained from the world." Here is something to provoke the liberal and something to provoke the conservative. James gets in the face of left-leaning Democrats, and James gets in the face of right-leaning Republicans. To the one, he says: "Care about private morality—chastity, honesty, fidelity, modesty, purity." To the other, he says: "Care about social justice and works of compassion."

So the stage is set: true religion—true Christianity—is moved by a

Christ-shaped heart of mercy. It bridles the tongue when talking about people created in God's image. It cares for the poor—the ones who can easily be taken advantage of and don't have any power to care for themselves. And it keeps itself free from the impurities of pornography and gluttony and greed. The stage is set.

THE MAIN POINT

The main point of the text comes in three different verses and is said in three different ways, moving from the most specific to the most general. I'll give it to you in reverse order from the most general to the most specific.

> James 2:12: *Live as those who will be judged under the law of liberty.*
> James 2:8: *Love your neighbor as you love yourself.*
> James 2:1: *Don't show partiality to people because of riches or race.*

All the rest of the text is argument—reasons why we should not show partiality. But before the arguments, let me say a word of explanation about the meaning of *partiality* and about the *law of liberty*.

Partiality

First, partiality (James 2:1) means that you base your treatment of someone—or your attitude toward someone—on something that should *not* be the basis of how you treat him. So here in the text, for example, the basis of how people get treated is riches and poverty. You see it in verses 2–3:

> For if a man wearing a gold ring and fine clothing comes into your assembly, and a poor man in shabby clothing also comes in, and if you pay attention to the one who wears the fine clothing and say, "You sit here in a good place," while you say to the poor man, "You stand over there," or, "Sit down at my feet."

This is what James calls partiality. Riches and poverty should *not* be the basis of how people get treated. So treating them differently on that basis is "partiality."

I am applying this text to race as well as riches. One of the main reasons is the way this word *partiality* is used elsewhere in the New

Testament. I'll give you an example from Romans 2. Here Paul is dealing with an ethnic and racial (and religious) issue, namely, Greeks and Jews. And he says that both are liable to judgment because of their sin. Then he gives the reason in verse 11: "For God shows no *partiality*"—which is the same word as here in James 2:1.

So I think James and Paul would be very happy for us to take this text that focuses on partiality based on riches and say that it also applies to partiality based on race. Good treatment and bad treatment, honor and dishonor, rejection and acceptance should not be based on riches or race.

Law of Liberty

Here's another word of explanation about the main point, namely, the words in James 2:12: "So speak and so act as those who are to be judged under the law of liberty." When you don't show partiality but love others as you love yourself, you are acting according to the law of liberty. What is that?

James uses the term *law of liberty* twice (James 1:25 and 2:12) and the term *royal law* once (James 2:8) but does not define them explicitly. He treats these terms as though they were common knowledge for the early Christians. So I am going to take the definition partly from a verse in Galatians where the language is very similar. Galatians 5:13–14 says, "For you were called to freedom, brothers. Only do not use your freedom as an opportunity for the flesh, but through love serve one another. For the whole law is fulfilled in one word: 'You shall love your neighbor as yourself.'"

James speaks of "liberty," and Paul speaks of "freedom" (same Greek word). Christians are set free from their sins. That is, we are forgiven and freed from the condemnation and dominion of sin. Now we are to live in that freedom—forgiven, not condemned by God. Does that liberty produce lawlessness? Both Paul and James answer no. It produces love.

For James, the summary of the law of liberty is given in verse 8: "You shall love your neighbor as yourself." And for Paul the summary of the law of liberty is given first in Galatians 5:13 ("Through love serve one another") and then again in verse 14 ("You shall love your neighbor as yourself").

For both James and Paul, love is the natural fruit, and the necessary evidence, of being justified by faith (Gal. 5:6 and James 2:17). Love is the kind of law that governs us when we are freed from condemnation by the blood and righteousness of Christ. And we will be judged under this law of liberty. If we have not loved, we will perish, because there will be no evidence that we are born again and justified by faith.

THE CONTEXT OF ETERNAL JUDGMENT

So you can see that James and Paul elevate the issue of partiality in an extraordinary way. They put partiality, based on riches and race, in the context of our eternal judgment. This is not a light thing. How we treat others is the evidence of our relation to Christ. If we have been set free from sin's condemnation and dominion by Christ, then we live in liberty. And in this liberty there is a law, the law of liberty—that is, the law of love. It is not written on stone, but on our hearts. We will be judged under this law. And this law says, *Do not show partiality on the basis of race or riches.*

SEVEN REASONS WHY WE SHOULD NOT SHOW PARTIALITY

The rest of James 1:26–2:13 is argument. It is all rooted in the understanding of reality that makes the royal law—life in step with the gospel—understandable. I see seven reasons that James gives for why we should not show partiality. God is good to us not merely to tell us *what* to do, as if he were only an authority, but also to tell us *why*. He has reasons. He wants us not only to submit to his commands but to submit with some understanding. He wants us to see the beauty and the wisdom and the goodness of his commands. So he gives us reasons to do what he says.

1) *Partiality reveals a judging heart and behind it evil thinking.*

> For if a man wearing a gold ring and fine clothing comes into your assembly, and a poor man in shabby clothing also comes in, and if you pay attention to the one who wears the fine clothing and say, "You sit here in a good place," while you say to the poor man, "You stand over there," or, "Sit down at my feet," have you not then made distinctions among yourselves and become judges with evil thoughts? (James 2:2–4)

185

The last words in verse 4 are the nub of the argument: "Have you not . . . become judges with evil thoughts?" James obviously thinks they have. The essence of the sin here is pride, that is, a desire to be seen as superior.

They have acted as "judges." But they are, in fact, *not* in the exalted place behind the bench in the courtroom with these other people. They are in the dock with all the other sinners. Only God is behind the bench. They are taking to themselves a role that only one can have. "There is only one lawgiver and judge, he who is able to save and to destroy. But who are you to judge your neighbor?" (James 4:12).

That is one sign of pride. The other is the "evil thoughts" they were having as they told the poor to sit in a lowly place and the rich to sit in an exalted place. Why would they do this? Because if the poor are prominent, your church may not look as important and powerful and attractive to rich people. But if the rich are prominent then your church might look important and influential. James says those are "evil thoughts." And the essence of them is pride. And pride is the opposite of what the gospel produces and what sustains the royal law of love.

2) *Partiality to the rich contradicts God's heart, because he has chosen many of the poor for himself.* The belittling of the poor by seating them inconspicuously, or in an inferior place ("Sit down at my feet"), is not just about the sin of pride but about the belittling of God. James says in James 2:5, "Listen, my beloved brothers, has not God chosen those who are poor in the world to be rich in faith and heirs of the kingdom, which he has promised to those who love him?" If we are ashamed of the poor, we are ashamed of God, because God is not ashamed to choose the poor. God leans toward the poor, not away. Therefore, if we lean away, we lean against God.

3) *Partiality dishonors people created in the image of God.* When the church is ashamed of the poor and seats them in an out-of-the-way place, not only is God indicted for his choosing the poor, but the poor themselves are dishonored. James says in James 2:6, "But you have dishonored the poor man." Even though the poor and the rich are all sinners, there are two problems with dishonoring the poor. One is that since I am a sinner, I have no business acting as though I am worthy of exaltation and the poor man is not. Neither of us is.

And if God has shown me grace that I don't deserve, I should treat the poor that way.

The other problem with dishonoring the poor is that, even though the poor man is a sinner, he is also created in the likeness of God. We know this matters to James because he laments in James 3:9, "We curse people *who are made in the likeness of God.*" Whether we curse men or seat them in lowly places, we do wrong against them and against God. They are not to be despised as humans, and they are to be pursued as possible fellow heirs of mercy—which is what God has done in the gospel.

4) *Partiality to the rich backfires and becomes your downfall.* James points out an irony in the sin of treating the rich with favoritism: "Are not the rich the ones who oppress you, and the ones who drag you into court? Are they not the ones who blaspheme the honorable name by which you were called?" (James 2:6–7). James gives an example of this behavior of the rich. The point is not that all rich people act this way. But at least in the experience of James and the churches he was writing to, riches were seen as corrupting. It was mainly the rich who made life miserable for the righteous.

> Behold, the wages of the laborers who mowed your fields, which you kept back by fraud, are crying out against you, and the cries of the harvesters have reached the ears of the Lord of hosts. You have lived on the earth in luxury and in self-indulgence. You have fattened your hearts in a day of slaughter. You have condemned and murdered the righteous person. He does not resist you. (James 5:4–6)

So James is pointing out in James 2:6–7 that the church is not only "evil" in her thoughts when she shows favoritism to the rich but also self-defeating. Why favor those who bring you down? Such a partiality would make it look like money is more valuable to you than Christ.

5) *Partiality makes you a transgressor of the law of liberty.* James says that partiality is law breaking. And law breaking is serious, not mainly because of the law but because of the lawgiver. Whatever point of the law we break, what makes it serious is that God spoke it, and we are in rebellion against him. But the sum of the law—the royal center of the law—is the command to love your neighbor as yourself. That is the

law that covers the sin of partiality. So realize what you are doing when you show partiality: you are breaking the royal law, the sum of the law, the center of the law, and you are assaulting God, who is the lawgiver. Here is the way James says it:

> If you really fulfill the royal law according to the Scripture, "You shall love your neighbor as yourself," you are doing well. But if you show partiality, you are committing sin and are convicted by the law as transgressors. For whoever keeps the whole law but fails in one point has become accountable for all of it. For he who said, "Do not commit adultery," also said, "Do not murder." If you do not commit adultery but do murder, you have become a transgressor of the law. So speak and so act as those who are to be judged under the law of liberty. (James 2:8–12)

His conclusion is "speak and act" with the expectation of divine judgment. And realize that it is not the Old Testament law per se that will be the final standard of judgment but the center of that law—loving your neighbor as yourself. This law will be used in the judgment not as a "law of bondage" but as a "law of liberty."

This means that James is not taking us back again to a yoke of slavery where we lived under law as the means of setting ourselves right with God. Rather the "royal law" (James 2:8)—love your neighbor—has become a "law of *liberty*" because it can only be fulfilled by those who have been *liberated* from having to fulfill it as the way to get right with God.

By believing in Christ to put us right with God because of his death and righteousness, we are set at "liberty" from law keeping as a way of getting right with God. Now the way we relate to the law is as a "law of liberty." In our liberty from the law as the ground of justification, we are enabled by the Spirit to walk in the law of Christ as confirmation that we are loved and forgiven and accepted by God.

So we will be "judged under the law of liberty." But the point of our final judgment will *not* be to determine if we kept the law to get right with God, but to determine if we loved our neighbor *because we had already been put right with God by grace alone through faith alone because of Christ alone.* The record of our love—our not showing partiality because of race and riches—will be brought out in the courtroom of heaven. It will not be the ground of our final vindication. Only Christ will be that. It will be the public evidence that we were united to Christ by faith, so that his righteousness counts as ours.

So walking in love and showing grace to the poor and the rich and every ethnic group is *not* the way God becomes 100 percent for us. That happens when we trust Christ, who is 100 percent of the perfection God demands for justification. Rather, walking in love and overcoming the racism and ethnocentrism of our hearts is possible precisely *because* by grace alone God is 100 percent for us in Christ. Our walking in love is not the foundation but the confirmation that God is for us.

6) *Partiality is not merciful, and if you don't show mercy, you will perish.* This is an extension of argument 5. There we were warned that we will be judged under the law of liberty, and here James describes how that judgment works: "For judgment is without mercy to one who has shown no mercy. Mercy triumphs over judgment" (James 2:13). The meaning here is plain. It's based on the words of Jesus: "Blessed are the merciful, for they shall receive mercy" (Matt. 5:7). If we don't show mercy, we have not known Christ in a saving way. We have not drunk his mercy down into our souls (see Matt. 18:23–34).

A Christian is a person who has seen and tasted, and lives on, the mercy of Christ. If there is no mercy in our lives—if we show partiality because of riches or race, and come to no remorse and no repentance because of it—we don't know him, and we will perish (1 John 2:3–4). But if we have tasted his mercy and treasure it, and live in the liberty of his love, then we will show mercy, and that mercy will be the evidence of our faith in Christ, whose life and death in our place carries us through the judgment.

7) *Partiality contradicts faith in Jesus Christ as the Lord of glory.* James begins his arguments with faith in Christ, the Lord of glory. And this is where we will end the chapter. He says in James 2:1: "My brothers, show no partiality *as you hold the faith in our Lord Jesus Christ, the Lord of glory.*"

The key emphasis here is on the word "glory." James chose to accent that Christians trust Christ, *the Lord of glory*. Why? Because the origin of partiality is either craving for human glory or fear of danger. When the craving for human glory controls us, we show partiality to the rich and powerful. When we are governed by fear, we show partiality to whomever we think will make us safer.

But James's point is this: if you know Christ as the Lord of glory—if you trust him as the one who is gloriously gracious and gloriously merciful and gloriously forgiving and gloriously strong and gloriously wise and gloriously loving—then you won't be controlled by this craving for human glory or by this fear that uses partiality to be safe. Christ will be your glory—all the glory you need. And Christ will be your security—all the security you need.

So the issue of partiality—because of riches or race—is a huge issue for the way we live as Christians. Are we partial in our attitudes or actions? Or are we trusting Jesus as the Lord of glory? If we are trusting Jesus, then his glory will put us in our rightfully humble place, and it will make us safe. And from that lowly and safe place will flow love, not partiality. Mercy, not racial disrespect.

SECTION THREE

THE ULTIMATE GOAL OF THE GOSPEL

He chose us in him before the foundation of the world, that we should be holy and blameless before him. In love he predestined us for adoption as sons through Jesus Christ, according to the purpose of his will, to the praise of his glorious grace.

EPHESIANS 1:4–6

Christ became a servant to the circumcised . . . in order that the Gentiles might glorify God for his mercy. As it is written, "Therefore I will praise you among the Gentiles, and sing to your name."

ROMANS 15:8–9

CHAPTER FOURTEEN

WHY IS IT WORTH
THE DEATH OF HIS SON?

The entire universe exists to display the greatness of the glory of the grace of God manifest supremely in Jesus Christ dying in the place of sinners. Paul says in Colossians 1:16, concerning Christ, "All things were created through him and *for him*." "For him" does not mean that Christ needed them. It does not mean that he was defective or deficient and that the creation of all things made up for this deficiency.

Rather, it means that all things exist *for his glory*. That is, they exist to display his greatness. This display is what we were made to enjoy supremely forever. Therefore, the purpose of the universe and the aim of history reach their climax in the supreme display of the glory of Christ for the everlasting enjoyment of his people.

THE INCOMPARABLE DISPLAY OF GLORY AT CALVARY

That supreme display happened at Calvary in the death of Christ. What happened there is that through Christ, God's eternal purpose to adopt sinners into his eternal family was secured. And God did it in a way that would make the glory of his grace the supreme focus of our praise. Here's the way Paul says it in Ephesians 1:5–6: "[God] predestined us for adoption as sons through Jesus Christ, according to the purpose of his will, *to the praise of his glorious grace.*"

"Through Jesus Christ" means through his blood, that is, through his death: "In him we have redemption through his blood" (Eph. 1:7). And the divine aim of Christ's death—what Paul calls "the purpose of his will"—is "to the praise of his glorious grace." God's ultimate aim in the death of Christ is "the praise of his glorious grace."

We can see all through the Old Testament, and into the New, that the ultimate purpose of God in creation and providence has been the display of his glory for the joyful admiration of all who would see and believe.[1] Now it has become clear that this purpose reaches its apex in the manifestation of the glory *of his grace*. More than that, we see now that the supreme manifestation of the glory of his grace is in the death of his Son for sinners.

This is why Paul connects the glory of God to the gospel. He does it in two ways. First, he says that the glory of *Christ* in the gospel is the glory of the *image of God*. The gospel is "the gospel of *the glory of Christ*, who is the image of God" (2 Cor. 4:4). Second, he says that *this glory* shines in the *face of Jesus Christ*. The gospel is "the knowledge of *the glory of God* in the *face of Jesus Christ*" (2 Cor. 4:6). In these two verses, Paul makes clear that what is happening in the events of the gospel is the manifestation of the glory of God through the person and work of Jesus Christ, supremely on the cross.

GOD'S PURSUIT OF DIVERSITY GLORIFIES HIS GRACE IN THE GOSPEL

Now what does all that have to do with the point of this book? What we have been arguing is that the gospel is the good news that by the death of Christ for sinners, God purchased and impels and empowers racial and ethnic diversity and harmony in the emerging people of God. We have seen it again and again in many different texts. Now we connect *this* aim of the gospel with the *ultimate* aim of the gospel to display the glory of the grace of God. What becomes clear is that racial and ethnic diversity and harmony among the redeemed is a God-ordained and blood-bought means of glorifying the grace of God. This is one of the ways that the glory of God's grace becomes strikingly visible through the gospel.

The reason God decreed that the gospel would obtain people from every tribe and people and nation is that the aim of the gospel is the glorification of his grace and this ingathering of diverse peoples into one Christ-exalting, unified people who would glorify the power and beauty of his grace more than if he had done things another way. There is a strong confirmation of this in noticing that several texts which command the pursuit of all ethnic groups are explicit that this pursuit is for the glory of Christ.

For example, in Romans 1:5, Paul says that his apostleship was given "to bring about the obedience of faith *for the sake of [Christ's] name among all the nations.*" In other words, the pursuit of "all nations" (all ethnic groups[2]) is for the glory of Christ. Similarly in Romans 15:9, Paul says that Christ did his own missionary work in coming into the world "in order that the Gentiles [or nations] *might glorify God* for his mercy." The aim of Christ's pursuit of the Gentiles (the ethnically different ones) is for the glory of God's mercy, which was shown supremely in the death of Christ.

Accordingly, the consummation of the missionary mandate to make disciples of all nations (Matt. 28:19) is described in Revelation 5:9 as persons from "every tribe and language and people and nation" worshiping the Lamb and declaring the infinite worth of his glory. So the apostolic vocation (Rom. 1:5) and the messianic example of Christ (Rom. 15:9) and the consummation of all missions (Rev. 5:9) have one explicit aim: to display the glory of Christ through the ingathering of a hugely diverse and unified redeemed people.

DIVERSITY IS FOREVER

And we should not think that God's aim to have this racial and ethnic diversity in his kingdom is a temporary one only for this age. In spite of the resistance of most English versions, the standard Greek texts of the New Testament agree that the original wording of Revelation 21:3 requires the translation: "And I heard a great voice from the throne saying, 'Behold the dwelling of God is with men, and he will dwell with them and they will be his *peoples.*"

Most versions translate it "they will be his *people.*" But what John is saying is that in the new heavens and the new earth, the ethnic diversity described in Revelation 5:9 will be preserved: persons ransomed by the blood of Christ "from every tribe and language and people and nation." This diversity will not disappear in the new heavens and the new earth. God willed it from the beginning. It has a permanent place in his plan.

HOW DIVERSITY MAGNIFIES THE GLORY OF GOD

We have now seen the answer to the question, "Why is ethnic and racial diversity and harmony worth the death of God's Son?" It's worth it because by this diversity and harmony, God displays the glory of his grace more brightly in the gospel. Which brings us now to the question, "How?" How does God's pursuit of racial and ethnic diversity through the death of Christ and the mission of his church accomplish his purpose to be glorified for his grace—supremely through Christ and the gospel? I see at least four answers to this question in Scripture.[3]

DIVERSE UNITY IS MORE GLORIOUS THAN THE UNITY OF SAMENESS

First, there is a beauty and power of praise that comes from unity in diversity that is greater than that which comes from unity alone. Psalm 96:3–4 connects the evangelizing of all the peoples with the quality of praise that God deserves. "Declare his glory among the nations, his marvelous works among all the peoples! *For great is the* LORD, and greatly to be praised; he is to be feared above all gods." Notice the word "For"—"*For* great is the LORD, and greatly to be praised."

Recall that Ephesians 1:6 says that God is redeeming his people through Jesus Christ "to the praise of his glorious grace." Psalm 96 adds that the extraordinary greatness of the praise that God aims to receive is the foundation (the word *for*) and impetus of his pursuit of the "nations"—the whole bewildering diversity of ethnic groups on the earth.

I infer from this that the beauty and power of praise that will come to the Lord from the diversity of these ethnic groups are greater than the beauty and power that would come to him if the chorus of the redeemed were culturally uniform. The reason for this can be seen in the analogy of a choir. More depth of beauty is felt from a choir that sings in parts than from a choir that sings only in unison. Unity in diversity is more beautiful and more powerful than the unity of uniformity.

This carries over to the untold differences that exist between the peoples of the world. When their diversity unites in worship to God, the beauty of their praise will echo the depth and greatness of God's beauty far more exceedingly than if the redeemed were from only a few different people groups.

PRAISE FROM DIVERSE PEOPLES POINTS TO DEEPER BEAUTY

Second, the fame and greatness and worth of an object of beauty increases in proportion to the diversity of those who recognize its beauty. If a work of art is regarded as great among a small and like-minded group of people, but not by anyone else, the art is probably not truly great. Its qualities are such that it does not appeal to the deep universals in our hearts but only to provincial biases. But if a work of art continues to win more and more admirers not only across cultures but also across decades and centuries, then its greatness is irresistibly manifested.

Thus when Paul says, "Praise the Lord, all you Gentiles [all ethnic groups], and let all the peoples extol him" (Rom. 15:11), he is saying that there is something about God that is so universally praiseworthy, and so profoundly beautiful, and so comprehensively worthy, and so deeply satisfying that God will find passionate admirers in every diverse people group in the world. And the focus of this admiration will be on the supreme manifestation of God's beauty in the display of his grace in the death of his Son. "Worthy are you . . . for you were slain" (Rev. 5:9). The "worth" of Christ shines supremely in being slain willingly for sinners. Therefore, all the peoples will praise God for the glory of his mercy above all other glories. Christ came to do his work "that the Gentiles might *glorify God for his mercy*" (Rom. 15:9).

Thus the true greatness and beauty of God, in the display of his grace through Christ in the gospel, will be manifest in the breadth of the diversity of those who perceive and cherish this beauty. His excellence will be shown to be higher and deeper than the parochial preferences that make us happy most of the time. His appeal will be to the deepest, highest, largest capacities of the human soul, awakened by the Holy Spirit. Thus the diversity of the source of admiration will testify to the incomparable glory of the God of grace.

A DIVERSITY OF FOLLOWERS POINTS TO
A GREATER LEADER

Third, the strength and wisdom and love of a leader are magnified in proportion to the diversity of people he can inspire to follow him with joy. If you can lead only a small, uniform group of people, your leadership qualities are not as great as if you can win a following from a large group of very diverse people.

Paul's understanding of what is happening in his missionary work among the ethnic peoples of the world is that Christ is demonstrating his greatness by winning obedience from all the diverse peoples on earth: "I will not venture to speak of anything except what *Christ has accomplished through me to bring the Gentiles [the ethnic groups] to obedience*" (Rom. 15:18). It is not Paul's missionary expertise that is being magnified when more and more diverse peoples choose to follow Christ. It is the greatness of Christ. He is showing himself superior to all other leaders.

The last phrase of Psalm 96:3–4 shows the leadership competition that is going on in world missions. "Declare his glory among the nations . . . *he is to be feared above all gods*." We should declare the glory of God's grace in the work of Christ among the nations because in this way he will show his superiority, and the glory of his Son, over all other gods that make pretentious claims to lead the peoples. The more diverse the people groups who forsake their gods to receive the grace of the true God and follow Christ, the more visible is the superior beauty and power of Christ over all his competitors.

DIVERSITY UNDERCUTS ETHNIC PRIDE AND
POINTS TO GRACE

Fourth, by focusing his redemption and his mission on all the people groups of the world, God undercuts ethnocentric pride and puts all peoples back upon his free grace rather than any distinctive of their own. In this way, God's pursuit of ethnic diversity humbles us and magnifies his free grace.

This humbling effect of diversity is what Paul was emphasizing in Acts 17:26 when he said to the proud citizens of Athens, "[God] made from one man every nation of mankind to live on all the face of the earth, having determined allotted periods and the boundaries of their dwelling place." F. F. Bruce points out that "the Athenians . . . pride themselves on being . . . sprung from the soil of their native Attica. . . . They were the only Greeks on the European mainland who had no tradition of their ancestors coming into Greece; they belonged to the earliest wave of Greek immigration."[4]

To this boast Paul countered: "You and the so-called *barbarians* and the Jews and the Romans all came from the same origin. And you came by God's will, not your own; and the time and place of your existence is in God's hand." When God focuses his redeeming work and missionary force on *all* the ethnic peoples, he cuts the nerve of ethnocentric pride. It's a humbling thing to discover that God does not choose *our* group because of any distinctives of our worth but, rather, chooses us with the aim that we glorify him *for his mercy*. He saves and he seeks the peoples "to the praise of his glorious grace" (Eph. 1:6).

Humility is the flip side of giving God all the glory. Humility means reveling in his grace, not in our goodness. In pressing us on to all the peoples, God is pressing us further into the humblest and deepest experience of his grace and weaning us more and more from our ingrained pride. In doing this, he is preparing for himself a people—from all the peoples— who will be able to worship him with free and white-hot admiration.

REVERENCE FOR THE CROSS AND LOVE FOR GOD'S GLORY

The upshot of this chapter for the aim of this book is to show that God's pursuit of racial and ethnic diversity through the work of Christ on the cross is part of the larger aim of the cross to display the supreme worth of the glory of God's grace. What we have seen is that these two aims of the cross (God's glory and racial harmony in diversity) are not incidentally related. The achievement of the cross in reconciling all ethnic groups through faith in Christ is part of *how* the work of Christ on the cross magnifies the greatness of God's grace. Therefore, what is at stake in our pursuit of racial and ethnic diversity and harmony (both locally and globally) is both our reverence for the cross and our love for the glory of God.

SECTION FOUR

TWO ISSUES: INTERRACIAL MARRIAGE AND PREJUDICE

Miriam and Aaron spoke against Moses because of the Cushite woman whom he had married, for he had married a Cushite woman. . . . And suddenly the Lord said to Moses and to Aaron and Miriam, "Come out, you three, to the tent of meeting." And the three of them came out. And the Lord came down in a pillar of cloud and stood at the entrance of the tent and called Aaron and Miriam, and they both came forward. And he said, "Hear my words: If there is a prophet among you, I the Lord make myself known to him in a vision; I speak with him in a dream. Not so with my servant Moses. He is faithful in all my house. With him I speak mouth to mouth, clearly, and not in riddles, and he beholds the form of the Lord. Why then were you not afraid to speak against my servant Moses?" And the anger of the Lord was kindled against them, and he departed. When the cloud removed from over the tent, behold, Miriam was leprous, like snow.

NUMBERS 12:1–10

CHAPTER FIFTEEN

INTERRACIAL MARRIAGE

My aim in this chapter is to argue from Scripture and experience that interracial marriage is not only permitted by God but is a positive good in our day. It is not just to be tolerated, but celebrated. America is ambivalent about this. On the one hand, interracial marriage has been advancing:

> Half of all Asians are now marrying non-Asians; by the third generation half of all Hispanics are also marrying outside the ethnic group. The black intermarriage rate is slowly but steadily rising. The categories "Hispanic," "Asian," and "white" (always questionable) are fast becoming a positive anachronism, and even "black" is a label that is fraying at the edges.[1]

On the other hand, the history of resistance, while changing, is still with us. There is opposition to interracial marriage from all sides.

LAWS AGAINST MISCEGENATION

Thankfully, this strange word, *miscegenation*, is not known the way it used to be. It means "the interbreeding of people considered to be of different racial types." It used to be found in the law books of many states—as prohibited.[2]

"As late as 1958, only 4 per cent of American whites approved of inter-racial marriage."[3] Interracial marriage was against the law in sixteen states in 1967 when the *Loving v. Virginia* Supreme Court decision struck down those laws.[4] Not until 1998 did South Carolina, the state I grew up in, remove from the state constitution language that prohibited "marriage of a white person with a Negro or mulatto or a person who shall have one-eighth or more Negro blood."[5] "According to a Mason-Dixon poll four months before the vote, 22 [percent] of South

Carolina voters were opposed to the removal of this clause. It had been introduced in 1895."[6]

The legislature in Alabama took until the year 2000 to remove from the state constitution Article IV, Section 102, which said, "The Legislature shall never pass any law to authorize or legalize any marriage between any white person and a Negro, or a descendant of a Negro."[7] That law had been introduced in 1901. "According to a poll conducted by the Mobile Register in September of 2000, 19 [percent] of voters said that they would not remove section 102. . . . However, 64 [percent] said that they would vote to remove it."[8]

That is very fresh historically. I spent the first eighteen years of my life growing up in a state where interracial marriage between white and black was illegal. When those laws were struck down by the *Loving* case in 1967, I was a senior in college. From a historical perspective, that is almost like yesterday. Laws reflect deep convictions. Often the change in conviction lags far behind the change in law. That is certainly the case with regard to interracial marriage.[9]

OPPOSITION TO INTERRACIAL MARRIAGE

When I was preparing to preach on this topic in January of 2005, the first website that came up on my Google search for Martin Luther King and interracial marriage was the website of the Ku Klux Klan, which still had this anachronistic quote: "Interracial marriage is a violation of God's Law and a communist ploy to weaken America." Communist?

Many African Americans believe interracial marriage erodes the solidarity of the African American community. Lawrence Otis Graham wrote that "interracial marriage undermines [African-Americans'] ability to introduce our children to black role models who accept their racial identity with pride."[10]

Some whites oppose interracial marriage for a different reason. Syndicated columnist H. Millard wrote:

> We are seeing the death of the American and his replacement with a
> non-European type who now has enough mass in our society to pervert
> European-American ways. . . . White people . . . are going to have to
> struggle mightily to survive the Neo-Melting Pot and avoid being part

of the one-size-fits-all human model. Call it what it is: Genocide and extinction of the white genotype.[11]

One personal letter I received from a white Christian man went like this:

> As individuals, they are precious souls for whom Christ died and whom we are to love and seek to win. As a race, however, they are unique and different and have their own culture. . . . I would never marry a black. Why? Because I believe God made the races, separated them and set the bounds of their habitation (Deuteronomy 32:8; Acts 17:26).
>
> He made them uniquely different and intended that these distinctions remain. God never intended the human race to become a mixed or mongrel race. So, while I am strongly opposed to segregation, I favor separation that the uniqueness with which God made them is maintained.

MY PERSONAL EXPERIENCE

To these opposing views, I would add my own experience. I was a Southern teenage racist (by almost any definition), and since I am a sinner still, I do not doubt that elements of it remain in me, to my dismay. For these lingering attitudes and actions, I repent and set my heart against them.

Racism is a very difficult reality to define. But let's again make use of the definition that the Presbyterian Church in America decided on in the summer of 2004: "Racism is an explicit or implicit belief or practice that qualitatively distinguishes or values one race over other races."[12] That is what I mean when I say I was a racist growing up in Greenville, South Carolina. My attitudes and actions were demeaning and disrespectful toward nonwhites, and blacks were the only nonwhites I knew. At the heart of those attitudes was opposition to interracial marriage.

As I mentioned in the introduction, my mother, who literally washed my mouth out with soap once for saying "Shut up!" to my sister, would have washed my mouth out with gasoline if she knew how foul my mouth was racially. She was, under God, the seed of my salvation in more ways than one. As I mentioned previously, after our church voted not to admit blacks in 1963, when I was seventeen, my mother ushered the black guests at my sister's wedding right into the main sanctuary herself because the ushers wouldn't do it. I was on my way to redemption.

In 1967 my wife, Noël, and I attended the Urbana Missions Conference. I was a senior at Wheaton College. There we heard Warren Webster, former missionary to Pakistan, answer a student's question: "What if your daughter falls in love with a Pakistani while you're on the mission field and wants to marry him?" With great forcefulness, he said something like, "Better a Christian Pakistani than a godless white American!" The impact on us was profound.

Four years later I wrote a paper called "The Ethics of Interracial Marriage" for Lewis Smedes in an ethics class at Fuller Seminary. I still have it. For me that was a biblical settling of the matter, and I have not gone back from what I saw there. The Bible does not oppose or forbid interracial marriages. And there are circumstances which together with biblical principles make interracial marriage in many cases a positive good.

Now I am a pastor at Bethlehem Baptist Church in Minneapolis. One quick walk through the pictorial directory of our church gives me a rough count of 203 non-Anglos pictured in the book. I am sure I missed some, and that more have joined since the directory was printed in 2005. And I am sure the definition of *Anglo* is so vague that someone will be bothered that I even tried to count. But the point is this: many of them are children and teenagers and single young men and women. This means very simply that we as a church need a clear place to stand on interracial marriage. Church is the most natural and proper place to find a spouse. And some of them will find each other across racial lines.

A PLACE TO STAND

That standing place is what I would like to provide in this chapter. First, we will make four textual observations and then draw out some concluding implications for our experience.

1) All Races Have One Ancestor, and All Humans Are Created in God's Image

The Bible portrays the human race as coming from one pair of human ancestors who were created in God's image, unlike all the animals, and that this image of God is passed on to all humans. Genesis 1:27: "So

God created man in his own image, in the image of God he created him; male and female he created them."

Again in Genesis 5:1–3: "When God created man, he made him in the likeness of God. Male and female he created them, and he blessed them and named them Man when they were created. When Adam had lived 130 years, he fathered a son in his own likeness, after his image." In other words, the magnificent image of God goes on from generation to generation.

Then Paul makes the sweeping statement in Acts 17:26, "And he made from one man every nation of mankind to live on all the face of the earth." In other words, Adam, who was created in God's image, is the father of all human beings in all ethnic groups. Therefore, all of them are dignified above the animals in this absolutely unique and glorious way: humans are created in the image of God. With all the beautiful, God-designed ethnic and cultural diversity in the world, that truth is paramount. That truth is decisive in setting priorities for how we respect and relate to each other.

The Bible's Restraint on Secularist Racist Doctrines

Colin Kidd, professor of modern history at the University of Glasgow, has shown in his book *The Forging of Races* the extensive influence of Christianity and the Bible in undermining certain teachings about race that served to uphold racism. The secular abandonment of the authority of Scripture was not a uniformly liberating experience for all the races. Hand in hand with the abandonment of Scripture also came the secularist views of the supremacy of the white race rooted in different evolutionary origins. The secularist Nazi and Communist governments of the twentieth century, for example, left unspeakably bloody tracks on the trail of their racist regimes.

For all the misuses that have been made of the Bible in supporting racism, there is, Kidd shows, a long history of the Bible's restraint upon such racism because of its unambiguous affirmation that we all have one historical father in Adam. "In large part, the message of the Christian Scriptures constrained the development of polygenist ideas of multiple human origins."[13]

That clear affirmation of the single origin of all humans in one human ancestor, Kidd observes, has been affirmed by the first UNESCO Statement on Race in such a way that it "exiled notions of racial polygenesis beyond the bounds of recognized science." It continues:

> Scientists have reached general agreement in recognizing that mankind is one: that all men belong to the same species, Homo sapiens. It is further generally agreed among scientists that all men are probably derived from the same common stock; and that such differences as exist between different groups of mankind are due to the operation of evolutionary factors of differentiation, such as isolation, the drift and random fixation of the material particles which control heredity (the genes), changes in the structure of these particles, hybridization, and natural selection.[14]

Sometimes the objection is raised that the early chapters of Genesis not only depict a single human origin but also God's will that there be separate ethnic groups. This objection then goes on to say that intermarriage between any of these groups is a contradiction of God's desire to create them.

Diluting God-Willed Differences?

What about intermarriage then? Does it contradict the diversity God wills? Some speak of intermarriage as the dilution of God-willed differences. Some speak of the offspring of interracial marriage as "half-breeds" and a "mongrel race." I cannot bring myself to believe that the mingling of racial traits in the children of interracial marriages is a "diluting" of the diversity God wills. The "races" have never been pure or well defined. The human lines that flowed from the sons of Noah (Shem, Ham, and Japheth) have flowed into far more diversity than three ethnic types of human beings. There is no reason to think that diversification has stopped.

Just one example: after the flood, Noah's three sons (Shem, Ham, and Japheth) become the fathers of the human race. But look what happens to these racial fountainheads. Genesis 10:6 says, "The sons of Ham [are] Cush, Egypt, Put, and Canaan." The ethnic and "racial" differences between Canaanites and Cushites and Egyptians were physiologically pronounced. In other words, "race" is a fluid concept with no clear boundaries.

God seems to delight not just in three but in thousands of variations of human beings. In fact, many today would argue that the concept of race is unhelpful altogether because there are no clear lines that can be drawn, and the ones that are drawn are not genetically or morally significant.

Moreover, the offspring of interethnic marriages *add* to the diversity of the human race rather than dilute it. The scope of the world's peoples is so huge that there is no serious possibility that intermarriage will reduce diversity of peoples. In fact, there is more likelihood that new ethnic types will emerge rather than that all will become the same—let alone "mongrel."

Canaanites (Arabs) and Cushites (black Africans) emerged from one line (Ham). At what point did intermarriage within this line become destructive to God's ordained diversity? It appears that God willed that the so-called three "races" should diversify increasingly rather than be preserved in purity. After the flood, God set in motion a process of increasing diversification of ethnicities (see Gen. 10:5). He is not concerned with limiting diversity to a few peoples. According to the text, he planned the multiplication of increasing numbers of peoples.

2) The Bible Forbids Intermarriage between Unbeliever and Believer—but Not between Races

One of the most celebrated marriages in the Bible, and one that gave rise to the line of king David, and finally to Jesus, was the marriage between a Jew and a Moabite—the marriage of Boaz and Ruth (Ruth 4:21–22). Ruth was the Moabite (Ruth 1:4). They were not only ethnically and religiously foreign; they were the offspring of incest: "Thus both the daughters of Lot became pregnant by their father. The firstborn bore a son and called his name Moab. He is the father of the Moabites to this day" (Gen. 19:36–37).

But in spite of these serious divisions, Ruth was a lover of the true God and came under the wings of his covenant with Israel (Ruth 2:12). This faith and this marriage and the offspring that came from it were so remarkable that the New Testament Gospel of Matthew included Ruth as one of the four women mentioned in the genealogy of Jesus (Matt. 1:5).

What the book of Ruth illustrates is that there was no absolute rule in God's Word forbidding marriage across racial and ethnic lines. What the Bible does forbid is the marriage of a believer and unbeliever. The apostle Paul says in 1 Corinthians 7:39, "A wife is bound to her husband as long as he lives. But if her husband dies, she is free to be married to whom she wishes, *only in the Lord*." Whom she wishes, only in the Lord. The man she marries must be *in the Lord*. He must be a believer in Jesus Christ.[15]

This was the main point of the Old Testament warnings about marrying those among the pagan nations. The point was not to protect racial purity. The point was to protect religious purity. For example, in Deuteronomy 7:3–4 Moses said:

> You shall not intermarry with them, giving your daughters to their sons or taking their daughters for your sons, for they would turn away your sons from following me, to serve other gods. Then the anger of the LORD would be kindled against you.

The issue is not color mixing, or customs mixing, or clan identity. The issue is: *will there be one common allegiance to the true God in this marriage or will there be divided affections?* The prohibition in God's Word is not against interracial marriage but against marriage between the true Israel, the church (from every people, tribe, and nation), and those who are not part of the true Israel.[16] That is, the Bible prohibits marriage between those who believe in Christ (the Messiah) and those who don't. "Do not be unequally yoked with unbelievers" (2 Cor. 6:14).

This is exactly what we would expect if the great ground of our identity is not our ethnic differences but our common humanity in the image of God and especially our new humanity in Christ. Which leads to the third biblical observation.

3) In Christ Our Oneness Is Profound and Transforms
Racial and Social Differences from Barriers to Blessings
In Christ ethnic and social differences cease to be obstacles to deep, personal, intimate fellowship, including marriage.

> You have put off the old self with its practices and have put on the new self, which is being renewed in knowledge after the image of its creator. Here there is not Greek and Jew, circumcised and uncircumcised, barbarian, Scythian, slave, free; but Christ is all, and in all. (Col. 3:9–11)

This does not mean that every minority culture gets swallowed up by the majority culture in the name of unity. God does not obliterate all ethnic and cultural differences in Christ. He redeems them and refines them and enriches them in the togetherness of his kingdom. The final image of heaven is "every tribe and language and people and nation" (Rev. 5:9; 7:9). God values the differences that reflect more fully his glory in man.[17]

The point of Colossians 3:11 is not that cultural, ethnic, and racial differences have no significance; they do. The point is that they are no barrier to profound, personal, intimate fellowship. Singing alto is different from singing bass. It's a significant difference. But that difference is no barrier to being in the choir. It's an asset.

When Christ is all and in all, differences take an important but subordinate place to fellowship—and, I will argue, marriage.

4) Criticizing One Interracial Marriage Was Severely Disciplined by God

The fourth observation is that Moses, a Jew, apparently married a black African and was approved by God. "Miriam and Aaron spoke against Moses because of the Cushite woman whom he had married, for he had married a Cushite woman" (Num. 12:1). "Cushite" means a woman from Cush, a region south of Egypt, and a people known for their black skin. We know this because of Jeremiah 13:23: "Can the Ethiopian [the very same Hebrew word translated *Cushite* in Num. 12:1] change his skin or the leopard his spots? Then also you can do good who are accustomed to do evil." So attention is drawn to the difference of the skin of the Cushite people.

J. Daniel Hays writes in his book *From Every People and Nation: A Biblical Theology of Race* that Cush "is used regularly to refer to the area south of Egypt, and above the cataracts on the Nile, where a Black African civilization flourished for over two thousand years. Thus it is quite clear that Moses marries a Black African woman."[18]

What is most significant about this context is that God does not

211

get angry at Moses; he gets angry at Miriam and Aaron for criticizing Moses. The criticism has to do with Moses's marriage and Moses's authority. The most explicit statement relates to the marriage: "Miriam and Aaron spoke against Moses *because of the Cushite woman whom he had married, for he had married a Cushite* woman." Typically commentators say that Miriam and Aaron's objections to Moses's marriage "were only a smokescreen for their challenge to Moses' spiritual authority."[19] Perhaps. But what you use for a smoke screen reveals your heart. And God was not pleased.

SO, YOU LIKE BEING WHITE, MIRIAM?

What happened next is startling. God is furious. First, he defends his servant Moses from false charges, and then he strikes Miriam with a terrible disease that turns her skin white—white as snow.

> [God said concerning Moses that] "he is faithful in all my house. With him I speak mouth to mouth, clearly, and not in riddles, and he beholds the form of the LORD. Why then were you not afraid to speak against my servant Moses?" And the anger of the LORD was kindled against them, and he departed. When the cloud removed from over the tent, behold, Miriam was leprous, like snow. And Aaron turned toward Miriam, and behold, she was leprous. (Num. 12:7–10)

Is there more here than mere punishment? Is there symbolism in the punishment? Consider this possibility: in God's anger at Miriam, Moses's sister, God says in effect, "Do you like being light-skinned, Miriam? Do you belittle the Cushite because she is dark-skinned and foreign? All right, I'll make you light-skinned." Verse 10: "Behold, Miriam was leprous, like snow."

God says not a critical word against Moses for marrying a black Cushite woman. But when Miriam criticizes God's chosen leader for this marriage, God strikes her skin with white leprosy. If you ever thought black was a biblical symbol for uncleanness, be careful how you use such an idea; a white uncleanness could come upon you.[20]

Those are my four biblical observations. (1) All races have one ancestor in the image of God, and all humans are in God's image. (2) The Bible forbids intermarriage between unbeliever and believer, but not between races. (3) In Christ our oneness is profound and transforms racial and social differences from barriers to blessings. (4) Criticizing one interracial marriage was severely disciplined by God.

CLOSING IMPLICATIONS

From my own experience and from many conversations, I would argue that *opposition to interracial marriage is one of the deepest roots of racial distance, disrespect, and hostility in the world.* Show me one place in the world where interracial or interethnic marriage is frowned upon and yet the two groups still have equal respect and honor and opportunity. I don't think it exists. It won't happen.[21]

Why? Because the supposed specter of interracial marriage demands that barrier after barrier must be put up to keep young people from knowing each other and falling in love. They can't fellowship in church youth groups. They can't go to the same schools. They can't belong to the same clubs. They probably won't live in the same neighborhoods. Everybody knows deep down what is going on here. It's the silent disapproval and fear of intermarriage.[22]

And as long as we disapprove of it, we will be pushing our children, and therefore ourselves, away from each other. The effect of that is not harmony, not respect, and not equality of opportunity. Separation has never produced mutual understanding and respect. It has produced ignorance, suspicion, impersonal stereotyping, demeaning innuendo, and corporate self-exaltation.

Where racial intermarriage is disapproved, the culture with money and power will always dominate and always oppress. They will see to it that those who will not make desirable spouses stay in their place. If your kids don't make desirable spouses, you don't make desirable neighbors.

CREATE A PROBLEM AND MAKE IT THE REASON FOR THE PROBLEM

And here is a great and sad irony. The very situation of separation and suspicion and distrust and dislike that is brought about (among other things) by the fear of intermarriage is used to justify the opposition to intermarriage. "It will make life hard for the couple and hard for the kids (they'll be called half-breeds)." Catch-22. It's like the army being defeated because there aren't enough troops, and the troops won't sign up because the army is being defeated. Oppose interracial marriage, and you will help create a situation of racial disrespect. And then, since there is a situation of disrespect, it will be prudent to avoid interracial marriage.

THE CALL OF CHRIST IS NOT COMFORT

Here is where Christ makes the difference. Christ does not call us to a prudent life but to a God-centered, Christ-exalting, justice-advancing, countercultural, risk-taking life of love and courage. Will it be harder to be married to another race, and will it be harder for the kids? Maybe. Maybe not. But since when is *that* the way a Christian thinks? Life is hard. And the more you love, the more painful it gets.

It's hard to take a child to the mission field. The risks are huge. It's hard to take a child and move into a mixed neighborhood where he may be teased or ridiculed. It's hard to help a child be a Christian in a secular world where his beliefs are mocked. It's hard to bring children up with standards: "You will not dress like that, and you will not be out that late." It's hard to raise children when Dad or Mom dies or divorces. And that's a real risk in *any* marriage. Whoever said that marrying and having children was supposed to be trouble-free? It's one of the hardest things in the world. It just happens to be right and rewarding.

Christians are people who move toward need and truth and justice, not toward comfort and security. Life is hard. But God is good. And Christ is strong to help.

THERE ARE MORE THAN PROBLEMS IN STORE

Who knows what blessings through pain God may have in store? Interracial marriage has an amazing potential for great joy and peace. Yes, there are exceptions—a white father may never speak to his black son-in-law. But another wonderful possibility exists. Indeed, it comes to pass over and over in interracial marriages. A once-bigoted group of relatives is forced to see *as a person* the "outsider" who just married their "insider."

The newcomer into the family is not just a race anymore. He or she is a person. Over time the suspicions and prejudices and hostilities die away, and something beautiful is born—reconciliation and respect and harmony, spreading out beyond the marriage in ways no one thought possible. The once angry father now views all his ethnic colleagues at work differently.

EMBRACING THE BEAUTY AND THE BURDEN

We conclude this chapter by returning to a central text on our newness in Christ, Colossians 3:11—"Here [in the church] there is not Greek and Jew, circumcised and uncircumcised, barbarian, Scythian, slave, free; *but Christ is all, and in all.*" We are not interested in diversity for diversity's sake. We are not interested in being popular or politically correct. We are interested in moving toward the visible experience of Colossians 3:11.

That means moving toward a more visible display of Christ being our all and Christ being manifestly in all. When Christ is our all, and when Christ is in all, ethnic differences change from being barriers to becoming blessings. Even "barbarians" and the most distant of them, "Scythians," are in the new "race"—the church. The head of this "race" is no longer Adam, but the "last Adam" (1 Cor. 15:45), Jesus Christ. God aims that in this new "race" of humans all ethnic groups in the world will be included (Matt. 24:14). Inter-ethnic marriage in this new humanity is one manifestation and one means of Christ being all in all.

We will not underestimate the challenges of interracial marriage and biracial children (and transracial adoption—they go closely together). Rather, we will strive to nurture churches where such marriages thrive. We will celebrate the beauty, and we will embrace the burden. Both will be good for us, and good for the world, and good for the spread of the gospel and the glory of God.

The next day Jesus decided to go to Galilee. He found Philip and said to him, "Follow me." Now Philip was from Bethsaida, the city of Andrew and Peter. Philip found Nathanael and said to him, "We have found him of whom Moses in the Law and also the prophets wrote, Jesus of Nazareth, the son of Joseph." Nathanael said to him, "Can anything good come out of Nazareth?" Philip said to him, "Come and see." Jesus saw Nathanael coming toward him and said of him, "Behold, an Israelite indeed, in whom there is no deceit!" Nathanael said to him, "How do you know me?" Jesus answered him, "Before Philip called you, when you were under the fig tree, I saw you." Nathanael answered him, "Rabbi, you are the Son of God! You are the King of Israel!" Jesus answered him, "Because I said to you, 'I saw you under the fig tree,' do you believe? You will see greater things than these." And he said to him, "Truly, truly, I say to you, you will see heaven opened, and the angels of God ascending and descending on the Son of Man."

JOHN 1:43–51

CHAPTER 16

PROBABILITY, PREJUDICE, AND CHRIST

When the eternal Son of God became flesh and dwelt among us (John 1:14), he crossed an infinite chasm—from the infinite to the finite, and from immortality to mortality. He left infinite moral perfection to live among moral corruption. Christ did not despise us. He came to us. He loved us. He died in our place to give us life. And he did all this when we were more alien to him than anyone has ever been alien to us.

When we feel or think or act with disdain or disrespect or avoidance or exclusion or malice toward a person simply because he or she is of another race or another ethnic group, we are, in effect, saying that Jesus acted in a foolish way toward us. You don't want to say that.

REMOVING A SUBTLE SELF-JUSTIFICATION

One of the ways we continue to fall short in diverse ethnic relationships is by using subtle self-justifications to protect the sinful prejudice in our hearts. In this chapter, I would like to describe and help remove one of those self-justifications. This is a self-justification that we all are tempted to use either consciously or subconsciously. Knowing what it is, and understanding the truth and error in it, will help us be free from its snare.

The gist of it is this: we know intuitively that we cannot live our lives without making generalizations about people and events and nature. (I will illustrate this in a moment.) But often we do not make clear distinctions between legitimate and necessary generalizations, on the one hand, and disrespectful stereotyping, on the other hand. One reason we don't make these distinctions is that it's not easy to do. Another is that not making these distinctions supports our unloving prejudices.

We can get at this issue through Nathanael's words in John 1:46— "Can anything good come out of Nazareth?" In John 1:43, Jesus calls Philip to be his disciple. In verse 45, Philip finds Nathanael and says to him, "We have found him of whom Moses in the Law and also the prophets wrote, Jesus of Nazareth, the son of Joseph." In other words, Philip has believed that Jesus is the Messiah and is eager for Nathanael to know him too. He identifies the Messiah as "Jesus of Nazareth." He identifies Jesus with a town and a group of people who live in that town.

Nazareth was a small town, no larger than two thousand people.[1] The Old Testament is clear that the Messiah would be from Bethlehem of Judea (Mic. 5:2), not from Nazareth. For whatever reason, Nathanael responds to Philip's announcement in verse 46, "Can anything good come out of Nazareth?" The answer that Nathanael expects is no. His question amounts to a foregone conclusion: nothing good can come out of Nazareth.

WHAT WAS NATHANAEL'S MISTAKE?

Nathanael is wrong. He has made a mistake. Jesus *does* come out of Nazareth, and he is good. Nathanael will have to eat his words very soon. But my question is, *What was the nature of Nathanael's mistake?* One of the reasons I am prompted to ponder this is that Jesus does not write off Nathanael as a hopeless bigot. In fact, Jesus surprises us by what he says in verse 47 when he sees Nathanael coming. He says, "Behold, an Israelite indeed, in whom there is no deceit!"

That is not a criticism. It's a commendation. Don't make it more positive than it is, however. It's not a statement that Nathanael is sinless or that what he said about the people of Nazareth is true or loving. He simply says, "Now here is someone who tells it like it is. What you see is what you get. He's not two-faced. He doesn't like the people of Nazareth. That may not be a good attitude, but at least he's not coy. He's not deceitful." Jesus knew this about Nathanael's heart before he ever met him.

But what then was the nature of Nathanael's mistake?

SINFUL PREJUDICE?

One way to describe it would be to say that it was sinful prejudice against the people of Nazareth. Perhaps he had what we call a *stereotype* of people from Nazareth. Perhaps he judged by appearances and not by truth. Jesus said, "Do not judge by appearances, but judge with right judgment" (John 7:24). We would say today: "Jesus said, *Don't judge by stereotypes.*"

In our ordinary use of language today, a *stereotype* is a generalization that is *not* built on what Jesus calls "right judgment." *Merriam-Webster* defines a *stereotype* as "a standardized mental picture that is held in common by members of a group and that represents an *oversimplified* opinion, *prejudiced* attitude, or *uncritical* judgment."[2] In other words, a *stereotype* is an unwarranted generalization. It's the kind of judgment that is unreliable to guide your life and tends to puff you up and hurt others.

Perhaps that is what Nathanael was doing—forming a judgment about Jesus based on that negative stereotype. We will come back in a moment and ask what is sinful about that.

PROBABILITY JUDGMENT?

But there is another way to describe his mistake. One might say Nathanael did what we all do every day: he made a generalization based on multiple experiences, and biblical evidences, and then formed a probability judgment based on that generalization. "My experience is that the folks of Nazareth are ordinary and even ornery, and I don't see in the Old Testament that the Messiah can come from Nazareth. Therefore, from those general observations, I think it highly improbable, if not impossible, that this Jesus is the Messiah."

LIFE DEPENDS ON GENERALIZING

Now this way of thinking—generalizing from the particulars of our experience and drawing probability judgments on that basis—is both inevitable and good. The human brain inevitably works this way. And, in fact, our life depends on it working this way.

You observe carefully that mushrooms with certain features are poisonous. So when someone offers you one like that, you turn it down.

You have never tasted or tested that individual mushroom, but you see it as belonging to the general class that in the past has been poisonous, and so you form a probability judgment that it could well be poisonous and so refuse to eat it. Your life depends on not treating this individual mushroom in isolation from your experience of others like it.

Sometimes your judgment seems totally legitimate but proves to be dead wrong. You form a generalization that the I-35 bridge over the Mississippi River in Minneapolis is safe. You have crossed it a thousand times. The state inspects it regularly. But on August 1, 2007, you make the judgment to cross in safety, and it collapses. Your probability judgment was wrong. But it was not a sinful judgment. It was well warranted.

If I pass a man with certain features and dressed a certain way in my neighborhood—at least for this season of our corporate life—I form the probability judgment that he is Somali and Muslim. I could be wrong. But that is what my brain does with the information that I have. Facial features, dress, language, gait, location—all these and more incline me to think he is part of the group of Somalis who live in my neighborhood. However, a conversation reveals he is from Ethiopia. I made a mistake.

I see a white car with red lights flashing behind me. From all my experience, I form the probability judgment that this is the police and not a criminal faking the lights to trap me. I could be wrong. But I pull over.

GENERALIZATIONS CAN BE HORRIBLY MISTAKEN

Oh, how horribly mistaken we can be. Years ago one of the doctors in our church working the emergency room at Hennepin County Medical Center told me of the most bizarre thing he had ever seen. A man was brought in from deer hunting with an arrow through his back straight through his heart and coming out his chest. One of his own hunting buddies had shot him by accident. How? He formed a probability judgment that something brown moving in the bushes must be a deer. And he was wrong. Dead wrong.

JESUS DOESN'T CONDEMN GENERALIZING

Nevertheless, we *must* think this way. Life is not really livable without interpreting specific experiences in terms of the more general experience we have had. Jesus once commended this way of thinking in a kind of backhanded way. The Pharisees came to him to test him by asking for a sign from heaven. Jesus was not happy about this because he had given them enough evidence of his identity. He knew their request was owing to their hardness of heart. So he said to them in Matthew 16:2–3:

> When it is evening, you say, "It will be fair weather, for the sky is red."
> And in the morning, "It will be stormy today, for the sky is red and threatening." You know how to interpret the appearance of the sky, but you cannot interpret the signs of the times.

In other words, you are really good at generalizing about the natural world and forming probability judgments from the way a red morning sky precedes a storm and a red evening sky precedes fair weather. You have studied the world, and you are good at this way of thinking. It works. But when it comes to seeing spiritual reality, you are blind. Jesus doesn't condemn this universal way that the human brain learns from experience and forms probability judgments.[3]

WHEN PROBABILITY JUDGMENTS BECOME SINFUL PREJUDICE

So what about Nathanael? Philip says in John 1:45, "We have found [the Messiah] . . . Jesus of Nazareth, the son of Joseph." And Nathanael answers, "Can anything good come out of Nazareth?" Is this a non-sinful, fully warranted probability judgment that proved to be wrong—like judging the I-35 bridge to be safe proved to be wrong? Or is Nathanael guilty of sinful prejudice?

I think he is guilty, because he doesn't say, "Can the Messiah come from Nazareth?" That would have been a legitimate skepticism, given all that he knows and what he knew about where the Messiah was to be born. But what he said was, "Can *anything good* come out of Nazareth?" If his heart were gracious, loving, patient, and hopeful toward the people of Nazareth, he might have been legitimately skeptical about whether the Messiah would come from Nazareth, but he would probably not have said, "Can *anything good* come out of Nazareth?"

Nathanael has moved from legitimate probability judgments to sinful prejudice. His view of these people is so negative that he sweeps all of them into the stereotype, including Jesus. His reaction is immediate. He does not seriously consider the possibility that Philip might know what he is talking about. He is temporarily blinded by his prejudice.

JUDGE HIM BY HIS GLORY, NOT HIS GROUP

Philip doesn't argue. He simply says in John 1:46, "Come and see." In other words, give this man a chance. Judge him by his glory, not his group—or, as Martin Luther King Jr. said, "by the content of his character."[4] In verse 47, Jesus sees Nathanael coming and says, "Behold, an Israelite indeed, in whom there is no deceit!" In other words, Jesus acknowledges that Nathanael is honest. He's not deceitful. What you see is what you get. So he is probably teachable.

Nathanael asks Jesus, "How do you know me?" And Jesus says, "Before Philip called you, when you were under the fig tree, I saw you." With that, the stereotype is shattered. Nathanael knows he was wrong. And he changes his mind. Verse 49: "Rabbi, you are the Son of God! You are the King of Israel!"

THE LINE BETWEEN PROBABILITY JUDGMENTS AND SINFUL PREJUDICE

Now here is my point: there is a fine line between legitimate probability judgments and sinful prejudice. It is a real line. God sees it even when we don't. And my concern in this chapter is to plead with you not to let the legitimacy of probability judgments function in your heart as a subtle self-justification for sinful prejudice.

To say what I am saying is very risky. It's risky because there will be some people who read this, and, in the hardness of their hearts, they will take my words about generalizing and probability judgments and use them as a cloak for their own prejudices. I know that.

But I take that risk because there is another group of people—most who are reading this book, I hope—who deep down know we already use this self-justification. We don't have names for it. We don't work at it. It just comes naturally, and it feels so legitimate. I am pleading with born-again people—real saints with remaining corruption in our hearts—I am pleading that you read this and say, "Yes, thank you for helping me see the subtlety of my own sin. I must put this to death."

THREE INDICATIONS OF A GOOD HEART

I draw this chapter to a close with five indications of a sinful disposition toward other groups and three indications of a good heart, as we struggle with the line between inevitable generalizations and sinful prejudice. By "good heart," I mean the heart that has received Christ, knows forgiveness, and is indwelt by the Holy Spirit, even though it is not yet perfect (Phil. 3:12–13). We have a sinful disposition when:

> We *want* a person to fit a negative generalization (accurate or inaccurate) that we have formed about a group.
>
> We assume that a statistically true negative *generalization* is true of a particular *person* in the face of individual evidence to the contrary.
>
> We treat all the members of a group as if *all* must be characterized by a negative (or positive) generalization.
>
> We speak negatively of a group based on a generalization without giving any evidence that we acknowledge and appreciate the *exceptions*.
>
> We speak disparagingly of an entire group on the basis of a negative generalization without any personal regard for *those in the group who don't fit* the generalization.[5]

The evidence for a *good heart* in relationship to others would, of course, be the renunciation of those five traits. But more positively this good heart . . .

> . . . desires to know people and treat people for who they really are as individuals, not simply as a representative of a class or a group. If this were not so, Jesus could never be recognized for who he really is. Do you desire—really desire—to know people and treat people as individuals not merely as samples of their group?
>
> . . . is willing to take risks to act against negative expectations and belittling stereotypes when dealing with a person. Paul said, "Love . . . believes all things, hopes all things" (1 Cor. 13:7). I think he meant that love strives to believe and hope for the best, not the worst.
>
> . . . is ready, like Nathanael, to repent quickly and fully, when we have made a mistake and judged someone wrongly.

GOD, HELP US

Our hearts are deceitful still. And corruption remains. We must constantly lean heavily on the gospel of the forgiveness of sins through Jesus (Col. 2:13–14). We must persistently conform our minds to Christ in the gospel (1 Cor. 2:16) and adjust our walk to be "in step with the truth of the gospel" (Gal. 2:14). We must continually "put to death . . . what is earthly" in us because we have died and our life is hidden with Christ in God (Col. 3:3, 5).

May the Lord give us absolute honesty with ourselves and with him. May he expose every remnant of sinful prejudice. May we never use the legitimacy of generalizing to cloak the sin of prejudice. May the glory of Christ shine in our lives. God, help us.

My beloved brothers, be steadfast, immovable, always abounding
in the work of the Lord, knowing that in the Lord your labor is
not in vain.

1 CORINTHIANS 15:58

CONFESSION, WARNING, PLEA

The aim of this book has been to encourage you to pursue Christ-exalting, gospel-driven racial and ethnic diversity and harmony—especially in the family of God, the church of Jesus Christ. I have tried to argue from Scripture that the blood of Christ was shed for this. It is not first a social issue, but a blood issue. The bloodline of Christ is deeper than the bloodlines of race.

I have tried to show that the gospel of Christ is more relevant for the American and global dimensions of ethnic disharmony than we can imagine. The great issue of the human race is that we are alienated from God. That is the first and deepest problem. Alienation from each other is next and is rooted in that first and deeper alienation. Only the Son of God, Jesus Christ, by his death and resurrection, can reconcile us to God. And only then can we pursue Christ-exalting, God-centered, gospel-driven diversity and harmony.

Our failures to love each other are rooted in our sin against God. When we are reconciled to God by the gospel of Christ, a new supernatural power enters our life, our family, our churches, and the world. This is the power of Jesus Christ alive within his people. The failings of the human heart that Jesus changes by the power of his gospel are the root causes of racial and ethnic disharmony—guilt, pride, hopelessness, paralyzing feelings of inferiority, greed, hate, fear, and apathy. Only one power in the world can conquer these and the supernatural influence of Satan, which is constantly at work in the world to escalate them to genocidal proportions—the power of the gospel.

I conclude by confessing sin, warning against chronological smugness, and pleading for persevering sacrifice.

CONFESSION

There is no point in trying to hide the fact that the Bible has been used by Americans to justify both race-based, demeaning slavery and its abolition. Mark Noll's book *God and Race in American Politics: A Short History* clarifies this painful confession.[1] With an eye for concrete (incarnational) stories and meticulous historical detail, Noll is above all a seer of the *both-and*. Or call it *paradox*. Or *historical conundrum*. There are no simple explanations.

The thesis of Noll's book is: "Together, race and religion make up, not only the nation's deepest and most enduring moral problem, but also its broadest and most enduring political influence."[2] That is provocative enough. But his working out of how race and religion are interwoven is where the puzzles come. For example, "Before the Civil War, religion drove abolitionist assaults upon slavery even as it under-girded influential defenses of slavery in both the North and the South."[3] Agonizingly *both-and*, not comfortably *either-or*.

> The Christian faith that has been so prominent in so many ways throughout American history has, again on balance, been a benefi-cent force at home and abroad. Christian altruism, Christian philan-thropy, Christian consolation, and Christian responsibility are not the only forces for good in American history, but they loom very large and have had very positive effects.
>
> And yet . . . and yet. . . . The American political system and the American practice of Christianity which has provided so much good for so many people for so many years, has never been able to over-come race.[4]

It is fitting that we frankly confess that Christians—we Christians—have often used our Bible to justify sinful attitudes and actions. We have done it in our personal lives, and we have done it in the larger structural dimensions of life.

If it were not for the gospel of Christ, we would—and we should—despair. What Noll points out is that this very gospel—this cross-centered view of history—contains an explanation of how the gospel itself can be so badly misused. Here is his summary, which penetrates to the bottom of the *both-and* nature of the God-loved, God-cursed world we live in:

To explain the simultaneous manifestation of superlative good and pervasive malevolence in the history of race and religion, neither simple trust in human nature nor simple cynicism about American hypocrisy is adequate . . . . [Something else must explain the pervasive commingling of opposites.]

That commingling has included domination with liberation, false consciousness with genuine idealism, altruism with greed, self-seeking with self-sacrifice, economic independence with economic exploitation, tribalism with universalism, hatred with love. Any final explanation for the conundrums of American history must be able to account for a mind-stretching conjunction of opposites.

It must evoke both the goodness of the human creation and the persistence of evil in all branches of humanity. . . . It must show how the best human creatures are sabotaged by their own hubris and the worst human depredations are enlightened by unexpected shafts of light. . . . It must be able to hold these contradictions, antinomies, and paradoxes in one cohesive vision.[5]

Is there such a vision? Noll believes there is. He calls it "historic Christian faith."

From the much used and much abused Scriptures, a long line of Christian readers have affirmed in varying accents and diverse emphases a transcendent account of profound complexity to take the measure of human nature and human achievement. . . .

God made humans, and the creation was good—yet at the same time, humankind is fallen and will never escape the effects of sin. Further, God offers in the work of his Son, Jesus Christ, and in the power of the Holy Spirit, the transforming prospect of redemption— yet redemption never equals perfection; the redeemed must always recognize their own shortcomings and be filled with gratitude for all the gifts of creation, including all other human creatures.

Ultimately, because the manifestation of God in Jesus Christ is, at the same time, so thoroughly human and so thoroughly divine, so completely infinite and so completely finite, the heart of the Christian faith offers the hint of an explanation for how the commingling of contradictions, antinomies, and paradoxes can occur in other spheres of life.[6]

Paradoxically, the very paradoxes of good and evil in history—and in imperfect Christian hearts—bear witness to the Christian vision as the best explanation of why things are the way they are. In the end, the true historian becomes an apologist.

The gospel is the power of God to save. But that power is working progressively—not with instantaneous perfection—in the lives of those who believe it, and therefore in the church and in the world. There is remaining sin in all of us and in all of our institutions. This is our confession. It humbles us and breaks our hearts, but because of Christ, it does not paralyze us in the pursuit of racial harmony.

WARNING

In this humility, every ethnic group should be warned against speaking with moral smugness about the sins of others, especially other generations. We are all prone to self-righteousness because of how clearly we see the sins of others, especially that of other generations. This weakness is a species of what C. S. Lewis calls "chronological snobbery."[7] In chronological smugness, we think we have progressed out of sins into greater righteousness, when in fact we are probably as soft on our own sins as the previous generation was on theirs.

We saw earlier how Shelby Steele illustrates this by comparing the typical sins of the 1950s with those of the 1990s and how each would have roundly condemned the sinfulness of the other while glossing over its own. What would have gotten Eisenhower impeached was glossed over by supporters of Bill Clinton, and what would have ended the presidency of Clinton was winked at in the 1950s. How many people today are indignant over the racism of the fifties but adapt easily to the sexual promiscuity of our day!

Here is the way Steele describes the dangers of our chronological smugness. He is reflecting on the Clinton-Lewinsky scandal compared to Dwight Eisenhower's reputed use of the n-word.

> I wondered if President Clinton would be defended with relativism if he had done what, according to gossip, Eisenhower was said to have done. Suppose that in a light moment he had slipped into a parody of an old Arkansas buddy from childhood and, to get the voice right, used the word "nigger" a few times. Suppose further that a tape of this came to light so that all day long in the media—from the unctuous morning shows to the freewheeling late-night shows to

the news every half hour on radio—we would hear the unmistakable presidential voice saying, "Take your average nigger. . . ."

Today in America there is no moral relativism around racism, no sophisticated public sentiment that recasts racism a mere quirk of character. Today America is puritanical rather than relativistic around racism, and if Clinton had been caught in this way, it is very likely that nothing would have saved him. . . .

The point is that President Clinton survived what would certainly have destroyed President Eisenhower, and Eisenhower could easily have survived what would almost certainly have destroyed Clinton. Each man, finally, was no more than indiscreet within the moral landscape of his era (again, Eisenhower's indiscretion is hypothetical here for purposes of discussion).

Neither racism in the fifties nor womanizing in the nineties was a profound enough sin to undermine completely the moral authority of a president. So it was the good luck of each president to sin into the moral relativism of his era rather than into its Puritanism. And, interestingly, the moral relativism of one era was the Puritanism of the other. Race simply replaced sex as the primary focus of America's moral seriousness.[8]

This is a sobering warning for all of us, lest we mount our self-righteous soapbox and condemn the sins of one generation while glossing the sins of our own. May God open our eyes to the implications of the gospel in our own day so that we can identify our own sins as well as the sins of others. Because of Christ, we need not fear that such honesty will paralyze us. It will in fact set us free.

PLEA

No lesson in the pursuit of racial and ethnic diversity and harmony has been more forceful than the lesson that it is easy to get so wounded and so tired that you decide to quit. This is true of every race and every ethnicity in whatever struggle they face. The most hopeless temptation is to give up—to say that there are other important things to work on (which is true), and I will let someone else worry about racial issues.

The main reason for the temptation to quit pursuing is that whatever strategy you try, you will be criticized by somebody. You didn't say the right thing, or you didn't say it in the right way, or you should have said it a long time ago, or you shouldn't say anything but get off your backside and *do* something, or, or, or. Just when you think you have made your best effort to do something healing, someone will point out the flaw in it. And when you try to talk about doing better, there are few things more maddening than to be told, "You just don't get it." Oh, how our back gets up, and we feel the power of self-pity rising in our hearts and want to say, "Okay, I've tried. I've done my best. See you later." And there ends our foray into racial harmony.

My plea is: never quit. Change. Step back. Get another strategy. Start over. But never quit. Langston Hughes, one of the twentieth century's most notable African American poets, expressed the cry for not giving up like this (titled "Mother to Son"):

> Well, son, I'll tell you:
> Life for me ain't been no crystal stair.
> It's had tacks in it,
> And splinters,
> And boards torn up,
> And places with no carpet on the floor—
> Bare.
> But all the time
> I'se been a-climbin' on,
> And reachin' landin's,
> And turnin' corners,
> And sometimes goin' in the dark
> Where there ain't been no light.
> So boy, don't you turn back.
> Don't you set down on the steps
> 'Cause you finds it's kinder hard.
> Don't you fall now—
> For I'se still goin', honey,
> I'se still climbin',
> And life for me ain't been no crystal stair.

To white or black—or any other race or ethnicity—that is my plea. I'm not saying you have to make it the number-one emphasis of your life. Some are called to that. Not all. But I am saying to make it *an* emphasis of your life. Again Shelby Steele, in his stirring book *The Content of Our Character*, issues the call in words that I find very moving.

What both black and white Americans fear are the sacrifices and risks that true racial harmony demands. This fear is the measure of our racial chasm. And though fear always seeks a thousand justifications, none is ever good enough, and the problems we run from only remain to haunt us. It would be right to suggest courage as an antidote to fear, but the glory of the word might only intimidate us into more fear. I prefer the word effort—relentless effort, moral effort. What I like most about this word are its connotations of everydayness, earnestness, and practical sacrifice.[9]

Amen. Earnest, practical, everyday effort. What I have tried to do in this book is show that the gospel of Jesus Christ—the death and the resurrection of the Son of God for sinners—is the only sufficient power for this effort, and the only power that in the end will bring the bloodlines of race into the single bloodline of the cross. It is the only power to bring about Christ-exalting harmony, which, in the end, is the only kind that matters, because all things were made through him and *for him* (Col. 1:16). To his grace, and his name, and his Father be glory forever. Amen.

IS THERE SUCH A THING AS RACE?

A WORD ABOUT TERMINOLOGY

And he made from one man every nation of mankind to live on all the face of the earth.

ACTS 17:26

It is a healthy sign to wish that the term *race* did not exist. It has not served well to enhance human relations. In general, the term *race* has been used to signify "a biological concept referring to the taxonomic (classificatory) unit immediately below the species."[1] We may not be able to communicate in our day without the term, but we can at least try to show why it is a fuzzy term that is minimally helpful and has often been hijacked by ideology for racist purposes.[2]

DOES RACIAL CLASSIFICATION HELP US RELATE TO EACH OTHER?

When you stand before a man who is manifestly different from you in skin color, hair type, and facial features, and you want to respectfully and intelligently take his significant differences into account in your interaction, it is generally more helpful to know that he is a Korean-American-third-generation-born-in-Philadelphia than to know that he belongs to the Asian race. Or if you are an African American standing before a "white" man whom you would like to interact with in an intelligent and respectful way, it will probably be more relevant to know that he is a Danish-international-student-studying-urban-trends than to know that he belongs to the Caucasian race.

This is true, unless, of course, you already have a controlling negative stereotype of people in these "races." If that stereotype is going to govern your relationship before you know more significant things about the person, then, of course, race classification is (regrettably) important to you up front. That is what I meant by ideology hijacking the concept of race for racist purposes.

But where racial stereotypes are not controlling, and someone really wants to encounter another person as an individual, while not being insensitive and disrespectful about relevant differences, the concept of *ethnicity* is more useful in human relationships than the concept of race. That is what the two relationships mentioned above were illustrating.

Ethnicity is bigger than race. Eloise Meneses defines it like this: "The term *ethnicity* is usually used to stress the cultural rather than the physical aspects of group identity. Ethnic groups share language, dress, food, customs, values, and sometimes religion."[3] Others also include physical traits as part of ethnicity, provided they are only part of the culturally relevant spectrum of a person's identity.[4]

WHY THE TERM *ETHNICITY* IS BETTER THAN *RACE*

There are numerous reasons why the term *ethnicity* is more helpful and less destructive than the term *race* in marking human identity. Here are some of them.

There Are No Clear Boundary Lines

First, the term *race* is imprecise and has very blurry edges. In other words, the dividing lines between the races are not discernible. Or another way to say it would be that there are so many variations of physical features in humankind that they defy any clear biological classification.

> Essentially all anthropologists have given up the attempt to identify races of human beings. This is very simply because the best evidence indicates that there are, physically, *no clear boundary lines* between the various communities of people around the world. Nearly all of the traits that distinguish human beings from one another are found in all communities, though in varying degrees.[5]

All Races Are Mixed Races

Second, the very fact that we have to talk about "mixed races" to make sense out of racial classifications shows the inadequacy of the classifications themselves. The possibilities of mixture are endless. There are countless degrees of racial traits that can be mixed in any given marriage. This means that there are no *pure* "races." There are only degrees of mixture, as the next point makes clear.[6]

We Are All Related in Adam

Third, we are all biologically related to one another and descended from one common ancestor. Once there was only Adam and Eve. As the apostle Paul said, "[God] made from one man every nation of mankind to live on all the face of the earth" (Acts 17:26).

The Historical Traits Used in Classifying Races Are Arbitrary

Fourth, other physical traits besides the usual more obvious ones (color, hair, facial features) produce different groupings than the traditional ones do. Colin Kidd shows that classifying humans according to fingerprints, type of earwax, body hair, possession of the lactase enzyme, blood groupings, sickle-cell gene mutation, stature, and body size produce different groupings that do not correspond to the groupings we usually come up with when we classify people by skin color.[7]

What this means is that the traits historically used in classifying races have been arbitrarily limited. This raises the question of whether the concept was emerging hand in hand with predispositions of preference for certain manifest features over others.

Physical Traits Are Comparatively Superficial

Fifth, the traits that traditionally define race groups are superficial when compared to the immeasurable value of the image of God in each person (Gen. 1:26–27) and when compared to the combination of physical, emotional, intellectual, spiritual, and relational aspects that give us the richness of our personal identity. "The biologist finds those observable racial differences which seem so obvious to the layperson to be superficial and misleading."[8]

Science Serves "the Superior"

Sixth, historically, the emergence of the anthropology of races in the modern world has gone hand in hand with assumptions of inferiority and superiority. Thus the science was bent from the beginning to serve "the superior." For example:

> The leading racial theorist of late eighteenth-century Europe was the Göttingen anatomist Johann Friedrich Blumenbach (1752–1840), who began his career by subscribing to a four-part division of humanity. . . . However, by the third edition of his canonical work of racial classification, *De generis humani varietate*, he had divided mankind into five basic racial types: Caucasian, Mongolian, Ethiopian, Malay and American.[9]

This in itself does not sound prejudicial. But the problem is that Blumenbach assumed a ranking of superior and inferior in the human classifications he proposed:

> The Caucasian, Blumenbach argued, had been the original racial form of mankind, of which the four later types were degenerations. The Ethiopian and the Mongolian stood at the two extremes of degeneration, with Malays intermediate between Caucasians and Ethiopians, and Americans, similarly, a point of racial degeneracy midway between the white Caucasian norm and the extreme of Mongolian degeneration.[10]

This historical use of the concept of race in the service of preferential description should give us pause and make us careful in the way we think and speak about race.

The Category of Race Is Not Found in the Bible

Seventh, the category of *race*, as a way of classifying humans according to physical features, is not found in the Bible.[11] The term never occurs in the King James Version in reference to people groups, but only to athletic races. Of the four places where it occurs in reference to people in the English Standard Version, it is referring to the elect people, either Jews or the church. The biblical way of talking about people groups leans heavily in the ethnicity direction, not the racial direction.

In the last day when the global mission of Christ is finished, there will be redeemed people "from every tribe and language and people and nation" (Rev. 5:9). These are not races. And none of them aligns with our usual concept of race. Nor is there any place in the Bible where people are grouped the way we often do.[12] So the Bible gives us little encouragement to make much of racial distinctions in the way we think about human beings.

Ethnicity Is More Helpful

Eighth, it follows from these points, especially point seven, that physical traits that we usually think of in defining race are biblically marginal, biologically ambiguous, superficial in relation to personhood, and not as helpful as the concept of ethnicity in helping us relate to each other with respect and understanding about the more significant differences that we bring to our relationships.

HOW I USE THE TERMS

So how then should you understand the terms *race/racial* and *ethnicity/ethnic* in this book? First, I have not tried to abandon the terms *race* and *racial*. As loaded as the terms are, they are too embedded in our language and in the thousands of books and articles and sermons and lectures and conversations that make up the world we must relate to. There is no escaping that historically, and in the present day, the problems we face are conceived along racial lines understood as color lines.

For example, in 1899 W. E. B. Du Bois delivered a speech to the First Pan-African Conference at Westminster Hall, London, and began like this:

> The problem of the twentieth century is the problem of the color line, the question as to how far differences of race—which show themselves chiefly in the color of the skin and the texture of the hair—will hereafter be made the basis of denying to over half the world the right of sharing to their utmost ability the opportunities and privileges of modern civilization.[13]

I will not begrudge Du Bois the use of *race* in this sense. This is history. And it is still the way the race issue is powerfully formulated today. So

I have used the terms *race* and *ethnicity* in ways that they have enough overlap with historical and contemporary usage to be understood. But I hope that the reader keeps in mind what I have written here.

Unless I explicitly differentiate *race* and *racial* from *ethnicity* and *ethnic*, I would like you to think of both when I mention either—that is, *ethnicity* with a physical component and *race* with a cultural component. Very often I have used the terms together to draw out this combination of ideas.

RACISM VALUES ONE RACE OVER ANOTHER

With regard to the term *racism*, it is possible to get oneself tied in so many knots that it feels hopeless to define. Several years ago, we spent months as a pastoral staff at our church trying to come up with a working definition. I never thought defining a word could be so difficult. But in this book I have simply cut the knot with a decision to work with someone else's definition.

As mentioned earlier, in the summer of 2004 the Presbyterian Church in America settled on the following definition, which I find helpful: "Racism is an explicit or implicit belief or practice that qualitatively distinguishes or values one race over other races."[14] Here I do make a distinction between *race* and *ethnicity*. If, as we have defined it, ethnicity includes beliefs and attitudes and behaviors, we are biblically and morally bound to value some aspects of some ethnicities over others. There are aspects of every culture, including our own, that are sinful and in need of transformation.

But *race* in the narrow sense, defined by physical traits, with all of its ambiguities and inadequacies, is still a perceived and powerful reality that must be dealt with. Hence I think this definition is helpful: "Racism is an explicit or implicit belief or practice that qualitatively distinguishes or values one race over other races."

The focus of this definition is on the heart and behavior of the racist. The *heart* that believes one race is more valuable than another is a sinful heart. And that sin is called *racism*. The *behavior* that distinguishes one race as more valuable than another is a sinful behavior. And that sin is called *racism*. This personal focus on the term *racism* does not exclude the expression of this sin in structural ways, for example, laws and policies that demean or exclude on the basis of race. (See chapter 5 where I wrestle with the issue of structural racism.)

ALL IN THE SERVICE OF THE GOSPEL

I hope this reflection on the terms *race, ethnicity,* and *racism* serves to make more clear and understandable and helpful the really crucial chapters in this book concerning the way the gospel of Christ provides the impulse and power for racial and ethnic diversity and harmony among the followers of Jesus.

THE SOVEREIGNTY OF GOD AND THE SOUL DYNAMIC

GOD-CENTERED THEOLOGY AND THE BLACK EXPERIENCE IN AMERICA

A MESSAGE DELIVERED ON FEBRUARY 4, 2002 AT THE DESIRING GOD CONFERENCE FOR PASTORS MINNEAPOLIS, MINNESOTA

I include here this message, with a few minor changes, in the form I gave it in 2002. You will see that both the message and the conference theme were inspired in large measure by Carl Ellis's book Free at Last: The Gospel in the African-American Experience. *In the subsequent years, I have some encouragement to believe that the dream it expresses is becoming a reality. There are a few repetitions in detail between this message and my story in the Introduction, but it seemed best to leave them than to restructure the message.*

My task tonight is to answer the question *Why this theme—The Sovereignty of God and the Soul Dynamic: God-centered Theology and the Black Experience in America, Past and Future?* And, if God would give me the grace to do it, my aim is to light a fire in you that would forge a link between the sovereignty of God and God-centered theology, on the one hand, and the soul dynamic and black experience in America, on the other hand. There is, I believe, an explosively powerful coming together of these that I want to advance and be a part of.

CAN THIS LINK BE FORGED?

I take the term *soul dynamic* from Carl Ellis's book *Free at Last: The Gospel in the African-American Experience*. He defines it like this:

> Soul Dynamic [refers to] the core of the African-American culture that developed in the context of White oppression and Black resistance to oppression. This dynamic is a combination of two main components: A theological dynamic—an oral tradition that emerged from historic African-American church experience. It captures nuggets of biblical truth in forceful, effective phrases and mental images out of life experience. A cultural dynamic—deeply moving expressions of African-American consciousness that emerged from the very roots of their humanity and experience, from levels where the image of God cannot be suppressed. Because these expressions are aligned with the power of God's Word, they have the power to deeply affect others who encounter them.[1]

Can a link be forged between such a rich and deep and living reality and the seemingly cerebral conceptuality of Reformed theology? The very terms seem in tension from the outset. The metals out of which I dream of forging such a link seem to be so different that they could never be welded together. The term *soul dynamic* points to a personal energy and life and deeply felt suffering and human kinship—unshakable soul-conviction—while the term *sovereignty of God*, in contrast, points to a divine, objective power outside ourselves imposing itself down from above, not up from within.

The term *black experience in America* points to the weight of history and tradition and suffering and passion and people and culture and warmth, but the term *God-centered theology*, in contrast, points to the burden of rationality and reflection and concepts and ideas. So from the outset, the prospect of forging a link between the sovereignty of God and God-centered theology, on the one hand, and the soul dynamic and black experience in America, on the other hand, looks dim.

> [A clarifying note to prevent misunderstanding: After I gave this message in 2002, one of the brothers asked me, "Were you saying that the whites bring the brains and the blacks bring the emotions?" My answer to him was: no, the point was that the Reformed tradition (mainly white) brings a long effort to *systematize* the sovereignty of

God. The black tradition brings a long experience of *suffering* without abandoning the sovereignty of God. It is the suffering with God, and without turning against God, that created a soul dynamic that may cohere with Reformed tradition and enrich it.]

THE LENS OF CHRISTIAN HEDONISM MAY MAKE THE WELDING POSSIBLE

Though the prospect looks dim, there is a very powerful reason why I dream in this direction and why I have strong hope that such a link is not only possible but, in fact, natural and crucial. And the reason is this: the vision of God's sovereignty and God-centered theology that drives the Desiring God Conference for Pastors, and hundreds of the pastors who come here, is not what many people—white or black—have in mind when they think of God-centeredness or the sovereignty of God, or Calvinism, or Reformed theology. There is a difference—a very significant difference that I think virtually demands a link between the soul dynamic and the black experience and the sovereignty of God and God-centered theology.

And here's the difference: we see the Reformed tradition—with its massive vision of the glory of God—through the lens of *Christian hedonism*; that is, we see it through the filter that *God is most glorified in us when we are most satisfied in him*. We see it through the almost overwhelming experience of suffering and sin in this world—an experience, however, that does not drive us *away* from God but *toward* God, who says to all our enemies (including ourselves), "You meant it for evil, but I meant it for good" (Gen. 50:20).

We see the sovereignty of God through the humanly impossible experience of the apostle Paul, whose wounds made him say, "[We are] sorrowful, yet always rejoicing" (2 Cor. 6:10). Is there any biblical phrase better suited to express the essence of the soul dynamic, or the taste of the triumphant spirit of black history in America, than "sorrowful yet always rejoicing"? And we see the sovereignty of God through the cross of Jesus, where God's love stoops down to give us all that we can know and enjoy of God at the infinite cost of God's own human life.

Now this is different from what most people feel when they hear the term *Calvinism*. But this is who we are, and what a whole stream of Christian history is. And this is what, I believe—what I pray—will forge a link between the sovereignty of God and the soul dynamic, God-centered theology and the black experience. These are ways of looking at the sovereignty of God and the centrality of God and the supremacy of God and the so-called Reformed tradition and Calvinism that transpose the key of the music of God's sovereignty into something that begins to sound like a Negro spiritual, or a freedom song, or a dirge from the Underground Railroad, or a lullaby for the babies after Daddy's lynching, or the misery and joy of the Delta Blues.[2]

MY DREAM

Therefore, I am not willing for the greatness of God and the supremacy of God and the centrality of God and "the preeminence of the glory of God" (which is the essence of the Reformed tradition[3]) to be hijacked by a white, Western, over-rationalized, cool tradition that alienates the black experience that has drunk so deeply at the wells of suffering and scorn. These great realities are not meant to be like planks in a party platform, or like the colors of competing teams, or like hostile signals between warring gangs. They are meant to be like the air we breathe and the earth we stand on and the galaxies we stare into.

So here's my thesis:

> Even though there are thousands of whites and thousands of blacks who stumble over the theological systems of dead white men from Geneva and Northampton and Princeton, and even though there are whites and blacks who ridicule the God-rooted soul dynamic of the black experience in America, nevertheless there is an untried vision to see the mountain streams of God's supremacy and sovereignty and centrality and glory, flowing from the Reformed tradition, on one side, together with the soul dynamic, flowing from the black experience in America, on the other side, to make a river—a single river—that runs deep with life and hope and joy through the valley of pain and death—a river of love that causes all who drink, not to make much of themselves, and not even to make much of others, but to lay down their lives to help others enjoy making much of our God, Jesus Christ. That's what I am pursuing.

THE HISTORY OF LIVING IN, AND MOVING OUT, OF RACISM

Now let me back up and give you some history and move toward a biblical foundation and explanation. I begin with some of the roots of my concern. I grew up in Greenville, South Carolina, and was manifestly racist in my assumptions and attitudes and actions as a child and a teenager. That is, I assumed the superiority of my race in almost every way without knowing or wanting to know anybody who was black, except Lucy, who came over on Saturdays to help my mother clean. I liked Lucy, but the whole structure of the relationship was demeaning. My attitude was not mainly my parents' fault. In fact, in some ways, it was in spite of my parents that I was guilty of racism. It was the air we breathed in Greenville, South Carolina.

In 1963, my home church voted not to allow blacks into the services. As I recall, my mother (who happened to grow up in Pennsylvania) was the lone voice on that Wednesday night to vote no on this motion. That December my sister was married in the church, and my mother invited Lucy's whole family to come. And they came. And when the ushers balked, my mother herself took them by the arm and seated them on the main floor of the sanctuary. So the seeds were sown in my conscience—as I watched that drama—that my attitudes were an offense to my mother and to her God.

I went to school in Illinois and then in Pasadena, California, and then in Germany; and I have lived in the Twin Cities since 1974. It has been a long journey, and my burdens today are 180 degrees from what they were in the early sixties growing up across town from Jesse Jackson, whose mother listened to the same Christian radio station my mother did but couldn't go to the local Christian college, which forbade blacks.

Several years ago our church here in Minneapolis wrote six fresh initiatives that still function to guide us. One of them read, "Against the rising spirit of indifference, alienation and hostility in our land, we will embrace the supremacy of God's love to take new steps personally and corporately toward racial reconciliation, expressed visibly in our community and in our church." That has had a very significant effect on us. We have a long way to go. But we have not let go of the vision.

Six years ago [as of 2002], as a part of a larger movement of transracial adoption and pro-life commitment, Noël and I, at age 50, adopted Talitha Ruth, who is ethnically African American. This was a huge thing for me to do, not only because I was fifty and would basically be starting my parenting life all over again, after the four boys were almost grown, but also because I had Southern relatives who looked on this with incredulity at best. And, of course, it was huge because the personal and cultural identity for Talitha and us will be critical no matter what we do to prepare for it.

READING *FREE AT LAST*

Then came the summer of 2001 on a porch in Asheville, North Carolina, while I was reading Carl Ellis's book, first published under the title *Beyond Liberation*, and now expanded and reissued as *Free at Last: The Gospel in the African-American Experience*. It was like one of those little magnets which, as you lower it slowly onto a table where there are thousands of tiny metal filings, the filings begin to turn and vibrate and orient in the same direction; and then you touch the table where they are and all of them come together and cling to that little magnet and dangle from it if you lift it up.

I felt, in reading this book about the soul dynamic and the black experience in America, that everything I had ever seen and savored of the sovereignty of God and the centrality of God and the supremacy of God was a preparation for being a part of this reality—that is, a God-centered, Christ-exalting, Bible-saturated rebuilding of black and white evangelical culture not primarily around color but around the triumphant, sovereign glory of the all-knowing, all-governing, crucified, suffering, and living Christ.

THE WHITE SECULARIZATION OF BLACK THEOLOGY

There are sentences in this book—so many of them I could not tell you—that made me feel like Ellis's vision for the rebuilding of a God-centered black culture was profoundly relevant for the rebuilding of a God-centered white American evangelicalism. For example, a sentence like this: "White historians had sold us a bill of goods by leaving Black folks out; Black secularists sold us a bill of goods by leaving God out."[4]

The reason that sentence cuts deeply both ways is not mainly that it criticizes white historians as bad historians, or black secularists as bad theologians, but mainly because it makes us focus on that particular weakness of the black community, which it had taken over straight from the dominant white culture, namely, secular humanism, in contradiction to the deeper, more authentic, God-soaked roots of the black culture in America—and, I would add, also in contradiction to the deeper, more authentic, God-soaked roots of the white evangelical culture in America.

And, oh, yes, I know that those white, Reformed, Puritan roots are contaminated with the poison of racist slavery; and I know that the deeper roots of black culture are contaminated by African paganism. But if we are willing to cut each other some slack here and see the working of God's providence in and through the imperfections of our histories, then the ax of Carl Ellis falls not only against the modern black tree of godlessness, but also against the modern white tree of godlessness.

BLACK IS BEAUTIFUL—BUT NOT AS A GOD

The trumpet that Carl Ellis is sounding in this book for the rebuilding of a God-centered African American culture is really, at root, the call for something even bigger and deeper—namely, the rebuilding of a God-centered Christianity, not "Christianity-ism,"[5] but authentic, God-centered, Christ-exalting, Bible-saturated Christianity out of white and black and every other color.

You feel the two-edged sword of Carl Ellis again in sentences like this (keep in mind, I am still on the porch in Asheville, North Carolina, in the summer of 2001 experiencing what brought this message into being):

> Black is truly beautiful, but it is not beautiful as a god. As a god it is too small. Afrocentrism is truly magnificent, but it is not magnificent as an absolute. As an absolute, it will infect us with the kind of bigotry we've struggled against in others for centuries. . . . Whenever we seek to understand our situation without [the] transcendent reference point [of the Word of God] we fail to find the answer to our crisis. The white

man's religion has failed us [namely, Christianity-ism]. The Arab ethnic religion has failed us and will fail us again.[6]

Yes, the trumpet is sounding to the black community in these words: We need a bigger vision than "black is beautiful." We need a bigger vision than "Afrocentrism." We need a transcendent reference point! We need the supremacy of God! The centrality of God! The Word of God!

What did I hear in this critique? There I was a white man, reading Ellis on a porch in July in Asheville and finding everything in me *not* crying, "Amen," about the *black* community, but about the so-called *white* church—my own puny-god, market-driven, materialistic, middle-class, comfort-seeking, truth-compromising, wishy-washy, white, evangelical, American church. And I had to ask there on that porch: Does not the burning of my heart beckon me to call Carl Ellis on the phone and say, would you come help me create a conference where God just might make it plain that what the black community needs *and* what the white community needs is a transcendent reference point in the sovereignty of God and the supremacy of God and the centrality of God in all things? So I called him, and he was willing to come. [That is how the conference in February 2002 came to be.]

BIBLICAL FUEL FOR THE LINK-FORGING FURNACE

Now let me take a few minutes to put some biblical foundations underneath what I mean by God-centeredness and God's supremacy, and add biblical fuel to the furnace that I pray will forge the link between the great realities of God-centeredness and God's supremacy, on the one hand, and the soul dynamic and the black experience, on the other hand, for the sake of rebuilding white and black Christian communities interlocked by the transcendent reference point of God's God-centered Word.

Here is where I am going: I want to exult with you in the God-centeredness of God—first, in his providence over all history; second, in the love of God for his people; third, in the suffering and death of Jesus Christ on the cross; and fourth, in our suffering and death with Jesus in this world of sin and pain. And at every point where I stress the radical God-centeredness of God, I want to show that this is the best news in all the world. This is what we were made for. This is our hope and salvation and everlasting joy—together.

1) THE GOD-CENTEREDNESS OF GOD IN HIS PROVIDENCE OVER ALL HISTORY

All of God's providence over history starts with creation, and we learn what that providential rule is about from what creation is about. Isaiah 43:6–7 tells us, "I will say to the north, Give up, and to the south, Do not withhold; bring my sons from afar and my daughters from the end of the earth, everyone who is called by my name, whom I *created for my glory.*" God created the world to display his glory. God's work in creation was about making God the center of creation.

Now we could do some logic here and say, *therefore*, it must be that God governs the world for the same reason. But let's not do the logic; let's just read the answer in the Bible. For what purpose does God rule the world he has made? Paul tells us in one of the most sweeping statements in the Bible about the God-centeredness of God. Ephesians 1:11–12: "[He] works all things according to the counsel of his will, so that we who were the first to hope in Christ might *be to the praise of his glory.*" Why does he work all things according to his will? So that his glory will be praised. He is absolutely God-centered in his providence.

This is good news if you are a God-centered person and love God's commitment to make himself the central reality in the universe where he will be enjoyed forever and ever with ever-increasing joy. But it is disappointing news to man-centered white and black communities that are controlled by the god of white supremacy or the god of the beauty of blackness. God does not rule the world to make us central—not as white, not as black, not as brown, and not as human beings, period. We are not absolute. We are not ultimate. *He* is absolute, and *he* is ultimate. He is central. Has been. Is now. Always will be.

Ellis at His Philosophical Best

If this sounds white to you, then play it on your own instrument. Here is Carl Ellis playing what may sound like white, Reformed God-centeredness (maybe even Van Tillian presuppositionalism), only he is playing it on his black instrument. Listen to him preaching!

[God's] existence is the most obvious and fundamental thing in human experience. There can be no *is* without God's *is*: and since *is* is, God is, because God is *is*. . . . The only way anyone can declare that God "ain't" is to declare that *is* ain't. And if *is* ain't, there never was a "God ain't" declaration in the first place. Without God even the atheist could not say "God ain't." He would not exist to say it.[7]

My black brothers, I beg of you, don't be hoodwinked into thinking that the supremacy of God in all things is a white man's vision. It is God's vision. And it must be played on both our instruments. As Carl Ellis explains in his twelfth chapter, it must be played by the black jazz preacher, and it must be played by the white classical preacher.[8] And, I would add, these preachers better learn from each other, because there are more white people longing for the soul of jazz preaching and more black people longing for the substance of classical preaching than we ever dreamed.

The point is this: in God's providence over all history, man is not at the top; man is not at the bottom; man is not at the center—God is. And he means to be. And I dream of standing on that granite foundation with you together.

2) THE GOD-CENTEREDNESS OF GOD IN THE LOVE OF GOD FOR HIS PEOPLE

Sometimes people who are saturated with the centrality of man—whether their own selves (which Ellis calls "me-ism") or their own kind (ethnocentrism)—do not feel that God's God-centeredness is a loving thing. How can God be loving if he does everything to display his own glory?

Well, what I have come to see is that God's commitment to the exaltation of his own glory is the essence of his love. Here is one place to see it—John 11:1–6:

> Now a certain man was ill, Lazarus of Bethany, the village of Mary and her sister Martha. It was Mary who anointed the Lord with ointment and wiped his feet with her hair, whose brother Lazarus was ill. So the sisters sent to him, saying, "Lord, he *whom you love* is ill." But when Jesus heard it he said, "This illness does not lead to death. It is *for the glory of God, so that the Son of God may be glorified* through it." Now *Jesus loved Martha and her sister and Lazarus. So,* when

he heard that Lazarus was ill, he stayed two days longer in the place where he was.

Notice three amazing things:

1) Jesus chose to let Lazarus die. Verse 6: "When he heard that Lazarus was ill, he stayed two days longer in the place where he was." There was no hurry. His intention was not to spare the family grief but to raise Lazarus from the dead.
2) He was motivated by a passion for the glory of God displayed in his own glorious power. Verse 4: "This illness does not lead to death. It is for the glory of God, so that the Son of God may be glorified through it."
3) Nevertheless, both the decision to let Lazarus die and the motivation to magnify God were expressions of *love* for Mary and Martha and Lazarus. Verse 5: "Now Jesus loved Martha and her sister and Lazarus . . . *so* . . . he stayed . . . where he was."

Oh, how many people today—even Christians—would murmur at Jesus for callously letting Lazarus die and putting him and Mary and Martha and others through the pain and misery of those days. And if they saw that this was motivated by Jesus's desire to magnify the glory of God, many would call this harsh or unloving. What this shows is how far above the glory of God most people value pain-free lives. For most people, love is whatever puts human value and human well-being at the center. So Jesus's behavior is unintelligible to them.

But let us not tell Jesus what love is. Let us not instruct him how he should love us and make us central. Let us learn from Jesus what love is and what our true well-being is. Love is doing whatever you need to do to help people see and savor the glory of God forever and ever. Love keeps God central. Because the soul was made for God.

NOT BLACK, NOT WHITE, NOT US, BUT GOD

We were not made to make much of blackness. We were not made to make much of whiteness. We were not made to make much of self or humanity in general. We were made to make much of God. And when God pursues this, he pursues what is best for us—what will satisfy us forever. And therefore God's self-exaltation is the essence of his love. He loves us not ultimately by making much of us but by freeing us from the bondage of self to enjoy making much of him forever.[9]

Jesus confirms that we are on the right track here by praying in John 17:24, "Father, I desire that they also, whom You have given Me, be with Me where I am, *so that they may see My glory* which You have given Me, for You loved Me before the foundation of the world" (NASB). The love of Jesus drives him to pray for us and then die for us, not that *our* value may be central but that *his glory* may be central, and we may see it and savor it for all eternity. "That they may see my glory!"—for that he let Lazarus die, and for that he went to the cross. And that, brothers, is a massive foundation for a great new vision of our common life—black and white, under God's loving God-centeredness.

3) THE GOD-CENTEREDNESS OF GOD IN THE SUFFERING AND DEATH OF JESUS CHRIST ON THE CROSS

The center of history and the center of salvation is the death of Jesus Christ. Why did he die? The Bible gives more than one answer. One is this: "Christ died for our sins" (1 Cor. 15:3). In other words, "the LORD has laid on him the iniquity of us all" (Isa. 53:6). Or you can say it another way: He died *for us*. Romans 5:8: "God shows his love for us in that while we were still sinners, Christ died *for us*." He died in our place (2 Cor. 5:14; 1 Thess. 5:10). "He bore our sins in his body" (2 Pet. 2:24).

But there is something deeper that explains the cross. If the only thing at stake were our lives, then he might have just said, "Let's let bygones be bygones." He might have forgiven us without the blood-shedding of his Son. He might have just declared us innocent and righteousness without the climactic act of perfect obedience and sin-bearing pardon. But Paul explains in Romans 3:25–26 why it could not be. The reason it could not happen that way is that God's own glory, his righteous commitment to uphold his name and worth and holiness, was at stake in passing over God-belittling sins:

God put [Christ] forward as a propitiation by his blood, to be received by faith. This was *to show God's righteousness*, because in his divine forbearance he had passed over former sins. It was *to show his righteousness* at the present time, so *that he might be just* and the justifier of the one who has faith in Jesus.

Our forgiveness and acceptance through the blood of Jesus hangs on God's commitment to be vindicated. God's zeal to be exalted as a righteous God is the foundation of his willingness to put his Son to death (Isa. 53:10). So the cross is a cry for us to make God central in our preaching of salvation.

Yes, oh, glorious yes, we are forgiven, and we are justified, and we will be glorified. But how do you speak of this? Do you not speak with the words of Psalm 25:11—"*For your name's sake*, O LORD, pardon my guilt, for it is great"? Are we pardoned to parade our worth and our glory? Or are we pardoned so that we might be freed to join the happiest parade that ever was—to spend eternity celebrating his worth and God's glory in Christ? I say, let us speak the way God speaks in Isaiah 43:25: "I, I am he who blots out your transgressions *for my own sake*, and I will not remember your sins."

The suffering and death of Jesus are not meant to make much of us. They are meant to free us from the bondage to mirrors, so we might enjoy making much of Christ forever. He died to "bring us to God" (1 Pet. 3:18) so that we might see and savor his glory forever (John 17:24).

4) FINALLY, THE GOD-CENTEREDNESS OF GOD IN OUR SUFFERING AND DEATH WITH JESUS IN THIS WORLD OF SIN AND PAIN

What does the pain of the black experience in America mean? What does the pain of white Christian martyrs in the reign of Bloody Mary mean? What does the suffering and death of thousands of Christians in China mean? None of these things has taken the all-seeing, all-knowing, risen, sovereign Christ off guard. In fact, he told us they would come:

> Behold, I am sending you out as sheep in the midst of wolves. . . . They will deliver you over to courts and flog you in their synagogues, and you will be dragged before governors and kings for my sake. . . . Brother will deliver brother over to death, and the father his child, and children will rise against parents and have them put to death, and you will be hated by all for my name's sake. But the one who endures to the end will be saved. . . . A disciple is not above his teacher, nor a servant above his master. . . . If they have called the master of the house Beelzebul, how much more will they malign those of his household. (Matt. 10:16–25)

Do you see what this means? It means that when we suffer for righteousness' sake, Jesus is shown to be a truth-teller. Paradoxically, his word is vindicated in the very experience that threatens our trust in him most deeply.

Paul picked up the theme and promised that the pain would come. "Indeed, all who desire to live a godly life in Christ Jesus will be persecuted" (2 Tim. 3:12). "Through many tribulations we must enter the kingdom of God" (Acts 14:22). And James: "Count it all joy, my brothers, when you meet trials of various kinds" (James 1:2). And Peter: "Beloved, do not be surprised at the fiery trial when it comes upon you to test you, as though something strange were happening to you" (1 Pet. 4:12).

SUFFERING FOR THE SAKE OF THE GLORY OF CHRIST

Now what does all this have to do with the supremacy of God and the centrality of God and the sovereignty of God? Let Paul answer from 2 Corinthians 12. After receiving indescribable visions Paul said, "To keep me from exalting myself, there was given me a thorn in the flesh, a messenger of Satan to torment me—to keep me from exalting myself!" (v. 7 NASB). He pleaded three times that the Lord would take it away. But the answer he received from Christ was this: "My grace is sufficient for you, for my power is made perfect in weakness" (v. 9).

The point of Paul's pain was to magnify the perfection of Christ's power. Here is a test, brothers. A hard test. How many in our white Christian community or in our black Christian community would hear this explanation of our pain and say, "I will be glad if Christ's power is to be magnified in my pain. That is enough for me." Or how many will rather say, "I don't care about this self-exalting, glory-seeking, Christ-centered Christ; I just want to be free from my pain!"?

What did Paul say when Christ said, "No, I will not take away your pain, but I will display the perfection of my power in it"? What did Paul say? He said (in 2 Cor. 12:9), "Therefore I will boast [Greek *krauchēsomai*] all the more gladly [*hēdista*] of my weaknesses, so that the power of Christ may rest upon me." How do you explain this man? He did not merely say, "I will endure this because Christ has appointed it for my good." He said, "I will exult with gladness in it because Christ will be made much of through it."

Is this not our aim brothers? Is this not the passion of our lives? To become so God-centered and so Christ-exalting and so consumed with a passion for the supremacy of God that anything that will show him to be the supreme treasure of our lives—above health, above wealth, above family, above success, above fame—any pain, any trial, any trouble, any loss, any grief, anything that will show him to be infinitely precious, we will embrace with joy. Because the love of God is not, at root, his making much of us, but his freeing us to enjoy making much of him forever?

ETHNICALLY INTERWOVEN GOD-CENTEREDNESS

"Sorrowful, yet always rejoicing"—in him! Is not this seed at the root of the soul dynamic? Is not this confidence, and this indomitable joy at the root of the black spiritual experience in America? Is not this the crying need of weightless, white evangelical Christianity with its man-centered God and flight from risk and suffering?

And if so, might it be—may it be!—that the link between the sovereignty of God and the soul dynamic, and between God-centered theology and the black experience, could become the awakening and the empowering, not just of a new black culture, and not just a new white culture, but a new ethnically interwoven culture, welded most deeply by a common passion for the centrality of God and the supremacy of God and the sovereignty of God and the glory of Christ, that frees us and carries us toward need and not comfort, ready to suffer, not running to safety, until we bring the neighborhoods and the nations into the joy of seeing and savoring the all-satisfying Christ forever?

HOW AND WHY BETHLEHEM BAPTIST CHURCH PURSUES ETHNIC DIVERSITY

I know that a book like this raises many practical questions about how a church carries out the implications of what I have written. To answer some of those questions I have chosen to provide a real-life example of one of our strategies in the pursuit of racial and ethnic diversity. On January 24, 2007, we made public on the web the following article. I have not changed a word in it. In the article, I mention some of the other things (besides writing articles like this) that we have done in the quest for more ethnic diversity and harmony. At the end of the article I will add a few more of those to fill out the picture.

The aim of this article is information and solicitation.

First, I want to *inform* the people of Bethlehem (and anyone else who cares to listen) how the staff and elders think about ethnic diversity in hiring pastoral staff and choosing elders.

Second, I want to solicit the help of any friend of Bethlehem or Desiring God in helping us know about African American, Asian, Latino, Native, or any other ethnic persons who might be a part of the pastoral staff at Bethlehem.

We realize that this kind of intentionality in seeking staff is controversial. Some would say, "Never consider ethnicity in hiring. Always be color-blind and focus only on competencies, doctrine, and faith." Here is the problem we see with that. Most people look at the ethnic diversity in the New Testament church and admire what they see. "There is *neither*

Jew nor Greek, there is neither slave nor free, there is no male and female, for you are all one in Christ Jesus" (Gal. 3:28).

It is right to admire this diversity for many reasons:

- It illustrates more clearly the truth that God created people of all races and ethnicities in his own image (Gen. 1:27).
- It displays more visibly the truth that Jesus is not a tribal deity but is the Lord of all races, nations, and ethnicities.
- It demonstrates more clearly the blood-bought destiny of the church to be "from every tribe and language and people and nation" (Rev. 5:9).
- It exhibits more compellingly the aim and power of the cross of Christ to "reconcile us both to God in one body through the cross, thereby killing the hostility" (Eph. 2:16).
- It expresses more forcefully the work of the Spirit to unite us in Christ. "For in one Spirit we were all baptized into one body—Jews or Greeks, slaves or free—and all were made to drink of one Spirit" (1 Cor. 12:13).

This list of blessings that come from biblically grounded ethnic diversity could be substantially lengthened. For example, every culture benefits from the insights into reality that other cultures bring. None of us has a corner on seeing things fully. "Now we see in a mirror dimly, but then face to face. Now I know in part; then I shall know fully, even as I have been fully known" (1 Cor. 13:12).

Therefore, it seems to us that the *admiration* we feel for this diversity in the New Testament should carry over into the *desires* we have for the visible church today. It seems to us that the local church should *want* these things to be true today at the local level where this diversity and harmony would have the greatest visible and relational impact. For us, this has implied *pursuit*. If we admire it and desire it, then it seems to us we should pursue it. What does that imply?

Four things: *Prayer. Preparation. Probing. Preferring.* These steps become increasingly controversial. They would be easier to simply avoid. We have chosen to take the risk.

Prayer: the leadership of the church prays privately and in public that God would have mercy on us and bless us with increased ethnic diversity.

Preparation: not all people desire or are ready for the pursuit of ethnic diversity. We all need gospel-centered preparation for this. Therefore, we preach on these things, and we hold roundtables, and read and recommend books, and bring in speakers who know more than we do, and have seminars, and encourage relationships across ethnic lines, and expose people in worship services to different kinds of cultural expressions, and more.

Probing: we search for candidates for pastors and elders who are from various ethnicities. We pursue the web of relationships that we have. We make the positions known on the web and in other ways. We write articles like this one.

Preferring: we intentionally take ethnicity into account when making choices about who we will call to the pastoral staff and eldership. This is the most controversial. It has been labeled "affirmative action" or "racial preferences." Here is how it works at Bethlehem and why we make decisions this way.

One guiding principle is this: to the degree that one of the aims of an organization is to experience and display racial diversity, to that degree the intentional consideration of race in hiring is warranted. If, for example, the *sole* aim of an organization is productive efficiency, it would be unwarranted for the hiring guidelines to contain racial preferences. Whether all the employees are black or Asian or white or Latino or Native is irrelevant. All that matters is maximum efficiency. So you don't consider race in hiring. The only thing you consider is competencies that maximize efficiency.

But if one of the stated aims of an organization is to experience and display the beauty of ethnic harmony in diversity, then it would be reasonable and warranted to consider race as part of the qualifications in hiring. An obvious example would be hiring actors for a dramatic production that has black, Asian, Latino, and white roles. One would consider race essential in the actors one hires for each role. One would not say: "Competency in acting is the only thing that matters," and then use makeup to create the impression of race. Of course, acting competency matters. But so does race. That's part of what the play is about. Hence, it is reasonable and warranted to take ethnicity into account when hiring actors.

Over ten years ago, we at Bethlehem set ourselves on a trajectory of intentional ethnic diversity. It coheres with the emphasis on "the joy of all peoples" in our mission statement: "We exist to spread a passion for the supremacy of God in all things *for the joy of all peoples* through Jesus Christ." But we did not make it easy for ourselves.

It would be easy if we said, "Diversity is the top priority that outweighs all others." Or: "Diversity at any cost." But there are things more important than ethnic diversity. For example, in hiring pastoral staff or choosing elders, there are theological and philosophical and personal commitments that are more important than ethnicity.

Embracing our *Elder Affirmation of Faith* is a nonnegotiable. Implied in this is a certain spirit of life and ministry captured by phrases such as *God-centered*, *Christ-exalting*, and *Bible-saturated*. This too is a nonnegotiable. Implicit in those expectations is a personal, authentic passion for Jesus—which is essential. And flowing out of all of those is a kind of commitment to marriage and childrearing that aims at radical, joyful obedience to Jesus.

All this means that the decision to call any particular pastor or elder is always made "on balance." Ethnicity never decides the case by itself, and competencies and commitments never decide the case by themselves. Many factors figure in the decision on each candidate.

We pray that the God of grace and wisdom will humble us and give us discernment and lead us into greater gospel-centered ethnic diversity and harmony for the glory of Christ and the good of all peoples. If you can help us forward in any way, we would be happy to hear from you.

A FEW ADDITIONS

MARCH 2009

This is a partial list of things we have done with a view to helping our church grow in ethnic diversity and understanding and harmony.

- We crafted a mission statement that included a reference to "peoples" and a series of "fresh initiatives" that included one about racial reconciliation.

    > Mission Statement: *We exist to spread a passion for the supremacy of God in all things for the joy of all peoples through Jesus Christ.*
    >
    > Fresh Initiative 3: *Against the rising spirit of indifference, alienation, and hostility in our land, we will embrace the supremacy of God's love to take new steps personally and corporately toward racial reconciliation expressed visibly in our community and in our church.*

- In the same Vision document, there were several "values" relating to racial harmony, one in particular under the section on worship: *Being more indigenous to the diversity of our metropolitan cultural setting, both urban and suburban.*
- With significant influence from Harold Best's *Music Through the Eyes of Faith*, we continually attempt to define our musical center in corporate worship in such a way that it includes a range of ethnic expressions and a combination of historic and contemporary lyrics and sounds. The key sections from Best have been these:

There is nothing un- or anti-Christian about any kind of music. By the same token there is no such thing as Christian music. . . . Indiscriminate musical choice for the sake of attracting everybody means that there is no real centeredness, no practitional authenticity. At first blush, this sounds like a refutation of everything said and defended so far about pluralism. It is not. It is, however a refutation of faceless pluralism, given these facts: (1) the best pluralists will always have limited, not infinite, choice; (2) pluralism never substitutes for the pursuit of excellence; (3) pluralism is the act of discovering and relating to the centeredness of others from the vantage point of one's own centeredness. . . . What [churches] cannot afford to do is to clone each other in order to keep up with each other, vying for souls. Rather, church "x," out of Spirit-driven conscience, chooses a certain musical profile, a certain combination of centeredness and diversity. Church "y" goes another way with the same integrity.[1]

- One revisiting of the issue of ethnicity and corporate worship found expression in a position paper entitled "Twenty-One Theses Relating to Corporate Worship Services, Ethnic Diversity, and Ministries of Mercy."
- We have put a very high emphasis on nurturing relationships of love, believing that public demonstrations of diversity in worship and programs cannot replace the personal touch of showing people that you care about them.
- We established a Racial Harmony Task Force to assist the elders in assessing our progress and making suggestions and interviewing staff candidates.
- We composed Racial Harmony competency questions for ourselves and for interviewing pastoral candidates.
- The Every Tribe and Tongue Choir was formed to specialize in ethnically diverse songs.
- We gave several concerts of spirituals, with historic readings from black history.
- For the last ten years or so, I have preached on the issue of racial diversity and harmony on Martin Luther King weekend.
- The Martin Luther King weekend often has a special seminar with a guest speaker.
- We established a monthly Racial Harmony Roundtable that focuses discussion on various issues related to racial harmony, usually followed by eating together.
- We have recently created a course on Racial Harmony for The Bethlehem Institute, which will cover a wide range of biblical and cultural issues.
- We seek to maintain informal fellowship in a network of theologically like-minded African American pastors.
- Together with an African American staff member and elder at Bethlehem, I have visited various black churches for Sunday morning services when I am on various leaves from preaching at Bethlehem.
- We devoted one of the Desiring God Conferences for Pastors to the issue of the Sovereignty of God and the Soul Dynamic. (See Appendix 2.)
- We try to include ethnic diversity among the speakers at our conferences.

- A Latino Fellowship within Bethlehem has grown up and recently begun to hold additional services.
- An intentionally diverse church plant was sent out from us called All Nations Christian Fellowship.
- We supported one of our African American elders in the establishing of an urban ministry center and church plant in St. Paul.
- We have held Native American Awareness seminars.
- The Somali Adult Literacy Training program reaches out to the largest urban Somali population in America.
- The Laotian Church of Peace meets in our building, and our relationship with the pastor and people goes back many years.
- We have devoted significant blocks of time as a staff to discuss the issues of racial diversity and harmony, seeking common understanding and strategies of progress.
- There is an All Nations fellowship in the church where a wide range of nationalities and ethnicities gather for closer fellowship.
- We have made book recommendations to our people and encouraged them to read a book together.
- We have held panel discussions with different ethnicities represented in order to explore in front of our people the kinds of experiences people have at Bethlehem and how we might be more welcoming.
- We have held celebrations several times by gathering over a dozen ethnic churches together to worship and hear preaching.
- Twice a year we gather with four other churches, including one African American church, to celebrate Good Friday and Thanksgiving.
- We connect regularly with the neighboring black Baptist church and hang out informally.
- Transracial adoption has become a huge part of our life at Bethlehem. The MICAH (Minority Infant and Children Adoption Help) and LYDIA (Let Youths be Delivered from Institutions by Adoption) funds provide money to help parents adopt.
- For several years, we published weekly articles on various biblical themes in the local black newspaper.
- We have held lunches for dozens of urban pastors when we have had guest speakers from out of town that we think they might appreciate.
- For many years, a good number of the pastoral staff at the Downtown Campus have lived in the very diverse neighborhood near the church. Over the thirty years I have been here, hundreds of our people have moved into the city to be a healing, reconciling presence.

WHAT ARE THE IMPLICATIONS OF NOAH'S CURSE?

The curse that Noah spoke over some of the descendants of his son Ham in Genesis 9:25 is irrelevant in deciding how the dark-skinned people are to be viewed and treated.

Over the centuries, some people have tried to prove that the black race is destined by God to be subservient to other races because of Noah's words over his son Ham, who was the father of the African peoples.[1] Let's look at the actual text of Scripture, and then I will give three reasons why it does not prescribe how the peoples of Africa are to be viewed and treated.

Recall that Noah had three sons: Shem, Ham, and Japheth. The key text is Genesis 9:21–25 (NASB):

> And [Noah] drank of the wine and became drunk, and uncovered himself inside his tent. And Ham, the father of Canaan, saw the nakedness of his father, and told his two brothers outside. But Shem and Japheth took a garment and laid it upon both their shoulders and walked backward and covered the nakedness of their father; and their faces were turned away, so that they did not see their father's nakedness. When Noah awoke from his wine, he knew what his youngest son had done to him. So he said, "Cursed be [or *will be*] Canaan; a servant of servants He shall be to his brothers."

Now notice three things.

1) Noah's Curse Falls upon Ham's Son Canaan

First, Noah takes this occasion of the sin of his son Ham, and uses it to make a prediction about the posterity of Ham's youngest son, Canaan.

Gordon Wenham asks, "Why should Noah have cursed Canaan, Ham's son, and not Ham himself?" He answers, "The question has baffled commentators for centuries, and there is no obvious answer."[2]

But Bruce Waltke seems to me to put the pieces together for a probable explanation.

> Why Canaan rather than Ham? Since the curses and blessings on the three sons have their descendants in view, it is not strange that the curse falls on Ham's son rather than on Ham himself (9:18–22), especially since God has already blessed this righteous survivor of the Flood (9:1). As the youngest son wrongs his father, so the curse will fall on his youngest son, who presumably inherits his moral decadence (see Lev. 18:3; Deut. 9:3).[3]

SHALL THE SONS BE PUNISHED FOR THE FATHER'S SINS?

Those last words are important: ". . . who presumably inherits his moral decadence." The reason they are important is that there are passages of Scripture that warn against punishing the son for the sins of the father. For example, "The son shall not suffer for the iniquity of the father, nor the father suffer for the iniquity of the son" (Ezek. 18:20, cf. Jer. 31:30; 2 Kings 14:6).

But, on the other hand, there are passages that say, "The LORD . . . [visits] the iniquity of the fathers on the children and the children's children, to the third and the fourth generation" (Ex. 34:6–7). The reasons these two passages are not a contradiction is that when God visits the sins of the fathers on a following generation, it happens because that generation becomes sinful like their fathers. They are real sinners.

That's why God says in Exodus 20:5, "I the LORD . . . [visit] the iniquity of the fathers on the children to the third and the fourth generation *of those who hate me.*" We are not told *how* the fathers' sins become the children's sins. But what we are told is that when the father's sins are visited on the children, it is because the children are really sinful. That is the form in which the fathers' sins are visited. Therefore, all judgment is really deserved by the person who is punished.

Moreover, the spread of condemnation from one generation to the next can be broken. Leviticus 26:40–42 reminds us, "If they confess *their iniquity and the iniquity of their fathers . . .* if then their uncircumcised heart is humbled and they make amends for their iniquity, then I will remember my covenant with Jacob." This is because of the precious words of Exodus 34:6–7, which are made possible finally because of the death of Christ, "The LORD, the LORD, a God merciful and gracious, slow to anger, and abounding in steadfast love and faithfulness, keeping steadfast love for thousands, *forgiving iniquity and transgression and sin.*"

When Waltke says that Ham's son Canaan inherits his father's moral decadence, he points to the fact that any punishments that will come upon Canaan for Ham's sin will be really deserved. There are mysteries in how sin moves from one generation to the next, but what we know from Scripture is that those who are punished by God deserve the punishment because of their own sin.

Thus the Jewish scholar Umberto Cassuto says of the descendants of Ham's son Canaan, "The Canaanites were to suffer the curse and the bondage not because of the sins of Ham, but because they themselves acted like Ham, because of their own transgressions, which resembled those attributed to Ham in this allegory."[4] Cassuto, I think, goes too far in saying "not because of the sins of Ham." But he is right to say, "but because they themselves acted like Ham." Mysterious as it is, both are true.

CANAAN WAS NOT THE FATHER OF AFRICA

So in sum, Ham had four sons, according to Genesis 10:6 (NASB): "The sons of Ham were Cush and Mizraim and Put and Canaan." Broadly speaking, Cush was probably the ancestor of the peoples of Ethiopia; Mizraim was the ancestor of the Egyptians; and Put was the ancestor of the peoples of northern Africa, the Libyans. But Canaan is the one son of the four who is not the ancestor of African peoples.

According to Genesis 10:15–18 (NASB), the descendants of Canaan were inhabitants of the land that took his name. "And Canaan became the father of Sidon, his first-born, and Heth and the Jebusite and the Amorite and the Girgashite and the Hivite and the Arkite and the Sinite and the Arvadite and the Zemarite and the Hamathite." All those peoples were the inhabitants of Canaan and its vicinity, not Africa. Thus the prediction of Noah came true when the Canaanite nations were driven out or subjugated by the Israelites because of their wickedness (Deut. 9:4–5).

AN UNWARRANTED SUPPOSITION

Nevertheless, a stream of interpretation continues to find in this text an explanation and even warrant for the slavery of Africans in history. For example, C. F. Keil stretches the curse on Canaan to cover all of Ham's heirs like this:

> Although this curse was expressly pronounced upon Canaan alone, the fact that Ham had no share in Noah's blessing, either for himself or his other sons [Gen. 9:26–27], was a sufficient proof that his whole family was included by implication in the curse, even if it was to fall chiefly upon Canaan. And history confirms the supposition. The Canaanites were partly exterminated, and partly subjected to the lowest form of slavery, by the Israelites, who belonged to the family of Shem. . . . The remainder of the Hamitic tribes either shared the same fate, or still sigh, like the negroes, for example, and other African tribes, beneath the yoke of the most crushing slavery.[5]

From what we have seen, this "supposition" of Keil is not warranted. The text focuses our attention on Canaan, not on the other sons of Ham, and the history of Israel in the conquest of the Promised Land (the land of Canaan) shows how relevant this focus was.

2) Noah's Curse Is Not about Individuals

Second, the predicted curse of Noah does not dictate how God's people should treat individual Canaanites—or any other group. For example, five chapters later, in Genesis 14:18, Abraham, the descendant of Seth, meets a native Canaanite named Melchizedek, who was a righteous man and "priest of God Most High" and who blessed Abraham. Abraham gave him a tenth of his spoils.

So not even the fact that God ordains to bring judgment on evil nations dictates for us how we are to treat individuals in those nations. Our treatment of others is based not on what God's sovereign providence designs but on what God's moral law commands and what the gospel of Jesus implies.

For example, even though God's providence designed that Jesus be betrayed, that does not give a warrant to anyone to betray him: "The Son of Man goes as it is written of him, but woe to that man by whom the

Son of Man is betrayed!" (Matt. 26:24). So God may destine a group of people, like the Canaanites, to experience idolatry and judgment, but that does not warrant anyone to commit idolatry or entice anyone to idolatry.

The fact that the Canaanites were appointed for subjugation does not justify any man to subjugate them. Whether that is permitted or commanded will depend on other factors. Divine providence does not define human duty.[6]

3) God Plans Redemption for All Nations

In Genesis 12, God sets in motion a great plan of redemption for all the nations to rescue them from this and every other curse of sin and judgment. He calls Abram from all the nations and makes a covenant with him and promises, "I will bless those who bless you, and the one who curses you I will curse. And in you a*ll the families of the earth* shall be blessed" (NASB). The phrase "all the families of the earth" includes the Canaanite families.

So what we see is that, with Abraham, God is setting in motion a plan of redemption that overturns every curse for everyone who receives the blessing of Abraham, namely, the forgiveness and acceptance of God that comes through Jesus Christ, the seed of Abraham (Gal. 3:13–14).

This implies for us, therefore, that every human being is seen primarily not as destined by providence for slavery or freedom but as offered by God the hope of full membership in God's family. "But to all who did receive him [Jesus], who believed in his name, he gave the right to become children of God" (John 1:12). The question we bring as Christians is *not*, "Are you a Canaanite and therefore subservient to me?" but, "Are you a believer and therefore brother to me?"

And if the answer is, "I do not believe on Jesus," then our response is, "I pray that you will one day believe. Until then, or until you die, I will love you, if necessary as my enemy, as Jesus commanded (Matt. 5:43–44). I will pray for you to be saved and become my brother in Christ (Rom. 10:1). And I will warn you that if you spurn God's grace in Jesus Christ, you will one day be brought forcefully into subjection to King Jesus and all his people. I pray that, instead, you will be part of that people. It would be my joy."

NOTES

A NOTE TO THE READER ON *RACE* AND *RACISM*

1. W. E. B. Du Bois, "To the Nations of the World," *Great Speeches by African Americans*, ed. James Daley (Mineola, NY: Dover, 2006), 85.

2. "Committee on Mission to North America, Pastoral Letter on Racism, Approved at the March 2004 MNA Committee Meeting as the Committee's Recommendation to the Thirty-Second General Assembly." http://www.pca-mna.org/churchplanting/PDFs/RacismPaper-Final%20Version%2004-09-04.pdf.

INTRODUCTION TO PART 1

1. Baby boomers are most commonly defined as the generation born from January 1946 to the end of 1964. The name comes from the population boom that happened when the troops came home after World War II. I was born January 11, 1946.

2. Stephan Thernstrom and Abigail Thernstrom, *America in Black and White: One Nation, Indivisible* (New York: Simon and Schuster, 1997), 101.

3. Stephen Oates, *Let the Trumpet Sound: The Life of Martin Luther King Jr.* (New York: Penguin, 1982), 222.

4. Martin Luther King Jr., *Letter from Birmingham Jail*, with an introduction by Paul Chaim Schenck (n.p., n.d.), 8–9. I have added paragraph breaks to what was originally one paragraph, but nothing has been omitted. The *Letter* may be found on many Internet websites by simply entering the title in a search engine; e.g., one site, accessed on March 19, 2010, is http://www.stanford.edu/group/King/frequentdocs/birmingham.pdf.

5. *Letter*, 14 (paragraph break added).

6. *Letter*, 17.

CHAPTER 1: MY STORY

1. Barack Obama, *Dreams from My Father: A Story of Race and Inheritance* (New York: Three Rivers Press, 2004), *ix*.

2. Ibid., *x*.

3. Ibid.

4. I take the term from Shelby Steele, *White Guilt: How Blacks and Whites Together Destroyed the Promise of the Civil Rights Era* (New York: HarperCollins, 2006).

5. Marshall Frady, *Jesse: The Life and Pilgrimage of Jesse Jackson* (New York: Simon and Schuster, 2006), 82.

6. We have tried to verify this from church records, but have been told that the church was not keeping minutes at this time. So this fact is based on my memory rather than confirmed documentation.

7. Silence concerning my father at this point is not to conceal anything. It is one of the facts of my upbringing that my father, as a traveling evangelist, was away from home so much that I seldom talked to him about such things. I assume he and my mother stood together. And, of course, neither was free from the marks of sinful culture and sinful hearts.

8. John Piper, *The Purifying Power of Living by Faith in Future Grace* (Sisters, OR: Multnomah, 1995), 51–53.

9. I tell the story of my intellectual and spiritual development in the chapter "The Pastor as Scholar: A Personal Journey and the Joyful Place of Scholarship," in *The Pastor as Scholar and the Scholar as Pastor: Reflections on Life and Ministry*, ed. David Mathis and Owen Strachan (Wheaton, IL: Crossway, 2011).

10. This syllabus of readings was simply loose-bound sheets, which, to my knowledge, was never published. It sits in front of me with its forty-two-year-old yellowed pages. The quote is from page *iv*. The sections were titled, by way of example, "Racial Prejudice in the Form of Physical Brutality"; "Racial Prejudice in the Form of Personal Indignities"; "Racial Prejudice and the Death of Incentive"; "Racial Prejudice and the Irrational"; "Racial Prejudice and the Black Woman"; "The Black Response to Racial Prejudice"; "Racial Prejudice and the White Psyche."

11. Lewis Smedes, *Love within Limits: A Realist's View of 1 Corinthians 13* (Grand Rapids, MI: Eerdmans, 1979).

12. The Minneapolis Planning Department, http://www.urbanventures.org/demo.pdf (accessed March 21, 2009).

CHAPTER 2: THE GOSPEL I LOVE

1. "'Greeks and Barbarians' represent the totality of the peoples of the nations, apart from the Jews. Centuries earlier when Greeks first heard the stammered guttural speech of foreigners, sounding as it did to them as 'bar bar bar,' they called such people *bararoi*, 'barbarians.' In time, however, because of the spread of Greek philosophy, literature and science among other peoples 'Greek' also came to mean 'wise' or 'cultured' and 'barbarian' to mean the 'ignorant' or 'uneducated.'" Paul Barnett, *Romans: The Revelation of God's Righteousness* (Fearn, Scotland: Christian Focus, 2003), 35–36.

2. "Harder Than Anyone Can Imagine," a *Christianity Today* forum responding to the book edited by Curtiss Paul DeYoung, Michael O. Emerson, George Yancey, and Karen Chai Kim, *United by Faith: The Multiracial Congregation as an Answer to the Problem of Race* (Oxford: Oxford University Press, 2003). *Christianity Today*, April 2005, 41.

3. Ibid., 37, 40.

4. "Evangelicals and Racism: The Lausanne II Press Conference," *Transformation*, January 1990, 29.

5. Quoted by Glen Kehrein and Raleigh Washington, in *Breaking Down Walls: A Model for Reconciliation in an Age of Racial Strife* (Chicago: Moody Press, 1994), 110.

6. David Michael, "A Double-Breasted Suit and Racial Reconciliation," unpublished position paper, January 17, 1994. The mentors he was referring to were Glen Kehrein and Raleigh Washington, *Breaking Down Walls*; Chris Rice and Spencer Perkins, *More Than Equals: Racial Healing for the Sake of the Gospel* (Downers Grove, IL: InterVarsity, 1993); and William Pannell, *The Coming Race Wars: A Cry for Reconciliation* (Grand Rapids, MI: Zondervan, 1993).

CHAPTER 3: GLOBAL SHIFTING AND THE NEW FACE OF THE CHURCH

1. http://www.census.gov/Press-Release/www/releases/archives/population/012496.html (accessed March 19, 2010).

2. http://www.guardian.co.uk/uk/2000/sep/03/race.world (accessed March 24, 2009).

3. http://www.fedstats.gov/qf/states/06000.html (accessed March 24, 2009).

4. The statistics are based on figures from the year 2000. http://www.prb.org/Educators/TeachersGuides/HumanPopulation/Urbanization.aspx (accessed March 24, 2009).

5. The *City View Report* may be ordered at http://www.cityvisiontc.org/shtml/cityview.shtml (accessed March 24, 2009).

6. I transcribed this from John Mayer's video at http://cityvisiontc.org/jam_video_short/streaming.shtml (accessed March 24, 2009). John Mayer sent a personal e-mail to some friends on October 15, 2008, and commented, "Today's *StarTribune* article in the South Metro Section for Wed. October 15 states that the Burnsville School district is now 38 [percent] non-White. Just two years ago I noted to you all that this number was at 29 [percent] and so has gone up by 9 [percent] in just two years. . . . We even have two mosques now as well as other ethnic/religious worship sites."

7. See esp. Philip Jenkins, *The Next Christendom: The Coming of Global Christianity* (Oxford: Oxford University Press, rev. and updated, 2007); and *The New Faces of Christianity: Believing the Bible in the Global South* (Oxford: Oxford University Press, 2006).

8. Dana L. Robert, "Shifting Southward: Global Christianity Since 1945," *International Bulletin of Missionary Research*, 24.2 (April 2000): 50.

9. Philip Jenkins, "Believing in the Global South," *First Things*, December 2006, 13.

10. Ibid., 12.

11. Ibid.

12. Robert, "Shifting Southward," 53.

CHAPTER 4: WHY THIS BOOK GIVES PROMINENCE TO BLACK-WHITE RELATIONSHIPS

1. You can read profiles of 16,306 ethnolinguistic people groups online at the Joshua Project website: http://www.joshuaproject.net/index.php.

2. Doris Kearns Goodwin, *Team of Rivals: The Political Genius of Abraham Lincoln* (New York: Simon & Schuster, 2006), 205.

3. Ibid., 204.

4. Ibid.

5. There is, in fact, significant debate as to whether Lincoln was a racist. Thomas L. Krannawitter defends Lincoln, arguing that public words like the ones I have cited here are a reflection of political realism in view of public opinion, not personal conviction. "However much one might lament or loathe public opinion, those who hope to bring about political change in America cannot ignore it. Lincoln concluded that 'we cannot, then, make [blacks] equals' precisely because he understood all too well the racial opinions of the vast majority of whites in America. . . . Rather than evincing racism . . . Lincoln's position demonstrates a prudential concern for the formation of public opinion, public policy, and the rule of law." *Vindicating Lincoln: Defending the Politics of Our Greatest President* (New York: Rowman & Littlefield, 2008), 33. Perhaps. I suspect, however, that when all is said and done, Lincoln will be seen—like every other great leader, except one—to be a flawed man, even in regard to his views of race.

6. Juan Williams, *Enough: The Phony Leaders, Dead-End Movements, and Culture of Failure That Are Undermining Black America—and What We Can Do About It* (New York: Crown, 2006).

7. Ibid., 94.

8. Bill Cosby and Alvin F. Poussaint, *Come On People: On the Path from Victims to Victors* (Nashville: Nelson, 2007).

9. Michael Eric Dyson, *Is Bill Cosby Right? Or Has the Black Middle Class Lost Its Mind?* (New York: Basic Civitas, 2005).

10. Ibid., 5.

11. Ibid.

12. Ibid.

13. Cosby and Poussaint, *Come On People*, 1–2.

14. Ibid., 8–9.

15. Williams, *Enough*, 121. For some of the raunchier lyrics, you can see pp. 127, 132. One of the milder lines (p. 132): "Can you control your ho? . . . Listen you've got to put that bitch in her place, even if it is slapping her in her face."

16. Ibid., 134.

17. Of course, not all rap is corrupt, and increasingly Christians are redeeming the genre for powerful Christian witness.

18. Williams, *Enough,* 135.

19. Ibid., 145.

20. Ibid., 135.

21. Not that there were no black leaders involved. "Black corporate captains have taken their pound of flesh, too. Robert Johnson's Black Entertainment Television (before it

was sold to Viacom) made its money with rap videos that relied heavily on half-naked black women and gangster violence." Ibid., 136.

22. Ibid., 127.

23. David F. Wells, *Losing Our Virtue: Why the Church Must Recover Its Moral Vision* (Grand Rapids, MI: Eerdmans, 1998).

24. Ibid., 59 (paragraph breaks added).

CHAPTER 5: PERSONAL RESPONSIBILITY AND SYSTEMIC INTERVENTION

1. Camille Cosby, "America Taught My Son's Killer to Hate African-Americans," *USA Today*, July 8, 1998, 15A. Ennis was shot to death while changing a flat tire on Interstate 495 in Los Angeles.

2. Quoted in Stephan and Abigail Thernstrom, *America in Black and White: One Nation, Indivisible* (New York: Simon & Schuster, 1999), 9.

3. On the twentieth anniversary of the 1967 riots in Detroit, Shelby Steele observed: "A comparison of the city then and now showed a decline in the quality of life. Residents feel less safe, drug trafficking is far worse, crimes by blacks against blacks are more frequent, housing remains substandard, and the teenage pregnancy rate has skyrocketed. Twenty years of decline in demoralization, even as opportunities for blacks to better themselves have increased. This paradox is not peculiar to Detroit. By many measures, the majority of blacks—those not yet in the middle class—are further behind whites today than before the victories of the civil rights movement." Shelby Steele, *The Content of Our Character: A New Vision of Race in America* (New York: HarperPerennial, 1990), 15.

4. "Today it is fashionable among blacks to say that integration was a failure, which is to imply that our true strength is in separatism. Today you can witness blacks everywhere enforcing on themselves the very separatism and community that segregation so recently imposed—like churches, civil rights confabs that are far more social than political, 'State of Black America' gatherings as if we still share a singular destiny, black professional associations by the hundreds, black student associations of every variety, or even a Congressional Black Caucus, not to mention black caucuses in many state legislatures. Now in the promised land of freedom we reach for the lost Eden of separatism." Shelby Steele, *White Guilt: How Blacks and Whites Together Destroyed the Promise of the Civil Rights Era* (New York: HarperCollins, 2006), 26.

5. Stephan and Abigail Thernstrom, *America in Black and White*, 10.

6. "The percentage of blacks in middle class occupations did not top 10 percent until 1960, whereas the white middle class constituted more than 20 percent of the total white population as early as 1910. . . . The United States experienced unprecedented economic growth and prosperity after 1950 up until the early 1970s. The coincidence of this growth with the Civil Rights Movement created a large swelling of the black middle class. Between 1980 and 1990, the percentage of blacks in middle class occupations grew from 39.6 percent to 44.9 percent." Mary Pattillo-McCoy, "Middle Class, Yet Black: A Review Essay," http://www.rcgd.isr.umich.edu/prba/perspectives/fall1999/mpattillo.pdf (accessed March 26, 2009).

7. http://en.wikipedia.org/wiki/African_American (accessed 3-26-09).

8. Stephan and Abigail Thernstrom, *America in Black and White*, 10.

9. Richard John Neuhaus, "Counting by Race," *First Things*, February 1996, 78.

10. Michael Eric Dyson, *Is Bill Cosby Right? Or Has the Black Middle Class Lost Its Mind?* (New York: Basic Civitas, 2005), 5.

11. Among academics, the solutions related to "personal responsibility" are frequently viewed in more corporate terms as "cultural" factors. See, e.g., William Julius Wilson, *More than Just Race: Being Black and Poor in the Inner City* (New York: W. W. Norton, 2009); and Barack Obama, *The Audacity of Hope: Thoughts on Reclaiming the American Dream* (New York: Three Rivers Press, 2006), 227–69.

12. Dyson, *Is Bill Cosby Right?*, 13.

13. Bill Cosby and Alvin F. Poussaint, *Come On People: On the Path from Victims to Victors* (Nashville: Nelson, 2007), 9.

14. Lawrence M. Mead, *Beyond Entitlement: The Social Obligations of Citizenship* (New York: Free Press, 1986), *viii.*

15. *How to Make Black America Better: Leading African Americans Speak Out*, comp. and ed. Tavis Smiley (New York: Anchor, 2001), 75–77.

16. Obama, *Audacity of Hope*, 244, 248.

17. Elijah Anderson, *Against the Wall: Poor, Young, Black, and Male* (Philadelphia: University of Pennsylvania Press, 2008), 25.

18. Orlando Patterson, "A Poverty of the Mind" in the *New York Times*, March 25, 2006, http://www.nytimes.com/2006/03/26/opinion/26patterson.html?_r=1.

19. Wilson, *More than Just Race*, 22–23.

20. Dyson, *Is Bill Cosby Right?*, *xiii.*

21. Ibid., 6.

22. Ibid., 7.

23. Ibid., 10.

24. Ibid., 8.

25. Michael O. Emerson and Christian Smith, *Divided by Faith: Evangelical Religion and the Problem of Race in America* (Oxford: Oxford University Press, 2000).

26. Perhaps the most common way of defining the term *evangelical* is to focus on the four traits laid out by David Bebbington in *Evangelicalism in Modern Britain: A History from the 1730s to the 1980s* (London: Unwin Hyman, 1989), 1–17; and in *The Dominance of Evangelicalism: The Age of Spurgeon and Moody* (Downers Grove, IL: InterVarsity, 2005), 23–40; and reaffirmed by Mark Noll, *The Rise of Evangelicalism: The Age of Edwards, Whitefield, and the Wesleys* (Downers Grove, IL: InterVarsity, 2003), 19. The four traits are: (1) an emphasis on the necessity of conversion; (2) an emphasis on the Bible as inspired, true, and authoritative in all it addresses; (3) a focus on the death of Jesus as essential in atoning for sin and acceptance with God; and (4) a call for all Christians, both lay people and clergy, to rise to action in spreading the gospel and doing good works.

27. By way of definition, they say that the racialized society is "a society wherein race matters profoundly for differences in life experiences, life opportunities, and social relationships . . . a society that allocates differential economic, political, social, and even psychological rewards to groups along racial lines; lines that are socially constructed." Emerson and Smith, *Divided by Faith*, 7.

28. Ibid., 75.

29. Ibid., 132.

30. Ibid., 90.

31. Ibid., 132.

32. Clarence Thomas, *Clarence Thomas, My Grandfather's Son, A Memoir* (New York: HarperCollins, 2007).

33. Thomas Sowell, *Black Rednecks and White Liberals* (San Francisco: Encounter, 2005); *Race and Culture: A World View* (New York: Basic Books, 1995).

34. Shelby Steele, *The Content of Our Character: A New Vision of Race in America* (New York: HarperPerennial, 1990); *A Dream Deferred: The Second Betrayal of Black Freedom in America* (New York: HarperPerennial, 1998); *White Guilt.*

35. John McWhorter, *Losing the Race: Self-Sabotage in Black America* (New York: Free Press, 2000); *Winning the Race: Beyond the Crisis in Black America* (New York: Gotham, 2005).

36. Ward Connerly, *Creating Equal: My Fight Against Race Preferences* (San Francisco: Encounter Books, 2000).

37. Dinesh D'Souza, *The End of Racism: Principles for a Multiracial Society* (New York: Free Press Paperbacks, 1995). I know that D'Souza is not African American. He was born in Mumbai in 1961 and came to the US first in 1978. I include him here for convenience as a nonwhite spokesman of this viewpoint.

38. Steele, *A Dream Deferred*, 15–16.

39. Williams, *Enough*, 105.

40. Ibid., 228.

41. Steele, *A Dream Deferred*, 18.

42. Ibid., 113.

43. Steele, *The Content of Our Character*, 117.

44. Ibid., 112.

45. Ibid., 113.

46. Ibid., 121.

47. Ibid., 116.

48. Ibid., 118.

49. Ibid.

50. John H. McWhorter, "What's Holding Blacks Back?" *The City Journal*, vol. 11 (Winter 2001): 6.

51. Quoted in Williams, *Enough*, 105. Henry Louis Gates Jr. wrote in 2001, "As crazy as this sounds, recent surveys of young Black kids reveal a distressing pattern. Far too many say that succeeding is 'white,' education is 'white,' aspiring and dream are 'white,' believing that you can make it is 'white.' Had any of us said this sort of thing when we were growing up, our families and friends would have checked us into a mental institution." Smiley, *How to Make Black America Better*, 75.

52. Williams, *Enough*, 91–92 (paragraph breaks added).

53. Ibid., 96.

54. Katherine Kerstine, "Teach Character to Cut Racial Gap in School Results," *Star-Tribune*, February 22, 2007, B1.

55. Steele, *The Content of Our Character*, 125.

56. Quoted in Neuhaus, "Counting by Race," 76.

CHAPTER 6: THE POWER OF THE GOSPEL AND THE ROOTS OF RACIAL STRIFE

1. Juan Williams, *Enough: The Phony Leaders, Dead-End Movements, and Culture of Failure That Are Undermining Black America—and What We Can Do About It* (New York: Crown, 2006), 215.

2. Shelby Steele, *The Content of Our Character: A New Vision of Race in America* (New York: HarperPerennial, 1990), 43–44.

3. Shelby Steele, *A Dream Deferred: The Second Betrayal of Black Freedom in America* (New York: HarperPerennial, 1998), 91.

4. Richard John Neuhaus, "Counting by Race," *First Things*, February 1996, 78.

5. Here is one expression of the gospel as Neuhaus spoke it. Ten years after his conversion, he wrote in his book *Death on a Friday Afternoon* (New York: Basic Books, 2000): "When I come before the judgment throne, I will plead the promise of God in the shed blood of Jesus Christ. I will not plead any work that I have done, although I will thank God that he has enabled me to do some good. I will plead no merits other than the merits of Christ, knowing that the merits of Mary and the saints are all from him; and for their company, their example, and their prayers throughout my earthly life I will give everlasting thanks. I will not plead that I had faith, for sometimes I was unsure of my faith, and in any event that would be to turn faith into a meritorious work of my own. I will not plead that I held the correct understanding of "justification by faith alone," although I will thank God that he led me to know ever more fully the great truth that much misunderstood formulation was intended to protect. Whatever little growth in holiness I have experienced, whatever strength I have received from the company of the saints, whatever understanding I have attained of God and his ways—these and all other gifts I have received I will bring gratefully to the throne. But in seeking entry to that heavenly kingdom, I will, with Dysmas, look to Christ and Christ alone. Then I hope to hear him say, 'Today you will be with me in paradise,' as I hope with all my being—because, although looking to him alone, I am not alone—he will say to all" (70).

6. Later that year welfare reform in America took a remarkable turn in the direction Neuhaus was pleading. The Personal Responsibility and Work Opportunity Reconciliation

Act was a cornerstone of the Republican Contract with America, and signed into law by Bill Clinton on August 22, 1996.

7. It has been a decade and a half since Neuhaus wrote, but he would, no doubt, still be concerned today about disparity between black graduation rates and white ones. The New York City Department of Education reported that for 2008, the gap in the high school graduation rate between white and black students was 20.1 percentage points, with 51.4 percent of black students in the class of 2008 graduating in four years. Cited February 8, 2011, at http://schools.nyc.gov/Offices/mediarelations/NewsandSpeeches/2008-2009/20090622_grad_rates.htm. In my city of Minneapolis, in 2008 there was a graduation rate of 87.31 percent of white students but only 68.48 for blacks.

8. Neuhaus, "Counting by Race," n.p.

9. William Wilberforce, *A Practical View of Christianity*, ed. Kevin Charles Belmonte (Peabody, MA: Hendrickson, 1996).

10. Ibid., 182.

11. Ibid., 198.

12. Ibid., 167.

13. Ibid., 66.

14. Ibid., 64.

15. Ibid., 166.

INTRODUCTION TO PART 2

1. Timothy George and Robert Smith, *A Mighty Long Journey: Reflections on Racial Reconciliation* (Nashville: Broadman, 2000). The title is taken from an African American chant (p. 7):

It's a mighty long journey,
But I'm on my way;
It's a mighty long journey,
But I'm on my way.

2. Edited by Kevin Charles Belmonte (Peabody, MA: Hendrickson, 1996).

3. Ibid, 79, emphasis added.

4. John Pollock, *Wilberforce* (London: Constable, 1977), 69.

CHAPTER 9: RANSOMED FOR GOD FROM EVERY TRIBE

1. It is of special relevance here to point out three African American pastors whose lives total 130 years of faithfulness to Christ in the context of loving the Reformed Faith: Lemuel Haynes (1753–1833), Daniel A. Payne (1811–1893), and Francis Grimké (1850–1937). Thabiti Anyabwile introduces them to us: "They were puritans. They committed themselves to sound theology in the pulpit, theologically informed practice in the church, and theologically reformed living in the world." Anyabwile's book is full of surprises and treasures for those who know little about this stream of black history. *The Faithful Preacher: Recapturing the Vision of Three African American Pastors* (Wheaton, IL: Crossway, 2007), 15. For the story of what has happened in African American theology since the time of Haynes, Payne, and Grimke, see Thabiti Anyabwile, *The Decline of African American Theology: From Biblical Faith to Cultural Captivity* (Downers Grove, IL: InterVarsity, 2007).

2. Kenneth J. Stewart, *Ten Myths about Calvinism: Recovering the Breadth of the Reformed Tradition* (Downers Grove, IL: InterVarsity, 2011), 247, 268.

3. See this thought expanded in the conclusion of this book with the help of Mark Noll's *God and Race in American Politics: A Short History* (Princeton, NJ: Princeton University Press, 2008).

4. Anthony Carter, *On Being Black and Reformed: A New Perspective on the African-American Christian Experience* (Phillipsburg, NJ: P&R, 2003).

5. Anthony Carter, ed., *Glory Road: The Journeys of 10 African Americans into Reformed Christianity* (Wheaton, IL: Crossway, 2009).

6. John Piper, *Spectacular Sins and Their Global Purpose in the Glory of Christ* (Wheaton, IL: Crossway, 2008), 48–49.

7. See John Piper, "I Will Not Give My Glory to Another: Preaching the Fullness of Definite Atonement," in *From Heaven He Came and Sought Her: Definite Atonement in Biblical, Theological, and Pastoral Perspective* (tentative title), ed. David Gibson and Jonathan Gibson (Wheaton, IL: Crossway, forthcoming).

8. Millard Erickson then says, "This is the view of all Arminians." *Systematic Theology* (Grand Rapids, MI: Baker, 1983), 829; emphasis added.

9. For a compelling and clear exegetical defense of the position I am building on here, see John Murray, *Redemption Accomplished and Applied* (Grand Rapids, MI: Eerdmans, 1955), 59–75.

10. For more on world missions, see John Piper, *Let the Nations Be Glad! The Supremacy of God in Missions*, 3rd ed. (Grand Rapids, MI: Baker, 2010).

11. For my effort to show the biblical extent of the meaning of these terms, see Piper, *Let the Nations Be Glad!*, 212–15.

12. The implication that God designed the cross and its fruit for his own glory is an expression of one of the greatest themes in all the Bible—God's passion for his glory and how such a passion is a great act of love toward us. I have tried to explore this biblical theme in John Piper, *God's Passion for His Glory: Living the Vision of Jonathan Edwards* (Wheaton, IL: Crossway, 1998); and John Piper, *The Pleasures of God: Meditations on God's Delight in Being God* (Sisters, OR: Multnomah, 2000).

13. For a much fuller explanation and biblical confirmation of the doctrine of unconditional election, see John Piper, "The Pleasure of God in Election," in *The Pleasures of God*, 121–56.

CHAPTER 10: EVERY PEOPLE JUSTIFIED THE SAME WAY

1. The most helpful effort to conceptualize the Trinity that I have found is Jonathan Edwards, *The Works of Jonathan Edwards*, vol. 21: *Discourse on the Trinity* (New Haven, CT: Yale University Press, 2003), 109–44.

2. F. F. Bruce, *The Book of Acts* (Grand Rapids, MI: Eerdmans, 1954), 357.

3. I love to recommend the book from which these two words, *accomplished* and *applied*, first entered my vocabulary: John Murray, *Redemption Accomplished and Applied* (Grand Rapids, MI: Eerdmans, 1984).

CHAPTER 11: DYING WITH CHRIST FOR THE SAKE OF CHRIST-EXALTING DIVERSITY

1. I have tried to unpack some of the depth and glory of the miracle of conversion in *Finally Alive: What Happens When We Are Born Again* (Fearn, Ross-Shire, Scotland: Christian Focus, 2009).

2. See chap. 9, n. 10.

CHAPTER 12: LIVING IN SYNC WITH GOSPEL FREEDOM

1. I have tried to lay out the wider biblical basis for understanding justification this way in two books: John Piper, *Counted Righteous in Christ: Should We Abandon the Imputation of Christ's Righteousness?* (Wheaton, IL: Crossway, 2002); and *The Future of Justification: A Response to N. T. Wright* (Wheaton, IL: Crossway, 2007).

2. This issue is so significant that Timothy George devotes an entire essay to it called "The Sin of Inhospitality," in Timothy George and Robert Smith Jr., *A Mighty Long Journey* (Nashville: Broadman, 2000), 141–49.

3. Quoted in Chris Rice and Spencer Perkins, *More Than Equals* (Downers Grove, IL: InterVarsity, 1993), 190.

4. Ibid., 190–91; emphasis added.

5. Dwight Perry, ed., *Building Unity in the Church of the New Millennium* (Chicago: Moody, 2002).

6. Ibid., 20.

CHAPTER 14: WHY IS IT WORTH THE DEATH OF HIS SON?

1. I have tried to give the foundation for this claim in several places. See John Piper, *Desiring God: Meditations of a Christian Hedonist*, 25th Anniversary Reference Edition (Sisters, OR: Multnomah, 2011), 313–26; John Piper, *The Pleasures of God: Meditations on God's Delight in Being God* (Sisters, OR: Multnomah, 2000), 25–120; John Piper, *Let the Nations Be Glad! The Supremacy of God in Missions* (Grand Rapids, MI: Baker, 2003), 21–29; John Piper, *God's Passion for His Glory: Living the Vision of Jonathan Edwards* (Wheaton, IL: Crossway, 1998).

2. For an extended exploration and explanation of the meaning of the relevant terms for *nation* and *people* and *Gentile* in the New Testament, see John Piper, *Let the Nations Be Glad!*, chap. 5, "The Supremacy of God among 'All the Nations.'"

3. What follows is adapted from John Piper, *Let the Nations Be Glad!*, 3rd ed., 221–24.

4. F. F. Bruce, *The Book of Acts* (Grand Rapids, MI: Eerdmans, 1954), 357–58.

CHAPTER 15: INTERRACIAL MARRIAGE

1. Stephan Thernstrom and Abigail Thernstrom, *America in Black and White: One Nation, Indivisible* (New York: Simon & Schuster, 1999), 12.

2. At http://www.lovingday.org/map.htm (accessed March 17, 2009), you can do a state-by-state study of which states had anti-miscegenation laws and when they were overturned.

3. Colin Kidd, *The Forging of Races: Race and Scripture in the Protestant Atlantic World, 1600–2000* (Cambridge, UK: Cambridge University Press, 2006), 275.

4. http://www.oyez.org/cases/1960-1969/1966/1966_395/ (accessed March 12, 2009). For the history of the *Loving* case and interracial marriage in America, see Peter Wallenstein, *Tell the Court I Love My Wife: Race, Marriage, and Law: An American History* (New York: Palagrave Macmillan, 2002); Phyl Newbeck, *Virginia Hasn't Always Been for Lovers: Interracial Marriage Bans and the Case of Richard and Mildred Loving* (Carbondale, IL: Southern Illinois University Press, 2004); Renee C. Romano, *Race Mixing: Black-White Marriage in Postwar America* (Cambridge, MA: Harvard University Press, 2003).

5. http://www.lovingday.org/courtroom.htm (accessed March 17, 2009).

6. Ibid. The 1912 South Carolina Criminal Code, Section 385, reads: "Sec. 385. Miscegenation—Punishment for—Penalty for Performing Ceremony.—It shall be unlawful for any white man to intermarry with any woman of either the Indian or negro races, or any mulatto, mestizo, or half-breed, or for any white woman to intermarry with any person other than a white man, or for any mulatto, half-breed, Indian, negro or mestizo to intermarry with a white woman; and any such marriage, or attempted marriage, shall be utterly null and void and of none effect; and any person who shall violate this Section, or any one of the provisions thereof, shall be guilty of a misdemeanor, and, on conviction thereof, shall be punished by a fine of not less than five hundred dollars, or imprisonment not less than twelve months, or both, in the discretion of the Court."

7. Ibid.

8. Ibid.

9. Even with the new legal status of interracial marriage since 1967 in all the states, the number of interracial couples is a small percentage. The census tells us that in 1990 there were 242,000 black-and-white married couples, which is double the number of those in 1980 and up 375 percent since 1960. However, that is still only 2.2 percent of the married population. Richard John Neuhaus, "Counting by Race," *First Things*, February 1996, 76.

10. Cited in "Interracial Relationships, Introduction," http://www.enotes.com/interracial-relationships-article/ (accessed March 17, 2009).

11. Ibid.

12. "Committee on Mission to North America, Pastoral Letter on Racism, approved at the March 2004 MNA Committee Meeting as the Committee's Recommendation to the Thirty-Second General Assembly," http://www.pca-mna.org/churchplanting/PDFs/RacismPaperFinal%20Version%2004-09-04.pdf.

13. Kidd, *The Forging of Races*, 271.

14. Quoted in Kidd, *The Forging of Races*, 271. This quote, of course, has evolutionary assumptions, but the point is that, in spite of these assumptions, the unity of the human race in one human ancestor is viewed as true—however that one ancestor came to be—whether as the end of billions of years of chance, or the direct creation of God, which is what I think the Bible teaches and what is true.

15. For more on Ruth, her surprising marriage to Boaz, and her place in the Messianic line of Jesus, see John Piper, *A Sweet and Bitter Providence: Sex, Race, and the Sovereignty of God* (Wheaton, IL: Crossway, 2010).

16. "So what theological conclusions should we draw? *I would suggest that interracial intermarriage is strongly affirmed by Scripture.* Marrying unbelievers, on the other hand, is strongly prohibited. The criteria for approving or disapproving of our children's selected spouses should be based on their faith in Christ and not at all on the color of their skin. This theological affirmation should have profound implications for the church today." J. Daniel Hays, "A Biblical Perspective on Interracial Marriage," in *Criswell Theological Review*, (Spring 2009): 22; emphasis original. Also available at http://criswell.files.wordpress.com/2009/03/ctrhaysformatted1.pdf.

17. See 194–95 earlier in the book on why differences give God more glory.

18. J. Daniel Hays, *From Every People and Nation: A Biblical Theology of Race* (Downers Grove, IL: InterVarsity, 2003), 71. Some have suggested, on the other hand that this woman really might be Moses's first wife, Zipporah the Midianite, and that the term *Cushite* might have been a slur against her. See Ronald Allen, "Numbers," in *Genesis, Exodus, Leviticus, Numbers*, The Expositor's Bible Commentary, vol. 2, ed. Frank E. Gaebelein (Grand Rapids, MI: Zondervan, 1990), 797. "It is possible that Moses' wife, Zipporah, is intended by this phrase (see Exod. 2:15–22). If so, then her foreign ancestry is attacked rhetorically by exaggeration." If this is so, the argument developed here would still be valid in its essence.

19. Gordon J. Wenham, *Numbers: An Introduction and Commentary*, Tyndale Old Testament Commentaries (Leicester, UK: Inter-Varsity, 1981), 111. Similarly, "Miriam's questioning of the Cushite origin of Moses' wife was but a smokescreen for her central concern." R. Dennis Cole, *Numbers*, The New American Commentary, vol. 3b (Nashville: Broadman, 2000), 200.

20. In fact, the word *black* in the Bible never refers to sin or moral evil. "Though your sins are like *scarlet*, they shall be as white as snow" (Isa. 1:18).

21. J. Daniel Hays comes to the same conclusion: "The common cultural ban on intermarriage lies at the heart of the racial division in the church. White Christians who say that they are not prejudiced but who vehemently oppose interracial marriages are not being honest. They are still prejudiced, and I would suggest that they are out of line with the biblical teaching on this subject. In addition, this theology applies not only to black/white interracial marriages, but equally to intermarriages between any two ethnic groups within the church throughout the world, especially in those regions where the church has inherited strong interracial animosities from the culture at large." "A Biblical Perspective on Interracial Marriage," 23.

22. You could see this thinking at work all over the country fifty years ago. For example, a leading Alabama attorney said in 1946, "Education causes the Negro to seek political equality because political equality leads to social equality and social equality leads to intermarriage." Quoted in Thernstrom and Thernstrom, *America in Black and White*, 39.

CHAPTER 16: PROBABILITY, PREJUDICE, AND CHRIST

1. Andreas Köstenberger, *John*, Baker Exegetical Commentary on the New Testament (Grand Rapids, MI: Baker Academic, 2004), 81.

2. Available at http://www.merriam-webster.com/dictionary/stereotypical; emphasis added.

3. For more on Matthew 16:2–4 and its implications for the life of the mind, see John Piper, *Think: The Life of the Mind and the Love of God* (Wheaton, IL: Crossway, 2010), 60–63.

4. Martin Luther King Jr., "I Have a Dream," in *The Norton Anthology of African American Literature* (New York: W. W. Norton, 1997), 82.

5. I assume that Jesus's generalizations about the Pharisees (Matthew 23) and Paul's generalization about the Cretans (Titus 1:12) are not sinful because they did have such regard and did appreciate the exceptions.

CONCLUSION

1. Mark Noll, *God and Race in American Politics: A Short History* (Princeton, NJ: Princeton University Press), 2008.

2. Ibid., 1.

3. Ibid.

4. Ibid., 177–78 (ellipses original).

5. Ibid., 179–80 (paragraph breaks added).

6. Ibid., 180–81.

7. C. S. Lewis, *Surprised by Joy* (New York: Harcourt, 1955), 207. ". . . the uncritical acceptance of the intellectual climate common to our own age and the assumption that whatever has gone out of date is on that account discredited."

8. Shelby Steele, *White Guilt: How Blacks and Whites Together Destroyed the Promise of the Civil Rights Era* (New York: HarperCollins, 2006), 5–6.

9. Shelby Steele, *The Content of Our Character: A New Vision of Race in America* (New York: HarperPerennial, 1990), 20.

APPENDIX 1

1. "Thus," the *World Christian Encyclopedia* continues, "mankind or the human race today consists of a single surviving species, Homo Sapiens, and 5 surviving subspecies or races or racial stocks: . . . Australoid, Capoid, Caucasoid, Mongoloid and Negroid." *World Christian Encyclopedia: A Comparative Study of Churches and Religions in the Modern World AD 1900–2000*, ed. David Barrett (Nairobi: Oxford University Press, 1982), 107.

2. I am indebted to Alex Kirk for his research and insights in helping me clarify and document the issues in this chapter. If I have made any poor judgments, they are my own, not his.

3. Eloise Hiebert Meneses, "Science and the Myth of Biological Race," in *This Side of Heaven: Race, Ethnicity, and Christian*, ed. Robert J. Priest and Alvaro Nieves (Oxford: Oxford University Press, 2006), 34.

4. "Ethnicity refers to selected cultural and *sometimes physical characteristics* used to classify people into groups or categories considered to be significantly different from others." http://anthro.palomar.edu/ethnicity/ethnic_1.htm (accessed March 23, 2009; emphasis added).

5. Meneses, "Science and the Myth of Biological Race," 34.

6. "Tellingly, there has been no consensus among race scientists as to the number of races of humanity. The answers range from three to over a hundred races." Colin Kidd, *The Forging of Races: Race Scripture and the Protestant Atlantic World* (Cambridge: Cambridge University Press, 2006), 9.

7. Ibid., 3–6. "Scientific observers of race have never been able to agree about the number of different races of humankind, nor about the characteristics that determine such groupings. Such disagreements do not mean that the scientific taxonomy of races is a holy grail which has still to be achieved, but that such a quest is, in fact, a fool's errand" (10).

8. Ibid., 3.

9. Ibid., 9.

10. Ibid. See also Jenell Williams Paris, "Race: Critical Thinking and Transformative Possibilities," in Priest and Nieves, *This Side of Heaven*, 22: "We have seen that race first emerged as a legitimation for colonialism, and developed informally through vocabulary, cultural norms, and legislation. Later, racially minded scientists formalized these cultural understandings, and race categories gained more credibility and authority."

11. Priest and Nieves write: "Contemporary racial identities diverge fundamentally from biblical ones. The peoples of Scripture did not identify themselves as 'white' to be contrasted with those who were 'black.' . . . When color language is applied to skin color in Scripture, we find white being associated with diseased skin, black being neutrally descriptive or sometimes descriptive of diseased unhealthy skin, and 'red' (translated 'ruddy') being the only color term applied positively to the color of people's skin. Even here, the color is not used as part of group identity. Our own practice of using black and white as core and contrasting identities for contemporary people has no equivalent in Scripture." "Conclusion," *This Side of Heaven*, 327.

12. See "Appendix 4: What Are the Implications of Noah's Curse?" for a discussion of how the sons of Noah relate to this question.

13. W. E. B. Du Bois, "To the Nations of the World," *Great Speeches by African Americans*, ed. James Daley (Mineola, NY: Dover, 2006), 85.

14. "Committee on Mission to North America, Pastoral Letter on Racism, approved at the March 2004 MNA Committee Meeting as the Committee's Recommendation to the Thirty-Second General Assembly," http://www.pca-mna.org/churchplanting/PDFs/RacismPaper-Final%20Version%2004-09-04.pdf.

APPENDIX 2

1. Carl Ellis Jr., *Free at Last: The Gospel in the African-American Experience* (Downers Grove, IL: InterVarsity, 1996), 266; see also 48.

2. "Anyone who has spent any time at all listening to the Blues knows it is not necessarily 'down' or 'depressing' or sad. It is soulful, without a doubt, and the lyrics are frequently concerned with misfortune and loss, but the Blues is really a complex combination of misery and high spirits. Often the musical accompaniment is joyous and arrogant, in apparent contradiction to the unhappiness of the lyrics. This fascinating ambiguity has more than anything else to do with the universal appeal of the Blues." http://afgen.com/aboutblu.html.

3. One of the great spokesmen in America for traditional Reformed theology was Geerhardus Vos, who said that the "root idea [of Reformed theology] which served as the key to unlock the rich treasuries of the Scriptures was the preeminence of God's glory in the consideration of all that has been created." "The Doctrine of the Covenant in Reformed Theology," in *Redemptive History and Biblical Interpretation: The Shorter Writings of Geerhardus Vos*, ed. Richard Gaffin Jr. (Phillipsburg, NJ: Presbyterian & Reformed, 1980), 241–42.

4. Ellis, *Free At Last*, 23.

5. The term is carefully chosen and defined by Carl Ellis in ibid., 214: "This ugly term is most fitting because of its ugliness, to refer to the negative or unchristian religious practices expressed in the language of Christianity."

6. Ibid., 154.

7. Ibid., 158.

8. In one of his most creative sections, Ellis compares typical white preaching to classical music and typical black preaching to jazz music: "There are essentially two approaches to music, the formal and the dynamic. We call them *classical* and *jazz*. We know what classical music is—the little dots, circles, lines of Beethoven and Brahms that come to life when a conductor stabs the air with a baton. These sounds that fill the air are not the conductor's or the violinists'. They belong to Beethoven and Brahms. The beauty of a classical piece is found in the mind of the composer, in the music as it is *written*. Thus the goal of the classical musician is to reproduce as faithfully as possible the sounds the great composers imagined. Only in rare moments and clearly marked cadences do classical musicians improvise. Their main task is not to improvise but to imitate. Jazz is different. The beauty of jazz is found in the soul of the musician and in the music as it is *performed*. Jazz is improvisational. Just as classical music has developed musical composition into a fine art, jazz has cultivated musical improvisation into a fine art. The notes that fill the air do not belong to a deceased composer; they issue from the vibrant souls of great performers like 'Diz,' 'Bird' and 'Lady Day.'" Ibid., 173–74.

9. For a discussion of the senses in which God does indeed make much of us, but only in such a way that enables us to enjoy most fully making much of him, see John Piper, *God*

Is the Gospel: Meditations on God's Love as the Gift of Himself (Wheaton, IL: Crossway, 2005), 147–62.

APPENDIX 3

1. Harold Best, *Music Through the Eyes of Faith* (New York: HarperOne, 1993), 190.

APPENDIX 4

1. For extensive studies of the history of this issue, see David M. Goldberg, *The Curse of Ham: Race and Slavery in Early Judaism, Christianity, and Islam* (Princeton, NJ: Princeton University Press, 2003); and Stephen R. Haynes, *Noah's Curse: The Biblical Justification of American Slavery* (New York: Oxford University Press, 2001).

2. Gordon Wenham, *Genesis 1–15*, Word Biblical Commentary (Nashville: Nelson Reference, 1987), 201.

3. Bruce Waltke, *Genesis: A Commentary* (Grand Rapids, MI: Zondervan, 2001), 150.

4. Umberto Cassuto, *A Commentary on the Book of Genesis* (Jerusalem: Magnes Press, 1949), 155. I would not say it exactly like this because there is a sense in which the curse is owing to Ham's sin, but it is not owing to it in a way that diminishes the accountability of the Canaanites for their own sin. C. F. Keil suggests that "the real reason [for why the curse fell on Ham's son Canaan] must either lie in the fact that Canaan was already walking in the steps of his father's impiety, or else be sought in the name *Canaan*, which Noah discerned, through the gift of prophecy, a significant *omen*; a supposition decidedly favoured by the analogy of the blessing pronounced upon Japhet, which is also founded upon the name. . . . The meaning of *Canaan* is 'the submissive one.'" *Biblical Commentary on the Old Testament*, vol. 1: *The Pentateuch* (Grand Rapids, MI: Eerdmans, 1968), 157.

5. Keil and Delitzsch, *Biblical Commentary on the Old Testament*, 158.

6. Old Testament scholar John Walton doubts that the curse from Noah's lips did in fact define God's plan: "A final observation [that] needs to be made about the nature of the pronouncement [of Noah against Canaan] is that it is not in the same category as prophecy. These pronouncements are never given as a message from God, nor are they presented as received revelation by the patriarch. In other words, God is under no obligation to fulfill these, and they do not necessarily reflect his will and plan." John Walton, *Genesis*, NIV Application Commentary (Grand Rapids, MI: Zondervan, 2001), 350. But it seems to me, and most commentators, that the author of Genesis wants us to see in this curse a real divine intention that will be seen later in Israel's history.

SUBJECT INDEX

NAME INDEX

SCRIPTURE INDEX

Psalms

16:2	165
22:27	14
25:7	30
25:11	253
49:7	134
49:15	134
67:4	50
73:25–26	165
96:1–4	154
96:3–4	196, 198

Isaiah

1:18	277
2:12	90
2:17	90
41:10	100
43:6–7	249
43:25	253
53:6	252
53:10	253
61:18–19	115

Jeremiah

4:2	154
13:23	211
31:30	264

Ezekiel

18:20	264

Amos

5:24	26

Micah

5:2	218

Matthew

1:5	209
2:1	119
5–7	117
5:5	97, 178
5:7	189
5:9	13
5:14–16	47
5:43–44	267
5:43–48	150
5:44	13, 26
6:33	96
7:12	13
7:16	134
8:1–4	117
8:5–13	117–18
8:11–12	50
10:6	119
10:16–25	253
10:28–31	100
15:24	119
16:2–3	221
16:2–4	277
18:23–34	189
21:33–43	119
21:43	119
23	278
23:3	134
23:12	90
24:14	215
26:24	266–67
28:19	119, 195

Mark

1:27	88
7:19	173
7:26	118
11:17	119

Luke

4:16–30	114–19
6:27	13

✖️ desiringGod

If you would like to explore further the vision of God and life presented in this book, we at Desiring God would love to serve you. We have thousands of resources to help you grow in your passion for Jesus Christ and help you spread that passion to others. At our website, www.desiringGod.org, you'll find almost everything John Piper has written and preached, including more than forty books. We've made over thirty years of his sermons available free online for you to read, listen to, download, and in some cases watch.

In addition, you can access hundreds of articles, find out where John Piper is speaking, learn about our conferences, and browse our online store. John Piper receives no royalties from the books he writes and no compensation from Desiring God. The funds are all reinvested into our gospel-spreading efforts. Desiring God also has a whatever-you-can-afford policy, designed for individuals with limited discretionary funds. If you'd like more information about this policy, please contact us at the address or phone number below. We exist to help you treasure Jesus Christ and his gospel above all things because he is most glorified in you when you are most satisfied in him. Let us know how we can serve you!

Desiring God
Post Office Box 2901 Minneapolis, Minnesota 55402
888.346.4700   mail@desiringGod.org

"All authority in heaven and on earth has been given to me."
Jesus

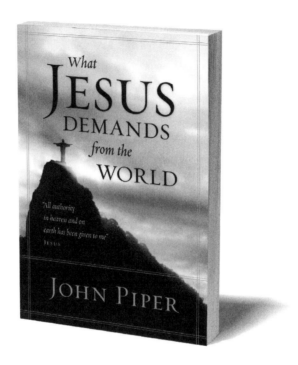

"Scholars, popularists, and now even novelists are falling over each other today in a blind passion to discover an alternative Jesus to the One so magnificently portrayed in the biblical Gospels. In stark and refreshing contrast John Piper clear-sightedly grasps the obvious-the biblical Jesus is worth living for and dying for."

SINCLAIR B. FERGUSON,
Senior Pastor, First Presbyterian Church, Columbia, SC

"This is now my favorite book by John Piper. In the best tradition of Adolf Schlatter's *Do We Know Jesus?* and his 'hermeneutic of perception,' *What Jesus Demands from the World* has changed my life and will certainly change yours because it is based on the pure words of Jesus as revealed in the four Gospels. A must-read for every true follower of Christ."

ANDREAS J. KÖSTENBERGER,
Editor, Journal of the Evangelical Theological Society;
Professor of New Testament and Director of PhD Studies,
Southeastern Baptist Theological Seminary

Now Available!

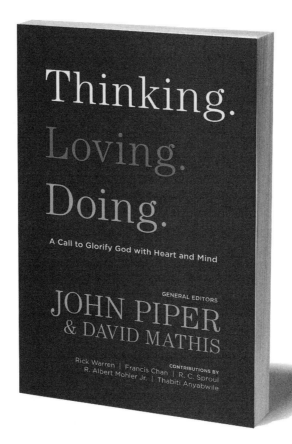

This new volume, built on the 2010 Desiring God National Conference and John Piper's recent book *Think: The Life of the Mind and the Love of God*, argues that thinking and the affections of the heart are inseparable. Our emotions fuel our thoughts for God. Likewise, hard thinking about God leads to deeper joy in our relationship with him. And both, in turn, help us focus outward as we express a greater love for others.

CONTRIBUTIONS BY Rick Warren, Francis Chan, John Piper, R. Albert Mohler Jr., R. C. Sproul, and Thabiti Anyabwile bring a wealth of perspective and experience in calling for readers to love God and others with heart and mind and hands.